Conversations with Margaret Walker

Literary Conversations Series

Peggy Whitman Prenshaw
General Editor

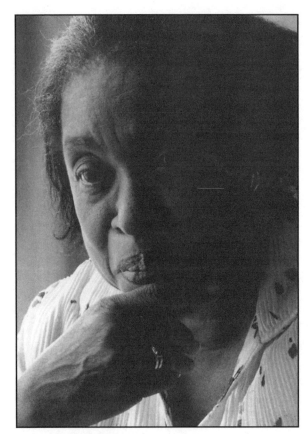

Photo credit: Diana Young

Conversations
with Margaret Walker

Edited by
Maryemma Graham

University Press of Mississippi
Jackson

Books by Margaret Walker

For My People. New Haven: Yale University Press, 1942.

Jubilee. Boston: Houghton Mifflin, 1966.

Prophets for a New Day. Detroit: Broadside Press, 1970.

How I Wrote Jubilee. Chicago: Third World Press, 1972.

October Journey. Detroit: Broadside Press, 1973.

A Poetic Equation: Conversations Between Nikki Giovanni and Margaret Walker. Washington: Howard University Press, 1974.

For Farish Street Green, February 27, 1986. Jackson, Mississippi: 1986.

Richard Wright, Daemonic Genius: A Portrait of the Man, A Critical Look at His Work. New York: Warner Books, 1988.

This Is My Century: New and Collected Poems. Athens: University of Georgia Press, 1989.

How I Wrote Jubilee *and Other Essays on Life and Literature.* Ed. Maryemma Graham. New York: Feminist Press at the City University of New York, 1990.

On Being Female, Black, and Free: Essays by Margaret Walker, 1932–1992. Ed. Maryemma Graham. Knoxville: University of Tennessee Press, 1997.

www.upress.state.ms.us

Copyright © 2002 by University Press of Mississippi
All rights reserved
Manufactured in the United States of America

10   09   08   07   06   05   04   03   02   4   3   2   1
⊗

Library of Congress Cataloging-in-Publication Data

Walker, Margaret, 1915–
    Conversations with Margaret Walker / edited by Maryemma Graham.
        p.   cm. — (Literary conversations series)
    Includes bibliographical references (p.) and index.
    ISBN 1-57806-511-9 (alk. paper) — ISBN 1-57806-512-7 (pbk. : alk. paper)
    1. Walker, Margaret, 1915—Interviews.   2. Authors, American—20th
century—Interviews.   3. African American authors—Interviews.   4. African Americans
in literature.   I. Graham, Maryemma.   II. Title.   III. Series.

PS3545.A517 Z468   2002
818'.5209—dc21   2002016898

British Library Cataloging-in-Publication Data available

Contents

Introduction

Margaret Walker created and lived by her own standards. "I read somewhere in *Newsweek* where Margaret Walker is one of those moral writers and that is supposed to be a form of derision," she told Ruth Campbell in a televised interview, "but to me, I could not have a greater compliment." This defiance of expectations is just one example of the dominant characteristic in these interviews with Margaret Walker. Describing herself to Marcia Greenlee as "a strange creature with a woman's body, a man's mind in a woman's body," Walker welcomed the opportunity to display her keen wit and love of language. Her passion came from her insatiable curiosity, a belief in Christian humanism, a hatred for irreverence, and an uncompromising commitment to social justice. Her geographic loyalty to the South in general and Mississippi in particular kept at least some of her critics at bay, believing her to be slightly crazy. An interviewer who encountered Walker, who was every bit the southern raconteur, found her entirely approachable, if somewhat intimidating. Combining the roles of preacher's daughter and southern matriarch, Walker's world embraced various kinds of intelligence, from the human and psychic to the divine. John Griffin Jones's preface to his 1982 interview evokes an all-to-familiar image of the late writer.

> She lives in a house at the end of Margaret Walker Alexander Drive in Jackson. Earlier on the day I came to call she'd attended a neighbor's wedding, and when the squad of young children who met me at the door brought me into the den to meet her, she was resting on the couch. She apologized, got to her feet and shooed away the kids, and suggested that we move to her study for the interview. There is nothing frail about her. It quickly became clear that ideas are her stimulant. When the issues we were discussing reached some level of complexity, she became animated. I realized in talking with her that, although she has behind her a distinguished literary career reaching back to the 1930s, her work is not done. She knows too many of the questions about black American experience to stop attempting to find answers in her work.

Walker began to ask the questions early in her life. They were there in her childhood and growing-up years. Some of the answers came when she moved to Chicago and encountered Marxism, which made possible an understanding of human history. She took from Marxism a new social perspective, especially around issues of race, and a way to integrate and synthesize ideas. A fanatical religious faith persisted, guiding her view on morality and spirituality. Neither could she give up her sense of public responsibility as she actively pursued personal and professional success. Painting her canvas in broad human terms, Walker reframes the familiar stride toward freedom as humanity striving toward divinity. To Walker, it's as if the writer is at war in the world, one "without heart, without soul," she remarks to Nikki Giovanni. Hence the writer's special calling. As she told me in an interview,

> Certainly this consists of telling the people—not only analyzing what is happening to us everyday, but showing the way we must go for a better life, a healthy economy, better education for our children, physical health and fitness. The writer seeks to inform the mass audience of his people for whom he writes of their human and spiritual destiny. He seeks to prepare them for the days ahead in which they may truly see a world of common humanity.

With such a strong sense of her own agency, Walker might easily have lived a very different kind of life. She tells us that she was most comfortable around ordinary people, as she liked to call them, and "the smell of fresh pine, with the trail of coon, warm skies and gulf blue streams";[1] repudiation of her traditional background, therefore, was never an option. In the interviews, conducted often in her beloved kitchen, Walker offers homespun wisdom in an authoritative voice, marked by the same biblical cadences that one finds in her poetry.

Despite the intellectualism of the interviews, they restore a sense of balance and perspective to a writer who endeared herself to many as a role model, a teacher, a mentor, and a poet's poet. Writing was not only discovery for Walker. It was the thing that could not be stopped. When asked to explain where the writing came from, Walker confesses to Campbell, "When I had nobody to talk to, I wrote to myself. I realize now that I did not talk to people. I was in conflict with those around me." Yet, the quiet, reflective child became the most talked-about writer for her people.

The life and times presented here invites the reader to journey into a world as dramatic as it is complex. Walker is as much guide as she is witness to America's social and cultural history, shared here from a deeply personal perspective. She is a writer whose voice we trust. "There are some of us

whom nobody can hush," Walker admonishes. "There are some of us whom
all kinds of persecution and oppression cannot keep quiet, not unless we are
dead itself."[2]

Walker's consciousness of her own literary biography is presented as a
fascinating progress narrative. At eleven, she began to write in journals and
diaries, her most prized possessions. At fifteen, she met Langston Hughes,
by which time she had already completed a manuscript that displayed remarkable talent. By seventeen, she was in Chicago finishing her education at
Northwestern. At twenty-one, she translated a vision—one of many guiding
her life—into her most famous poem, "For My People." A 1937 appearance
in *Poetry* confirmed her relationship to the social realists and linked the
young poet to an international avant garde.

In the interview with Joanne Gabbin, Walker provides a more detailed
assessment of the period and a movement that harnessed the energy of a
group of young black intellectuals who became the Southside Writers Group.
Under the leadership of Richard Wright, they tackled issues of race, politics,
and art. There Walker not only found her voice, but also the poetic form
which became her signature. By 1942—still under thirty—she had an award-
winning volume and fame at her doorstep. She lived under the shadow of the
book for years, twenty-four in fact, before her next book was published. That
book, like its title, was her *Jubilee*, a celebration and lifetime achievement.
Her themes were moral ones: love conquers violence and hatred; suffering
makes us strong; the search for home and community prevails over all else.

Walker's conversations belong to a genre of nonfiction to which the writer
turned in the last phase of her career. She was an established writer by the
time she gave her first interview. Sixteen interviews included here were com-
piled from an assortment of television, radio, and print interviews she conducted between 1973, the date of the first included here, and 1997, a year
before she died. Some of interviews have been transcribed and appear in print
for the first time in this edition. To assure the impact of Walker's words in
the context of their own time, I have preserved original texts and done mini-
mal editing of the transcriptions.

A somewhat auspicious beginning for Walker as a popular interviewee
bears repeating here. The controversy surrounding the authenticity of *Jubliee*
had convinced Walker of the importance of sharing with readers how and
why a writer works. Her first public conversation became, therefore, *How I
Wrote Jubilee* in 1972, where she detailed the painstaking journey of discovery, honoring a promise she kept to her grandmother, the inspiration behind

the book. If emphasis upon the folkloric aspects of the novel prefigured a new dialogue about black language and culture, it also validated a new role for women as subjects and authors of their own stories, as makers of their own history. With her novel as with her poetry published in the '60s and '70s, Walker found herself a participant in two corresponding revolutions, a black one and a feminist one. Readers became interested in what she had to say about *Jubilee*'s relationship to fact and fiction, and about her relationship to the *Black Power* phenomenon that was sweeping the nation. Walker may not have been conscious of liberating the modern black writer—and black writing—by her return to the painful subject of slavery and by restoring a sense of dignity to black vernacular culture in this first modern novel to treat a controversial subject. She, nevertheless, enjoyed the attention it brought. A succession of interviews followed, naming Walker as an elder for a new generation of writers for the explosive Black Arts Movement, on the heels of the bicentennial decade and the Civil Rights movement. Historical blindness and racial intolerance became the targets in a nation that needed new stories. Walker became a popular storyteller, a foremother, and a visionary. For Walker, there was nothing faddish about the period. From Mississippi, where violence and rage tied for dominance, Walker's preacherly exhortations represented a voice crying in the wilderness. Reading these interviews confirms for us that Walker was always in control, in a period woefully out of control, displaying her own artistry by balancing her decided strengths—the succinctness of the poet, the insight of a historian, and the critical acumen of a literary scholar.

Walker seems acutely aware that her readers, as well as critics, have identified her with multiple generations, and she is compelled to speak about her own difference as a writer and a woman. Her peers, Richard Wright, James Baldwin, Frank Yerby, Chester Himes, and William Gardner Smith all made Europe their homes, while Ralph Ellison and Albert Murray claimed Harlem and Gwendolyn Brooks, Chicago. Walker is a loner among them, the single woman who established a successful career as a fierce defender of the South. The South's "climate for genius" has a peculiar richness, Walker notes to Campbell. "The social ferment has been so horrible that out of it, you were bound to get great writers like Faulkner, Wright. You were bound to get very great writers like Tennessee Williams." Yet it does not mean that all southern writers write with the same vision, and Walker points to Wright's anger and Faulkner's gothicism as examples, taking care to distinguish her own style from theirs.

Walker's perceptions guide us through the contradictions in the southern landscape to the multiple literary traditions informing her work. She lays claim to a tradition of classical rhetoric and an African-based oral tradition. Her ability to translate these traditions was dependent upon the extent to which she remained a vital part of both. Stephen Vincent Benét well understood this when he introduced her book to the literary world. As is made clear in the interviews, Walker attributes her discovery to Benét, the then reigning dean of American poetry—and not to Wright—as is commonly held. It was Benét who first praised the biblical imagery that derived as much from her grandfather's folk sermons as from her father's standard English ones. If there were a label, Walker would have to claim humanist, but quickly qualifies her meaning. "Today, we speak of academic humanists," Walker tells Charles Rowell. "I am a working humanist. I teach, live, work, write purely in what I consider the humanist and humanistic tradition. I think it is more important now to emphasize humanism in a technological age than ever before because it is only in terms of humanism that the society can redeem itself." Writing with heightened cultural awareness, Walker sees these redemptive qualities as part of the gift of black folk to America.

Walker's relationship to the South remains, nevertheless, problematic. She became a writer in order to dispel the myths and lies in books she read as a child. Yet, as she confesses to Jerry Ward, it is the power of ancestral history that drew her back to the South. "This is where I put in from the sea. I put down roots here; I came to stay here. After going from place to place and literally tossing on the sea of life, I put in at this harbor. And it has sometimes seemed like a dead-end street, that I'm going no farther. This is my place." And it was always from this place that Walker wrote and talked consistently about the need for change, while enduring decades of resistance from the same white southerners who read and praised her books.

To understand Walker's worldview is to understand that there is little room for vacillation, no place for uncertainty. "I was born when [the century] was barely fifteen years old; a historical point of view is central to the development of black people," she told me as *For My People* turned fifty. Such a sustained interest in the past, one that faced not one but three wars, intensified by the race wars at home, magnifies the importance of understanding the political complexity of our times. For Walker, the point is more than academic; holding to one's convictions is more than principle. It is a way of life. For her, it meant having to be radically honest, to maintain a life inseparable from the art that it engages. Margaret Walker required no less of others than she required of herself. It meant speaking up when unpopular, challenging the status quo. Her public criticism of Richard Wright and the suit against Alex Haley brought endless challenges to her credibility. But it is the survivor who can bear to speak her own truth, as Walker does here, fiercely defending her beliefs often in the presence of opposing realities.

Much controversy surrounds the Walker-Wright relationship even today. References to Wright have been repeated to suggest the importance Walker placed upon these responses. Although she was reputed to be Wright's lover, there is no evidence to support anything other than an intense platonic relationship. They shared an intellectual curiosity; creative passion drew them together as much as it drove them apart. Only years later was Walker able to speak about that turbulent relationship; the pain of that aborted relationship is still very much apparent.

The Walker-Giovanni interview, the longest in the volume, foregrounds the most significant generational difference between Walker and those writers who came of age in the '70s. No two women could be more unlike than Margaret Walker and Nikki Giovanni, and yet both are passionately committed to an artistic enterprise that has not treated African American women favorably. Walker insists on maintaining her matronly status in her debate with Giovanni, claiming age before wisdom.

Generational differences might also account for much of Walker's thinking about contemporary feminism and gender. Walker's tendency to accept in principle something that she might not fully approve of in practice is applicable to feminism. By today's standards, Walker's "feminism" appears essentialist when she argues the primacy of the feminine in the biological and spiritual domain to Greenlee: "Men are far more objective and less emotional than women. And I'm an emotional creature so that creates a problem. The organization that men have, I have." And yet, Walker's sophisticated reading of the social positionality of women—"daughter, sister, mother," as she relates to Lucy Friebert—prefigures important discussions among feminist theorists today. Walker voices concerns for the historical oppression of women in *Jubilee,* based on her understanding that slavery was the source of a kind of triple oppression. About women writers, Walker mimics "she could get religion and a little emotion, but she couldn't write poetry."[3]

What defines Walker both in relation to and against those eras she represents is her preoccupation with historical synthesis. A child of the New Negro Renaissance, she was part of every literary movement that followed. Living as a believer, a Christian humanist in a century that denied the grounds for such faith made her a visionary. If any subject fascinates her more than the autobiographical and biographical roots for her work, it is the legacy that must be passed on to our youth. In the interview in *Black Nation* in 1982, Walker cuts through the tape of ideological dissension as she renders her judgment on the Civil Rights movement:

> You had two revolutions in the '60s, one led by Martin Luther King, Jr., and one led by Malcolm X. Both of those revolutions were quite liberating in their intentions, and insofar as they went, they were very good, they just didn't go far enough. King's revolution brought very definite social change because it brought social legislation that outlawed segregation. Malcolm X's revolution was a more inter-nationalized thing of changing the attitudes of black people towards themselves. Of recovering a sense of manhood and womanhood for black people. A sense of pride and of unity and power. But, that was purely on a moral and aesthetic, and shall we say, a kind of sociological level. It did not quite seriously deal with economic and political problems which of themselves determine our lives.[4]

Walker conducted at least three interviews in 1992, all prompted by the anniversary of *For My People*. Looking back at her own life is a priority in most of these interviews. Through them, we consolidate the image of Walker that will be long remembered: a strong, able-bodied humanist with none of the revolutionary fervor diminished, compelled to bear witness to her century. Fortuitously perhaps, Walker chose as the title of her last book of poetry *This Is My Century,* as if preparing us for her departure. These interviews direct us to examine another world the writer occupied: the world of the mind, the place where the rational and the metaphysical can coexist. In one of the interviews toward the end of her life, following a stroke that would end her writing career, she is unmoved by the inevitability of death. Once again she chooses to remind us of our responsibility. "We owe our children another world," she tells us, "we owe them another mind to face the future." Walker was a consummate artist; her aesthetic beliefs and cultural practice highlight her own struggle to make her art and life one. "The artist sees color, line, and movement in building a composition," Walker said to Jones. "The musician has a motif, and he hears the certain musical sounds and patterns together. The writer has nothing but words."

Notes

1. "Sorrow Home," *This Is My Century: New and Collected Poems* (Athens: University of Georgia, 1989), 12.

2. Michael Simanga, *"Black Nation* Interviews Margaret Walker," *Black Nation V 2: 1* (Fall/Winter 1982), 14.

3. Phanuel Egejuru and Robert Elliot Fox, "An Interview with Margaret Walker, *Callaloo* 6 (May 1979), 35.

4. Michael Simanga, 12.

Chronology

1915   Margaret Abigail Walker born 7 July in Birmingham, Alabama, the first of four children to Rev. Sigismund Constantine Walker, a Methodist minister originally from Jamaica, and Marion Dozier, a musician and teacher; Grandmother Elvira Ware Dozier moves to Birmingham to live with family and care for her first grandchild.

1932   Publishes first essay, "What Is to Become of Us" in *Our Youth,* a New Orleans magazine; meets James Weldon Johnson, Marian Anderson, and Langston Hughes; enrolls in Northwestern University as junior.

1935   Drafts first 300 pages of *Jubilee* for creative writing class; graduates from NU with B.A. in English in June.

1936   Begins work with the Federal Writers' Project in Chicago with Frank Yerby, Gwendolyn Brooks, and Richard Wright.

1937   Publishes "For My People" in *Poetry* in October; Southside Writers group disbands.

1940   Graduates from Iowa with M.A. in creative writing; publishes short story in *Anvil* and *Creative Writing;* returns to New Orleans for eighteen months; suffers depression and burn-out.

1941   "For My People" published in *Negro Caravan.*

1942   Wins Yale Younger Poet Award for poetry collection *For My People,* subsequently published by Yale University Press.

1943   Marries Firnist James Alexander; moves to High Point, N.C.; first of four children born.

1949   Becomes English professor at Jackson State University.

1965   Receives Ph.D. in English from Iowa.

1966   *Jubilee* is published 25 September; wins Houghton Mifflin literary award, Mable Carney Student National Education Association plaque for scholar-teacher of the year, and Alpha Kappa Alpha Sorority Citation for Advancement of Knowledge; is honored at New York produc-

tion *A Hand Is on the Gate;* meets Ruby Dee, Ossie Davis, Cicely
Tyson, Moses Gunn, Roscoe Brown, James Earl Jones, and Gloria
Foster (who performs Walker's poetry); attends party at home of
Langston Hughes.

1968   Establishes Institute for the Study of History, Life, and Culture of
Black People at Jackson State University, now the Margaret Walker
Alexander National Research Center. Retires from teaching at Jack-
son State University.

1970   *Prophets for a New Day* published by Third World Press, marking a
shift from mainstream publishers; publishes "The Humanistic Tradition of Afro-American Literature"; massacre at Jackson State inspires
poem; serves as witness before President's Commission on Campus
Unrest.

1972   Receives National Endowment for the Humanities senior fellowship
for independent study; conducts seminar at Atlanta's Institute of the
Black World; *How I Wrote Jubilee* later published as monograph by
Third World Press; speaks at centennial of Paul Laurence Dunbar's
birth in Dayton and conceives idea for festival of black women writers
to honor Phillis Wheatley; delivers speech "Agenda for Action: Black
Arts and Letters" at Black Academy Conference to Assess the State
of Black Arts and Letters in the United States, sponsored by Johnson
Publishing Company, Chicago; writes "Humanities with a Black
Focus: A Black Paradigm" distributed by the Institute for Services to
Education in *Curriculum Changes in Black Colleges III,* published by
U.S. Department of Education; delivers speech commemorating JSU
massacre.

1973   *October Journey* published by Broadside Press; hosts Phillis Wheatley (bicentennial) Poetry Festival at JSU in October; gathering of
black women helps inaugurate the black women's literary renaissance; appears before Federal Communications Commission regarding racial discrimination in media; participates in Library of Congress
conference on Teaching Creative Writing; presents "The Writer and
Her Craft."

1974   *Poetic Equation: Conversations with Nikki Giovanni and Margaret
Walker* published by Howard University Press; hospitalized for diabe-
tes; outlines sequel to *Jubilee* in hospital; goes on speaking tour in
Northeast; receives honorary degrees from Denison University,
Northwestern University, Rust College (Mississippi).

1977   Files suit against Alex Haley for plagiarism; judge rules in favor of Haley; Conference on Africa and African Affairs sponsored by Black Studies Institute.

1980   Publishes essay "On Being Female, Black and Free"; "Mississippi and the Nation" speech given at Governor's Inaugural Symposium; "Margaret Walker Alexander Day" proclaimed by Mississippi Governor William Winter, 12 July; husband Alex dies in November; Siggy (son) and family move in with Walker; conducts lengthy interview with Claudia Tate for book *Black Women Writers.*

1982   Receives W. E. B. Du Bois award from Association of Social and Behavioral Scientists; delivers lecture "Education and the Seminal Mind;" completes new book of poetry; reads excerpts to overflow crowd at Lincoln University (Pennsylvania).

1988   *Richard Wright: Daemonic Genius* published after long battle with Wright's widow; celebration held at Old Capital Museum, Jackson; serves as delegate from Fourth District to National Democratic Convention in Atlanta; branch of Hinds County library named in her honor.

1989   *This Is My Century: New and Collected Poems* published; Institute at Jackson State becomes Margaret Walker Alexander National Research Center for the Study of the Twentieth-Century African American, introduced into legislation as HR Bill 3252; receives three-year fellowship from Lyndhurst Foundation (1989–1992); goes on East Coast and West Coast book promotion/lecture tour; attends Federal Writers Project reunion in Chicago; opening of "I Dream a World" Exhibition (Brian Lanker) featuring Walker and other women at Corcoran Gallery; appears on CBS "Nightwatch" with Charlie Rose.

1990   Receives Living Legend Award for Literature from National Black Arts Festival, Atlanta; *How I Wrote* Jubilee *and Other Essays on Life and Literature* published by Feminist Press; U.S. Court of Appeals rules in favor of Walker's use of Wright's letters in biography and against the Richard Wright estate; unveils historic marker at Richard Wright's home site for Natchez Literary Festival.

1992   Celebrates seventy-fifth birthday in gala event at home; interviewed by Jack Switzer for national airing of "Open Air" (Mississippi Educational TV); fiftieth anniversary edition of *For My People* issued by Limited Editions and celebrated at Limited Editions Club, New York, 18 September; receives [Kirk Fordice's] Governor's Award for Excellence in the Arts, Lifetime Achievement Award from the College Language Association, Golden Soror Award from AKA Sorority, and together with Ralph Ellison, a tribute from Modern Language Association; participates in five-day conference on "Black Women Writers and Magic Realism" sponsored by MWA National Research Center; Roland Freeman publishes *For My People: A Tribute,* a book of photographs in honor of Walker; is hospitalized for minor stroke.

1993   Receives National Book Award for Lifetime Achievement; accepts honorary degree from Spelman College (Atlanta); delivers keynote address "Discovering Our Connections: Race, Gender, and the Law" at Washington College of Law, published in *American University Journal of Gender and Law.*

1995   Margaret Walker Alexander National Research Center for the Study of Twentieth-Century African Americans hosts Margaret Walker Alexander Week 27 November–2 December; listed by *Ebony* magazine as one of "Fifty Most Important Women in the Past Fifty Years"; publishes "Whose 'Boy' Is This?" on Clarence Thomas in *African American Women Speak Out* (Geneva Smitherman, ed.); completed first draft of autobiography.

1997   *On Being Female, Black, and Free* published by University of Tennessee; reads poetry at Atlanta Arts Festival in July; Margaret Walker Alexander Research Center moves into remodeled Ayers Hall at JSU.

1998   Honored at Zora Neale Hurston International Festival, Eatonville, Florida, in January; reads poetry and is honored at George Moses Horton Society at UNC in April; is diagnosed with cancer in June and undergoes radiation treatment, decides against surgery; receives Major Arts Achievement award in Jackson, Mississippi, in July; inducted into the African American Literary Hall of Fame at the Gwendolyn Brooks Writers Conference in October; dies in Chicago at home of oldest daughter, 30 November; funeral held in Jackson on 4 December.

Conversations with Margaret Walker

Margaret Walker and Nikki Giovanni: Two Women, Two Views

Nikki Giovanni / 1972

Excerpted from *A Poetic Equation: Conversations between Nikki Giovanni and Margaret Walker.* Washington, D.C.: Howard University Press, 1974. Reprinted by permission of Nikki Giovanni.

MW: You know, Nikki, you and I belong to a mutual admiration society. I know a lot of people who think you are a brazen hussy. I happen to like you—hussy and all!

NG: I'll tell you this. I will tell you a difference between us. I grew up in a world that said the exception is the exception. You grew up in a world that said the exception is the rule.

MW: The exception *proves* the rule is what I say.

NG: O.K., let me explain what I mean. If *you* met two white people who were nice you'd say there were some of them worth saving. If *I* met two white people that were nice, I'd say, Hmm, too bad when we have to act against them to save ourselves. That's what I mean. To me an exception is an exception.

MW: That *is* a very great difference between us. There may be something vacillatory about my position, and I hate vacillation, I don't like it at all. I like honesty. I like what *you* represent. I couldn't think of white people that way though, because I really genuinely believe in people everywhere. I know what the struggle of black people has been. I'm black, and I have been through some terrible stuff. Stuff that I cannot bear repeating because it is too painful, you understand? . . . The things that I see happening to black people across the country are just tearing me apart.

Before I die I want to make a certain statement about what our life is like here, but I want to add something that's not just about black people. I believe deeply in a common humanity. The black man belongs to the family of man. One part of that family is out of control—like a virus or cancer—and that is the white man. He and his technological society are bent on destroying the world. Everywhere the white man has gone with his empire, he has destroyed people, races, societies, cultures, and in the course of it, has sterilized him-

3

self. He is completely the mechanical man: without heart, without soul. He is the Tin Man of *The Wizard of Oz.*

But I *don't* believe that all the white people in the world are no good. There are some people of good will. I don't know what this country as a whole feels except what I see in the political elections, and I see the country going fascist. We have been going that route a long, long time. A lot of things the country has done from its inception were fascist. But now, now I think we are in the face of a terrible fascist dictatorship.

Now the difference between us, is well—I cannot exclude even the evil man from this business of common humanity.

NG: Well, I'm pleased that I know you, because I think that's a *rare* position. . . .

MW: I may have thought in my generation that I was an emancipated person because I didn't think the way my mother thought. And you don't think the way your mother's generation thought, because I'm of her generation and I say the answer to life is not always in getting what I want. When you talk about what you want, you mean what you want for your child.

NG: Yes, and for myself.

MW: And for yourself. The answer is that happiness is not a thing that comes just by getting everything you want.

NG: I never said that, Margaret.

MW: What do you mean by knowing what you want?

NG: The first thing you have to be concerned with is your own functional existence. You cannot throw your life away, and if there's anything that I would want for my child, I would want him to value his life. That is what I am trying in my own little screwed-up way to do, to teach him to value his own feelings so that if he had to decide whether or not he was going to fight some dumb-ass war, he would say, "You've got to be kidding—"

MW: Would you stop a minute?

NG: Go on.

MW: I don't understand how you proceeded and arrived at the conclusions that you did from the premise you made. You know what you said? You said something about him thinking about his feelings and your thinking about your feelings so that he will know not to go to war. Those are not the same. How do you come to a conclusion like this? I want to ask you. You are saying *my* feelings, *his* feeling—what about other people's feelings?

NG: What about them?

MW: You don't give a damn? I do and I figure you've got to think about other people as much as yourself.

NG: Don't. I mean, I resent the level of this conversation. I think it is unfair to say that because I would place my feelings—

MW: Above everything else.

NG: Wait, Margaret, can I finish my own sentence?

MW: *(impatiently)* Yes, I'm waiting.

NG: That I would place my feelings into perspective—

MW: That's another thing.

NG: You never gave me a chance because you kept screaming at me.

MW: I'm sorry.

NG: The first thing I think anybody has to do is to think about what they want as they face a situation. Now, my son—

MW: *(opens her mouth as if to say something)*

NG: Wait, wait, wait. My son may want to go to war and that will be his choice. What I don't want, and I'm just using that as an example, Margaret, which you well know, to say that he will have to make up his mind what he thinks is best for him. I would try to train him to always think of how he feels himself so that he will not blindly follow even me, which is one thing I am proud of about the three years Tommy has been on earth: he does not blindly obey me and I am pleased with that.

MW: *(quickly)* Wait a minute, Nikki, wait a minute, hold it, just one second—stick a pin in it. It is one thing to develop a child to be self-reliant and an entirely different thing to teach him that selfishness is the highest law of life.

NG: I didn't say that!

MW: When you think only of yourself and you teach your child to respect only his feelings you are teaching him selfishness.

NG: I see nothing wrong with selfishness.

MW: Well, now, there are degrees of selfishness. I used to hear someone talk about the higher art of selfishness. There are certain times, yes, when you need to be selfish. But I contend that you cannot base a life—yours, your son's, or anyone else's—purely on one's personal wishes, wants, and desires.

NG: Well, if we're going to pursue this—

MW: And I think this is important. You see, this business of permissiveness—and we are facing this in the schools today—this is the problem that we have, and in an age of revolution this is a danger. A danger because we have been restricted so long, been repressed and oppressed and will not continue to be suppressed and we misunderstand the meaning of true freedom. We misunderstand the meaning of true personal freedom and we take it to such an extreme that the child coming into the classroom cannot be handled by another soul—only his mother, and sometimes not even his mother can do anything with him, and what happens is this: the mother comes and says I don't want you doing such and such to my child. I want my child to speak his own mind. I want my child to have the right to think the way he wants to think. I want my child to believe what he wants to believe. I want my child to be free and to act in any way he wants to act. Do you see where we're going there? Do you understand what is happening to us?

NG: That is corrupt logic you're presenting to me.

MW: *(challengingly)* Corrupt logic? Well, you correct the logic that I have and show me what will happen to a child who is undisciplined, who believes that he has the right to do anything he feels like doing and his mother tells him the most important thing is to fulfill his personal wishes. You tell me what you mean by that. Qualify it or modify it and tell me where that leads.

NG: O.K., I'm going to try. I'll stick with my example because maybe I can make sense out of it. I want my son to test things against himself. In order to be free, one must be able to take care of oneself as best one can. That doesn't say that everybody goes out and starts a little Mom and Pop Goodness Store. But one must function in this society with the people with whom one finds oneself. I want my son, Thomas, particularly my son, Thomas, and I think every child, to be able to function wherever he may be.

MW: When you say "function," what do you mean?

NG: I mean—that's why I hate intellectual discussions. I mean that wherever he goes I want him to feel that he is still Thomas Giovanni. That he comes from someplace and is going someplace.

MW: That's important, that's very important.

NG: That he is competent to judge and make decisions.

MW: That is right, all of that is right.

NG: Now, in my opinion—to try to make it intellectual or something—in my opinion one of the things he needs is familiarity with skills and I would be in error as a mother if I did not insist that he acquire them.

MW: And learning to read is one.

NG: Wait, wait, wait.

MW: But as soon as I join an issue, you see—

NG: I'm just trying to deal with things one at a time as you keep bringing them up.

MW: All right.

NG: In terms of discipline, he must know that in order to be free, he will have to be able to make decisions.

MW: That is not the logical conclusion. Freedom and decision, Nikki, those are not analogous.

NG: *(change in tone and said aggressively)* You know, niggers are not free because they could not decide what to do when the war was over!

MW: Is that the reason?

NG: That's three-fourths of it. They had no skills with which to accomplish anything.

MW: But, here again, we're dealing with the kind of reasoning that differs from generation to generation. And I am not criticizing yours anymore than I would accept criticism of mine.

NG: How many people, how many young men in Jackson are dead today because they couldn't make a decision about the damned war, because they had no skills, because they had no alternatives to saying, O.K., I'll join the Army?

MW: Which war are you talking about—Vietnam?

NG: All of them, because it's stupid for a black man to have been in any of America's wars except the Civil War and they never completed what *that* began. After shooting on those Southerners they should have turned on those Northerners and then just fought it all out. But that's not what we have. What we have is a situation of black people, especially black men, particularly those who don't have the skills to make judgments, to make decisions about their own lives and their own life-styles. They are a dependent people.

MW: Whom do you blame for this?

NG: I'm not blaming anybody.

MW: Where is the trouble, then?

NG: The trouble is that they must learn—

MW: Where? Learn where? Their mamas should teach 'em? You're saying their mothers didn't teach 'em.

NG: Their mothers gave them what they had; their mothers didn't have much.

MW: Well, I disagree with you. I disagree with you on several grounds. I go back to what I consider the strength in that black woman way before the Civil War when she was just a slave. And I go back to the strength of what I think was in that black soldier who fought in the Civil War and what he tried to do after the war. I do not blame what happened to him on his basic inability to decide.

NG: I do.

MW: Then I think what you are saying is that the society, that the economy and the politics and the labor problem, the government, none of these things are determinants.

NG: Of course they are determinants, don't don't—

MW: But I'm saying this, those black people who lived a hundred and fifty or a hundred years ago faced odds they could not overcome. In the Reconstruction period, look at the men who went from these various Southern states into government halls—what did they face? When you talk about what they should have done, how many of them died doing just what you said they should have done? A lot of them died shooting it out; a lot of black people were killed in that period. Why? Because the Civil War was not over when Lee surrendered. The Southern whites turned on those blacks with everything, and that's why they intimidated them away from the polls with guns. Lynching was the law. And what was the decision the black man might have been able to make against that? How could he decide not to be lynched? How could he decide not to be killed?

In terms of labor, he actually tried to do a lot of things. He tried to go West; he was in the cowboy business, he was out there squatting on the land and homesteading just like everybody else. He struggled against the odds of poverty and ignorance just like everybody else. He wasn't just a weakling and namby-pamby who couldn't make any decisions. That's wrong, and when you say it you have to go back and think about what you're saying because that was not entirely true. Our situation today is not wholly of our own making. And it hasn't been. Black people, you must remember, came in chains, the majority of us. Some did not come in chains, but they did very little for those who were in chains. And yet the Abolitionists were not all white. The Abolitionists were black too. There was an anti-slavery struggle that black people belonged to. Don't underestimate us and don't just sell us down the road and say we didn't do anything because we did.

NG: Now, Margaret—

MW: You know that. You know too that what happened in Africa wasn't all white or all black. It was a human situation. Blacks in tribal wars. Whites buying and selling and killing—all that was a part of it. History is not just one solid page of black and white. Teaching your child how to come up in the society is your prerogative. But don't blame the black man back in the

Civil War years even for being indecisive. He had as much brains as the next fellow. He was a pawn in the social struggle and always remember that. I'm not trying to teach again; I sound like the teacher. I'm no Miss Teacher; but I sound like Miss Teacher.

But, I want to get back to this business of the child, because I think, Nikki, what happens to us as mothers is very important. Yes, it's extremely important. You have a wonderful child. You have a beautiful baby and you want to do everything you can for that child so that when he grows up he can face the world and he can be a man, and he can make decisions. But you want to be careful in your own logic that you do not confuse your affection and your love and your devotion for this child and your desire to do what is right for him in such a way that he becomes an anti-social, anti-people person.

How do I bring him up so that he remains lovable and desirable? How do I raise him so that he can insulate himself? That's what you want, you want him insulated against the hurts that even *you* have experienced. You want him able to stand on his own feet, and the last thing in the world that's important is being able to make a living, because you figure his instincts are going to help him find out a way to make money. That's not the important thing. You want the personality of your child developed the best way you possibly can.

We as black people today, and especially in this generation, are in an age that threatens to be an age of anarchy. Because we have undergone such tyranny the danger is great of our going to an extreme—an extreme of anarchy in order to resolve and dissolve the tyranny. And when you talk about decision-making—control is what I'm talking about, how much control, because you see we've had too much control and you are afraid of that. You don't want too much control, but I say there's got to be some.

NG: Do I get a chance? I resent the whole emotional level of this discussion.

MW: Emotional level! Well, now, do you want to put it on another level? You say you can't stand intellectual stuff. You don't want to get into something intellectual. Now you are resentful of the emotional thing. Just which level do you want to put this on?

NG: *(sighs and smiles)* I'm a woman, I can change my mind.

MW: You're a woman is right. So am I and—

NG: And I think it's unfair for you to sit here—

MW: And lecture you in this fashion.

NG: No, I don't mind your lecturing me, you've earned that right. But I think it's unfair to say that I have no respect for the Civil War story; that's not what I'm saying.

MW: *(in a quieter and almost motherly tone)* Well, I didn't say that, honey. I think you have a lot of respect, but you did say this: The trouble was that they didn't know what to do.

NG: I said that part of it was that they did not.

MW: What do you think they should have done?

NG: No, see, I cannot—I mean I can tell you what I think they should have done because—

MW: But then you were—

NG: *(voice rises)* Can I tell you what I think they should have done?

MW: *(quietly)* Yes.

NG: When they passed a law that said that black men must turn in their weapons, they should have fought.

MW: They shouldn't have turned them in?

NG: No, they shouldn't have.

MW: *(sarcastically)* They could have killed 'em off like that.

NG: You asked what I thought should happen. Did I answer it? Now I didn't rhetorize behind what you said with satirical remarks.

MW: Now, how am I making satirical remarks? I apologize.

NG: That did not happen and I do not have any less respect for the decisions made. The decisions made now must be used to—

MW: That's happened. Now, we're in another day.

NG: In another day. The young men coming back from Vietnam, which is a war that I have deplored, are not turning in their weapons!

MW: They're not going to have the same attitude they did after World War I, the Civil War—

NG: Not even Korea. The men come back here—Somebody is shooting cops all over this country, which I'm sure you've read about.

MW: I've been watching it, looking at it.

NG: But the thing that I'm saying is that today, and this is what I'm trying to impress upon you—at least give me the respect for my viewpoint—

MW: I want to, I want to—

NG: Without being nasty about it.

MW: *(good-heartedly)* Well, now wait a minute, wait a minute. I am wholly in respect of your viewpoint, and if I am nasty that's my disposition.

NG: I know you, Margaret, I'm not going to let you do that to me. What I'm trying to say is that today we must draw upon all the strengths.

MW: That's the word—the strengths, not the weaknesses.

NG: I didn't say it was a weakness. I said that there was an inability to make decisions.

MW: That was weak, wasn't it?

NG: No, if you don't have the skills to make a decision, if you don't feel you are enough of a person to make a decision, you will not make decisions. For example, I can't believe that Mark Essex climbed up on top of that Howard Johnson's Motel because he hated.[1] I cannot believe that, and his mother won't say that. She said, "My son was tired."

MW: Of all the trouble.

NG: His mother said, "My son will be a man." If *my* son, whom I love dearly and would hate the thought of having any bullet in him, let alone a hundred, decided to climb atop a building, I want to have that much strength to know that I reared him to be a man. That was Mark's decision. His mother did not tell him, "Son, go climb up there and shoot some folk." He made a decision and she backed him afterwards and that's the kind of woman I hope I am. With any man in my life.

MW: Wait a minute. There's some confusion here.

NG: There's no confusion to me.

MW: No, there's some confusion. In my mind I'm confused, if you're not. I feel this way. Again, there is a great difference, a gulf, between our ages and minds; between the thirties and the sixties. I said five years ago, the very week that Martin Luther King, Jr., was killed, that Vietnam is an immoral war and I'd rather see my son go to jail than fight in that war.

NG: But you couldn't make that decision for Siggy.[2]

MW: I didn't. To my consternation, he volunteered for the marines and I thank God he got home. This is the thing that I felt: While my son was away, I was sick unto death. A tick was in my face. I just looked something frightful and I was so nervous I couldn't sleep more than four hours a night. I made napkins, I made flowers, I embroidered, I couldn't sleep at night. I would wake up hearing him say, "This time I'm dead, Mama, I know I'm dead." I'd see him down in marshy places—he was actually in those places. He was actually saying that. He told me that one time he saw a man point a gun at

[1] In January of 1973 Mark Essex climbed upon a rooftop of a Howard Johnson Motel in New Orleans, Louisiana, and fired his gun at people below. There were seven killed and twenty-one wounded. However there is speculation as to the number shot by Essex, and the number shot by the police in their pursuance of him.

[2] Margaret Walker's son, Siggy Alexander.

him and he ducked and felt the heat as the bullet went by. That close. Another time three buddies were sitting down on the ground and he looks at this buddy and he looks at that buddy, and when he looks at the third buddy he sees him blown to pieces ten feet in front of him. I haven't begun to tell it—the horror, the horrendous experience. And now I realize—and it's not just my weakness—I had this great fear that if my son got in a battle he would be killed. My son got into plenty of battles and he didn't get killed. That's wonderful.

But I'd love to stop and analyze something you said and see if I understand it correctly. I said this is the difference, the great distinction between us. You know how I feel about that boy Essex? I don't feel that he was a great hero at all. Getting up there and killing all of those people and being riddled. He might have been in *your* estimation a man.

NG: Yes.

MW: I also feel that the boy was in great turmoil and emotionally sick of the stuff he had seen. And I think this: I'm not so sure that that is a sign of strength. I am not so sure. Now, I don't believe everything I read in the papers about how filthy his room was and all the dirty words and all the hate that he had written on the walls there. But I do know that every black man who comes back from Vietnam is inoculated with a virus of hate for the white man in this country. I know he has it. I don't know that that's necessarily great spiritual strength, to have deep hatred and feel that the only thing he can do is kill some of these "honkies." I am not so sure that it is, I am not so sure.

NG: I respect Essex.

MW: I think that any time a person is so completely, completely disjointed from the world in which he lives that he feels the only way out for him is to shoot and kill, there is not only something wrong with the society but there has to be something wrong with him, too.

NG: May I say something about Nikki Giovanni?

MW: Yes.

NG: O.K. I have a habit; I'm twenty-nine years old now so it's pretty much ingrained in me. I generally look at things as a choice, as it's either-or, you know? That I am pro-abortion because for one thing I hate child abuse.

MW: That's—

NG: Wait—I'm just trying to say something about my own logical faculties.

MW: I'm not following you.

NG: You're not following me, O.K. I look at things in terms of what would happen "if," and I look for the widest possible freedom for the individual to make a decision, Essex, I think, had limited choices to begin with. From what I can understand about the young man, he seemed to be very sensitive, he seemed to have come from a wonderful family. He dropped out of college and enlisted in the navy. He was less than honorably discharged. He came out and identified what bothered him. What he *could* have done is beat his wife, if he had one.

MW: Which would have been much more immoral and cruel and ugly.

NG: Because he wasn't mad at his wife. He could have had a bunch of kids, that he—

MW: Couldn't feed.

NG: Not only couldn't feed, but hated. He could have become a fearful young man in his community. He could have been one of those guys that every Friday night has to go down and kill a nigger.

MW: Are they the only choices he had, Nikki?

NG: No, I'm not saying that, Margaret. I'm just saying what I looked at was a young man that could have been all those things we've seen so many times before with *us* absorbing his anger. Essex made a decision. He made a decision and he carried it through and on that level, which is why I'm saying that I have ultimate respect for him. Black people today, young black people—my generation if you want to call it—are saying that if you want to play Nazi, we will not play Jew. And I think that the events that we're seeing are possibly going to make the whole community much more repressed. For we have put the world on notice that we are not going to be lined up and I think that that is very significant because I don't think America gives a damn about lining us up. They would like to. We have said, you can try, but we are fighting back. And our young men are in the forefront of this battle.

MW: I don't believe individual defiant acts like these will make for the revolution you want.

NG: No, don't ever misunderstand me and use of the term "revolution." I could never believe that having an organization was going to cause a revolution. America is known for absorbing and infiltrating. One thing the papers keep saying about this so-called Black Liberation Army is that the Establishment can't infiltrate it, and, you know, they can't infiltrate it because it does not exist. There is really no such thing as a Black Liberation Army. There are people they have trained to be their killers who are now back to kill them.

MW: I admire your generation. I know that I could not at all be the same as your generation. I wouldn't want to be. I lived and came of age in a time that I thought was exciting. It certainly wasn't as highly tensioned as the time we're living in now.

But, I think both of us have this concern, what is going to happen to our people in this country? I don't know that any of us can come up with a solution, just as we are never able completely to state all the ramifications of the problem. But, it seems to me that if we could formulate our different ideologies to come up with our different points of view and just stand them up there and stack 'em up where we could look at them, that we would discover that the whole racial picture has not only changed amazingly in the last thirty years but that our technological society has given it a completely different twist. My feeling for Essex is one of great sympathy and, I would hope, for understanding, but I also feel a great deal of pity for what society has done to that young man. I don't feel his life is wasted. I just have never believed that solutions come in isolated, individual packages. Roles may. The role-playing may be individual, but the solutions are not. Maybe he's part of the solution. Maybe the answer is in the violent outbursts and maybe in this racial confrontation and conflict. Well, now, how otherwise would you respect his action? You figure, well at least he made a decision, he was able to stand up to the decision, he carried it out and you respect him for that.

NG: If that young man had died in Vietnam, with the waste, with the same hundred bullets in him for having shot seven Vietnamese—

MW: Nobody would think anything about it.

NG: We would not be discussing it. He would still be dead. He made a statement. He made a decision and he made a statement. Let me put it another way. Someone once said that history was the biography of great men. I don't believe that. And, on the other hand, history is not just a chronicle of events, either.

MW: It's people.

NG: People are a part of it.

MW: Michael Harper says history is your own heartbeat, whereas Jay Wright says it's death.[3] Death is history.

NG: I can't believe that. What I have seen and the way I read history—and we all read history to suit ourselves—is that certain individuals have taken certain tasks upon themselves. In some cases, they were successful, in some cases, unsuccessful in their own terms, but they have helped to shape the way people think.

---

[3] Two black poets.

For example, we were speaking of Thurgood Marshall before we started taping. Who would have thought when that young man was a lawyer coming out of Howard, taking school desegregation cases, that he would one day sit on the Supreme Court; that he would have won his case and received the accolade he did? And just as Thurgood has a place in history, so does Essex. Because Thurgood made a decision to fight that way, you understand what I'm saying?

MW: I understand you.

NG: And Essex made a decision to fight his way.

MW: I understand that.

NG: And to me we can not take away either. And there are people, as you well know, who would take away what Thurgood did. There are people who would take away what Martin Luther King did. There are people who would take away what Malcolm X did. And I think that we, as people who try to give voice or meaning to some of these actions, must know that we must put them all together to make a history of the people. And what I fear today, what I deeply fear today, is that if we do not have what you call these isolated incidents, we as a people would be in even more serious trouble. It is not the trouble of lynching the nigger today that we went through in the 1890s up to World War I. It is not the urban decay that we went through after that war and going into World War II. It is not just the Depression, it is not just sending some black people over to Korea or something. We're talking about the possibility of annihilating people. It's always been on that level, you know. Some people have always felt that there was a good chance that we would be annihilated.

MW: I never have believed it's going to come off.

NG: I don't believe it and I think that history will bear that out, that you cannot wipe out a people. A blood line is a very strong thing. But I believe that it is difficult for anyone, any group, to exist with ten or twelve million of its members stacked up. One of the reasons I think war in the Middle East continues is that the Jews are trying to show the world that they have balls. Had they stood up in Germany against the Germans, who were killing them, the way they now stand up against the Arabs, with whom they possibly—as far as I read—could have made peace, the world would be different.

What we know is that American blacks have no place to go. We speak of Africa, we speak of getting out. Some of us will, most of us will not. Most of us will live and die here and I say that I have ultimate respect for people who are making decisions and saying you are on notice, we will fight back.

Because a war has been going on. The Panthers were wiped out. Those were nice young men, by any standard. They were not hurting anybody. Mark Clark and Fred Hampton were in bed when the police came in to shoot them.[4] You understand what I mean? They were just young men trying to respond to a problem. They can infiltrate the Panthers and they did, because they were organized, they put on their berets and their jackets, they said we are Panthers and this is our program. They cannot do anything with those Vietnam veterans except pray for them.

MW: I said the other day I really don't believe that the government is going to bring 'em back in here en masse. I don't believe they'd dare.

NG: Well, they claim that there's only six hundred POWs. They can bring back 600 men if they can get them on dope, which is what they've been trying to do—Vietnam is the second Opium War. You know, I would not want Essex to have been my son, but if he had been, I would pray that I carried myself as well as his mother has.

MW: Well, I think the woman acted with dignity.

NG: And I think that she shows an understanding of her son and the times in which he lived. And all she could say was if this would help someone to understand the terrible burdens that we all must carry, that perhaps it would not have been in vain.

MW: That's all very well, but I am not willing for the benefit of the young black who's coming along and who faces this terrible kind of death every day, I'm not willing to set up a heroic example of violence in any form.

NG: But see—that is a real disagreement. That is a real disagreement.

MW: Between us, yes.

NG: *(intensely)* Yes, indeed, because we have been subject to some of the most horrendous violence. We find that love is not the opposite of violence. Love does not stop violence. Nonviolence is not the antithesis of violence. It does not stop violence.

MW: And love is not the opposite of hate?

NG: No.

MW: What, then, would you say is the antithesis of nonviolence and what's the antithesis of love?

NG: The antithesis of love is indifference.

MW: Well, then, you and I don't agree on anything.

NG: And I think that the answer to violence is a response.

---

[4] Black Panthers killed by police in Chicago on December 4, 1969.

MW: A violent response to violence?

NG: One must respond.

MW: But, baby, you're not going to tell me that violence is the opposite of violence, are you?

NG: No, I'm not.

MW: Our reasoning process just don't go the same way.

NG: That's a word game. Don't misunderstand what I mean. Because that's a word game that *we're* playing. *(voice sharpens)* I know that if you stand in here beating the living shit out of me that the only way that I can stop you is to beat you back. Frederick Douglass said it much more eloquently—even if I lose, I have hurt you. Even if I lose, you will think twice.

That boy Frazier, poor Frazier, stood there and won that fight from Ali and Ali beat him down and put him in the hospital for two months and by the time he got to Foreman, he had to think twice before Foreman floored him. You fight and you fight. Maybe if someone were to come in this door right now and my son would be there, you understand, and I would be protecting him maybe I would get hurt. Maybe I wouldn't be able to protect him completely, but I would do enough damage so that the next time when he had to go up against them they're a little bit weaker. And that's the whole situation of blacks against whites, because if I am reading the situation right, now we are admitting maybe we cannot win. But goddamn, if you are going to drag us like bleeding sheep we are not going to go out loving you. It won't happen, those days are *over!* They have had our love and they didn't know what to do with it.

MW: I think people misunderstand this whole business of what my generation felt and feels about hatred and violence and love and nonviolence. My integrity is violated by my own hate, by my own bitterness, and by my own violence. It isn't what I do to the other fellow that hurts me so much as what I do to myself when I do something to the other fellow.

NG: Well, *I* can take that burden. I can take that weight.

MW: Well, I don't want it.

NG: I'll take it for you!

MW: I'm not going to teach my child that the only way you can answer tyranny is with hatred and violence. . . .

NG: I'm not going to disagree, but I'm going to say that if I were attacked, I would defend myself, and if you were going to sit here and say, "Well, Nikki, you were violent," I'm going to say, right! . . . I said the responses to the police and you said that's violence and I said if that's violence, fine. I'm not going to debate what to call it. . . .

MW: Where do you think all the killings and the hatred is going to go and how much of it has got to come off before it's all over?

NG: I will not accept a combination of killing and hatred. I say again, I don't think that Essex was hate-ridden. Because I think if he had been hate-ridden, he would have gone in there and shot his mama and daddy.

MW: He sure as hell wasn't love-ridden. . . .

MW: I think that when all the fighting and killing are done there's got to be some kind of reconciliation on some kind of basis other than a gun. I think there's got to be some kind of understanding.

NG: I am existential enough to say we cannot have reconciliation until *all* the killing is done.

MW: That's why we're very different.

Poetry, History, and Humanism: An Interview with Margaret Walker

Charles H. Rowell / 1973

From *Black World* 25:2 (1975): 4–17. Reprinted by permission of Charles H. Rowell.

CR: At the Second Annual Black Poetry Festival at Southern University (May, 1973),[1] you read your first published poem, "Daydream," which was later entitled "I Want to Write." It was published during the Thirties in *Crisis*.[2] The poem has, in my opinion, all of the beauty and grandeur of your later poetry in *For My People* and *Prophets for a New Day*. In fact, I think it is one of your most beautiful poems. When did you first start writing?

MW: I date the publication of that poem to be 1934, so I must have written it a year or two before then. But I actually began writing poetry when I was 12 or 13 years old. I wrote prose before then. My earliest poetry, I believe, must have been written in the late Twenties.

CR: What would you say is the most important literary influence on you during your early writing career?

MW: There were many influences. When I look back upon it, the earliest influences were in my home—my father, as a minister, and my mother, as a music teacher. My father had many books, and my mother read poetry to me when I was a child. My mother read such diverse poetry as that of Paul Laurence Dunbar and John Whittier's "Snowbound." My father taught us bits of doggerel. I memorized pieces from the Bible and from Shakespeare. But when I think back on it, I remember I read Langston Hughes' poetry when I was about 11 or 12 years old. The president of the college gave my mother and father a little brochure of the Four Lincoln Poets. That was the first time I had ever heard of the Harlem Renaissance poets. Langston Hughes was in that little brochure. In 1927, when I was about twelve, my father and mother brought home from Chicago, where they had been studying at Northwestern, a copy of Countee Cullen's *Copper Sun*. They gave it to my sister and gave me Edgar Guest's poetry. I was disgusted. I really felt they should have given me Countee Cullen's book, but my sister held on to it, and through the years when I would try to claim the book, she would remind me it was

her book. We memorized those poems. We read Countee Cullen. In the late
Twenties, I was actually reading the Harlem Renaissance poets. They greatly
influenced me, particularly Langston Hughes. I think Langston's poetry and
his life have influenced me remarkably from the time I was a child. I saw him
first when I was about 16 years old and halfway through college. He read my
poetry and encouraged me to write. So you see, my earliest influences include
Black poetry.

CR: Both *Jubilee* and *For My People* are grounded in the Black folk tradition: Black oratory, folk heroes, folk beliefs, music, *etc.* In fact, in *How I
Wrote Jubilee* you said, "I always intended *Jubilee* to be a folk novel based
on folk material, folk sayings, folk beliefs, folkways." If you had to discuss
the conscious or unconscious influences of the folk tradition on your work,
how much would you say you owe, so to speak, to it?

MW: A great deal. I never shall forget my first realization that I had this
quality in my own work. I had read people like Zora Neale Hurston in the
Twenties and the Thirties. I read Zora Neale Hurston's *Jonah's Gourd Vine*
before I went off to Northwestern. In later years I read everything she had
written. I was tremendously impressed with her grasp of folk material. A
number of books I read used the folk tradition. I remember a book by a
Mississippi writer that was a pure folk novel. I liked it very much. I always
liked Dunbar's dialect poems. I liked all of the poetry that Langston wrote
using the themes and idioms of the blues, and the street tradition—the folk
material from the streets. I read Sterling Brown. Even stories I heard from
my grandmother and folk tales I read influenced me. I was always taken by
the folk tradition. When I was in school, I don't suppose it was encouraged
by my white teachers in those two years at Northwestern. But when I went
out to Iowa almost accidentally Paul Engle reminded me of it and struck that
vein again. It was he who first encouraged me to use the ballad form in my
poetry. He and I fussed all the time, and he irritated me into writing, but that
I owe to him. I began writing ballads out in Iowa. I had put a number of folk
things down in little tales of vignettes, but I had not yet really translated them
into poetry. And there in Iowa in the late Thirties I began to write a great
deal in the folk tradition. I realized that *Jubilee* needed to be a folk story. I
read the thesis of Dr. Nick Aaron Ford, his doctoral thesis in the library at
the University of Iowa.[3] I suppose he did that in the Forties. I went back to
Iowa in the Sixties and just almost unconsciously—I don't think it was accidentally—I looked up Nick Aaron Ford's thesis. He said that the folk tradi-

tion in my poetry was one of the strongest points I had and that if I would develop that, I would make a mark with that folk tradition. Then I began to think of it in terms of almost everything I wrote. As you say, I have used the folk tradition in my poetry, but I was not too well aware of this in the Thirties. In the Thirties, I knew writers on the Writers' Project in Chicago, and for the first time I was writing not in isolation, but with other writers all around me—young Black and white writers on that project—and a form that I had always tried to develop suddenly stabilized itself then. I found my voice in what some people called the public statement poem or the long line of free verse, but what Stephen Vincent Benét described as the reflection of my growing up as the daughter of a minister and the granddaughter of preachers of the folk sermon.

CR: Eugene Redmond has described some of your poems in *For My People* as a celebration of Black people's strength, our stoicism.[4] In the title poem, for example, we are represented as a people of much strength. Do you agree with Redmond's comment on your poems?

MW: I agree with what a number of people have said. A great part of that poem just came out unconsciously—that is, the first part, but the last stanza, of course, is a conscious thing. The resolution is revolutionary. I do agree that it represents a kind of historical line—it gives a kind of panoramic picture of Black life.

CR: Is it a stoic picture of Black life?

MW: Yes. I think really "We Have Been Believers" does it better than "For My People." "We Have Been Believers" tells what we have come out of, what we have come to, how much we have done for other people and what we need. I think our strength—I say in there somewhere "out of our / strength have they wrung the necessities of a nation. / Our song has filled the twilight and our hope has / heralded the dawn." Do you remember that? That's in "We Have Been Believers."

CR: Am I accurate in assuming that the pronoun "I" in some of your poems in *For My People* is a communal "I" as opposed to the private or personal "I"?

MW: I think some of the poems are quite personal though they grow into a larger identity. They really begin with a very personal expression of my love for the South. "There were bizarre beginnings in old lands for the making of me," "my grandmothers," "I sing of slum scabs on city faces"—all of them began with the personal beauty, but they move out beyond the personal.

CR: When I read a poem like "Dark Blood," I, too, feel that I have "bizarre beginnings." I, too, feel that "Someday I shall go to the tropical lands of my birth."

MW: Yes, because you identify with the same things in the same way. The identity grows. It isn't just personal any longer, but it begins there.

CR: In stanza three of "For My People," you refer to "my playmates of Alabama backyards playing hair and Miss Choomby and company." Will you explain that reference?

MW: Yes. People always ask what does "Miss Choomby" mean. "Miss Choomby," my father said, is an African word. Miss Ann is the white lady, but Miss Choomby is the Black lady. My sister and I played Miss Choomby.

CR: Will you also comment on the symbolism and the meaning of the poem, "People of Unrest?"

MW: It is as if we were supine or sleeping or lying down. That is the way I felt Black people were largely in the Thirties. We were apathetic, we were not militant, we were not socially conscious, we were not altogether articulate. In the Sixties Black people became very conscious, very articulate, very militant, very vocal. And all of the consciousness grew, and it has grown and continues to grow in the Seventies. When I wrote that poem during the Thirties, there was no such consciousness among Black people.

CR: According to biographical sketches of you, and according to what you say in *How I Wrote* Jubilee, you lived for some time in New Orleans. Was the poem, "Molly Means," informed by your new Orleans experience?

MW: My grandmother told me that story of this witch or this woman who put a spell on this young girl who was just a bride. That is a part of my folk heritage and is not limited to a particular place as the way "Hoppy Toad" was told to me in North Carolina. Yes, New Orleans has all of the juju and the conjure tradition, but I never remembered much of it in New Orleans. I heard some there, but not very much.

CR: In his anthology of Black American literature, *Black Insights,* Dr. Nick Aaron Ford commented on your ode to the President of Jackson State, Dr. John Peoples. Dr. Ford asserts that it is not only a tribute to that Black educator, but "a tribute and a testimony to the dedicated administrators and teachers who have served without adequate salaries and recognition in more than a hundred Black colleges in the South, in states that more often than not were negligent and hostile instead of helpful and cooperative."

MW: I think that he is saying in part some of what I was doing, but the main thing is that it does go to these Black colleges, and it would include all of the students who came to learn, to know what it means to live in the South, to try to find out the meaning of life for Black people in this southern land. That's what I'm saying in the poem. This man is from the South, but he had gone to war and had come home without any hero's welcoming and his destiny was the destiny of his people.

CR: Am I accurate in describing the poems in *Prophets for a New Day*— all of them except "Ballad of the Hoppy Toad" and "Elegy" as your civil rights poems?

MW: I wrote these poems in the Sixties, and most of them were written in 1963, even the one, "Ballad of the Free, Bold Nat Turner by the Blood of God." I wrote that first stanza in 1943, I think, or even earlier, and I didn't finish that poem—that chorus that ties it together—until 1963. I wrote a number of those poems to Birmingham. Only one is in there. I wrote two poems to Medgar Evers and only one is in *Prophets for a New Day*. I wrote a great deal in 1963—and they are the civil rights poems.

CR: What was your main objective in your novel, *Jubilee?*

MW: I wanted to tell the story that my grandmother had told me, and to set the record straight where Black people are concerned in terms of the Civil War, of slavery, segregation and in Reconstruction. I believe that the role of the novelist can be, and largely is for me, the role of a historian. More people will read fiction than will history, and history is slanted just as fiction may seem to be. People will learn about a time and a place through a historical novel.

CR: What is your reaction to critics' assertion that *Jubilee* is the Black *Gone With the Wind?* Your book is far more humanistic than Margaret Mitchell's.

MW: I am sometimes amused at the comparison, though there are a number of things alike. I was writing about the backwoods of Georgia, and so was she. I was writing about the same period. So we were dealing with the same time and place, and her language, I find, is fairly accurate. The difference is, or the distortion is, that she does not distinguish between her culti-

vated whites and uncultivated whites. She has all the Blacks speaking one
way and all the whites another. That is wrong for the South. But I don't wish
to be compared with her turgid expository passages, which would have been
better left out of the book. Neither do I have the romantic nostalgia that she
has in her book. I am not a romanticist in *Jubilee.* It is a realistic book. You
are quite right—she was not concerned with humanistic and realistic standards. In some respects I suppose we could compare superficially the two
Margarets—Margaret Mitchell and Margaret Walker. But she was coming
out of the front door, and I was coming out of the back door.

CR: In your representation of Vyry and Randall Ware, did you intention-
ally try to show two different Black sensibilities during slavery in order to
give a balanced view of Black Americans during the period?
MW: They were different. A woman in the plantation tradition and a free
artisan just do not think the same way.

CR: When William Styron's *Confessions of Nat Turner* first appeared,
several Black scholars attacked the novel. What do you think of Styron's
novel?
MW: I think that what he does to a famous Black hero is unpardonable.
The racism in that book is the damage that he does to the hero for the Black
child. Nat Turner represents to Black people, first of all, a preacher, and that
is one of our heroes—you see, folk heroes; and then he represents a leader—a
slave leader and a man, an insurrectionist. He was fighting against all of the
tyranny and hatred and dominance of the society and of a feudal system that
was doomed. Styron maligned Nat Turner in every possible way. Styron attacks his personality. He attacks him as a folk hero. He deliberately destroys
the image of Nat Turner as a hero. That is unfortunate for Black people. That
is why the novel appears to Black people as a racist book and as an anathema.
Nat Turner is one of our great heroes.

CR: In your speech to the American Library Association, you spoke of
Black humanism as a tradition in Afro-American literature. Humanism is
also a recurring word in your speech to the National Urban League Conference in New Orleans.[5] Will you talk at length about what Black humanism
is?
MW: For the past five years, humanism, and Black humanism, particularly, has been my theme. I suppose in assessing my philosophy as an adult—
ever since I have been an adult—I considered myself a humanist—I suppose

various kinds of humanists in this sense. I grew up in the Judeo-Christian heritage with a minister for a father. My early years were largely influenced by this Christian philosophy. I have not ever completely gotten away from that, and I remember once that I did speak of myself as a Christian humanist. Then, of course, I went through a period of reading a great deal of materialistic philosophy, but I never could become a materialist. You understand? Today when we speak of academic humanists, I classify myself in that sense. I am a working humanist, you understand? I live, teach, work, write purely in what I consider the humanist and humanistic tradition. My concepts of humanism have broadened greatly in the past 20 to 25 years. There was a time when humanism had a tinge of materialism for me. In my speeches, frequently I do not emphasize Christian humanism because Christianity in America has taken such a terrible beating. The institutionalized church, the Christian Church, has become the tool of a very vicious racist society and system—a system that we see crumbling in front of our eyes. There are rumblings of the economic system crumbling. We have long since recognized that many other parts of our society have been in decay because we were not moving forward with the technological advancements of our time. I think it is more important now to emphasize humanism in a technological age than ever before, because it is only in terms of humanism that the society can redeem itself. Even the highest peaks of religious understanding must come in a humanistic understanding—the appreciation of every human being for his own spiritual way. I think of this in my own respect because I believe that mankind is only one race—the human race. There are many strands in the family of man—many races. The world has yet to learn to appreciate the deep reservoirs of humanism in all races, and particularly in the Black race.

CR: Since you gave your National Urban League speech, have you seen any efforts on the part of American educators at large to build a new educational system which will help liberate all peoples?

MW: With reference to revolutions in education in 1968, I went the next year in the spring to teach at Northwestern University. That was in the wake of the demand of the Black students for more recognition of the Black Experience in America. The demands of Black students spread all over this country—at Cornell, at Columbia, at Berkeley. Black students set in motion a kind of intellectual revolution in American education. This was different from the electronic revolution, and it was different from the revolution in methods of teaching. We have in the last 10 years observed all of these revolutions, and they are still going on.

CR: In your essay, "New Poets," which appeared in Phylon in 1950,[6] you made the following statement about Harlem Renaissance poets—"They lack social perspective and suffer from a kind of literary myopia." Later in the essay, however, you seem more positive toward Langston Hughes. Will you discuss the statement further?

MW: I feel this: that it is an interesting philosophy that Black people had of themselves and Langston accepted it and typified it in his novel, *Not Without Laughter.* At that time, there was a kind of euphoric belief among Blacks that we may have a tough time in life, that we may suffer, and that they may mistreat us, but we know how to live and laugh. We know how to laugh, we know how to enjoy life and nothing gets us down because we live with laughter. That was also the belief of Black and white people at the time when the Black person was a kind of exotic and peculiar or novel toy, a plaything from which whites got amusement. That was the attitude of the whites in the Twenties toward the genius of black writers. Now, Langston went through that period, but he grew out of it. In the Thirties, he developed a strong mode of social protest which was typical of the Thirties. In the Forties, he was a war poet. In the Fifties, he was fighting the witch-hunting and the race-baiting and the Cold War tactics of a post-war country. And in the Sixties, he, too, was ready to join the Civil Rights activities with the idea that Black is beautiful because he was one of the first to say it.

CR: What do you think of Dr. Alain Locke as a kind of leader of the Harlem Renaissance group?

MW: I thought Alain Locke was one of the brightest jewels in the Black crown. I knew him personally. As a philosopher, he was not only a trained scholarly man; he was discerning and understanding of what was authentic in the Black Experience. He understood the Twenties in its deepest meaning, and he encouraged this. He had a broad knowledge of Black culture.

CR: What do you think of the present day Black Arts Movement—*e.g.,* some of the leading writers, such as Don L. Lee,[7] Amiri Baraka and Sonia Sanchez?[8]

MW: I hesitate to make comments on either of them. I do not necessarily agree with all of their ideas. I think Baraka is the leader of Black revolutionary drama. He established that when he won the Obie Award with *Dutchman.* I think his early poetry was better than what he is doing now. As a philosopher, he may be ripening into something of very great value. I believe that his contributions to Black Drama in the Sixties will go down as permanent contributions, and they will be immortal. I will not say I understand all of the doctrines of his new religious sect and belief. The same thing is true with Don L. Lee. I think Don's early poetry shows that he is a brilliant poet. He has some poems that I regard as the work of pure genius. I am not sure that Don, as a critic, is on solid ground. I am not at all certain that I understand and accept what he is saying. With Sonia, I think she is a bright young woman. I have often compared myself to some of these young poets, like Nikki Giovanni, Alice Walker and Sonia Sanchez. They are near the age of my own daughter who has written some poetry, and I feel almost motherly toward all three of them. I recognize that I am a generation apart from them. Their boldness is not exactly what would have been boldness for me. I am sure people thought of me, when I was their age, as a bold new poet, but I am not at all certain that I had their kind of courage or even their kind of boldness. All of them are very talented young people.

CR: More poetry and drama seem to be coming out of the Black Arts Movement than fiction. What do you think accounts for this?

MW: The writing of fiction takes more time. Alice Walker is an excellent fiction writer. I don't agree with all of Alice's statements or some of her attitudes, but she is a good craftswoman in prose. I think Nikki Giovanni is developing a fine prose style. She certainly shows it in *Gemini.* I don't know too much of what Sonia Sanchez has done in fiction, but she is a good playwright, an excellent dramatist. Where fiction is concerned, the two most exciting people—I don't know if any have come up since them—are Ishmael Reed and Sam Greenlee. But fiction takes time and energy and care. You just don't throw it out. You can write a poem—dash off a poem—and you may not revise it and refine it, but you will have to work at fiction. Langston Hughes wrote some very fine fiction, and so did Arna Bontemps. Countee Cullen said he wrote one novel and he wouldn't write another because, he said, he was just too lazy. It took too much time. You have to sit at the typewriter for hours and hours, days on end, with no interruptions, week after week, month after month, to turn out a novel. It is hard work. People don't work at fiction because they don't have the time, or they don't take the time, or they are lazy. That's it.

CR: In your essay on Richard Wright in *New Letters,* you discussed some of your experiences with the Writers' Project of the WPA.[9] I think the Writers' Project is a part of our literary history which has not received adequate attention. Will you say some more about the Writers' Project—its objectives and impact on Black writers?

MW: Several things have been written about that project. I haven't seen Jerry Mangione's book, *The Dream and the Deal,* and neither have I read Studs Terkel, but both of them belong to that period. I read a book many years ago—I think in a woman's magazine—that was a novel about the Thirties. It talked briefly about that period. It was one of the few that captured the excitement and the mood of the Thirties when we were trying to pull out of the Depression. The government, for the first time, was underwriting the arts in this country. Not only creative writing, but music, the dance, drama, and the graphic or plastic arts—painting and sculpture. The government was paying thousands and thousands of amateur writers, as well as professional writers, down on their luck, writers who may have published a book or two, but could hardly eat. These people were put on these projects and were paid a subsistence check every two weeks that allowed them to eat and have a place to stay. This gave those of us who were writers some time to write. It was a wonderful time, and I was a very young writer then, but I remember the comradeship of the people on the project. It seems to me that was the wonderful thing. Also, the getting to know writers whom you never would have known otherwise. Out of that group came some very distinguished writers. I knew some people on the project in New Orleans and in New York, but I never felt that those projects were as exciting. Unlike the project in Chicago, those certainly weren't for me because I wasn't on them.

CR: Two colleagues of mine at Southern University studied with Langston Hughes at Atlanta University. They describe him as a man of his people. You knew him. In your opinion, did he impress you as such a man?

MW: Yes—a man who loved his people deeply, who was always proud of being a part of this segment of the human race. But Langston was a man who could love all people. He had a magnificent personality. He had a beautiful disposition. I never saw him angry. I knew him across 35 years, and he was one of the most wonderful persons I knew—in fact, I cannot think of anyone outside of my family who was more wonderful to me than Langston. He certainly influenced my whole writing career. I am sure that, added to him, would be W. E. B. Du Bois and Richard Wright. Those are the three famous writers who touched my life and had something to do with my writing.

CR: From your essay on Richard Wright in *New Letters,* one gets the impression that Wright was not a man of his people.

MW: He loved white. I think that Wright had a kind of hatred of himself as a Black man and that he could not conceive of a Black man in terms of greatness and heroism. If you look at his characters, you will discover that all of his Black men have more than one tragic flaw. They seem always to be lacking in some of the qualities you feel all human beings need. He is a naturalistic writer, and he shows Black men as corrupted by the society, but he never sees them in an idealistic or romantic way. He sees them always as deteriorating. He never visualizes a Black man as a great man. Almost always, his stories are full of violence, murder and vengeance, and frequently these Black men are killing women. They kill Black and white women. Think of the novels—I think there are four or five of them—*Native Son, Savage Holiday, The Outsider,* which I think is the most autobiographical of all, and *The Long Dream.* All of these show great hostility not only toward women, but toward Black men also. Can you think of one in which the Black man is a whole man?

CR: Another disturbing discovery I made from your essay on Wright is that he had no great respect for the literary achievements of Black people.

MW: Not even a man like Langston or a man like Du Bois whom he probably had read. I never heard him speak in the great tones about them as he would have a man like Hemingway, who is not my idea of a great writer at all, or a person like Faulkner, who he read and liked very much. He enjoyed all of the white literary greats that he associated with. But he never felt that any of the Black writers could do as much as he could do and certainly nobody could do it any better.

CR: Did he ever make disparaging comments about black writers?

MW: Personally, to me, about a man like Langston. Not about Arna. He had more respect for Arna than he had for Langston. Wright was two-faced about some people. Some were supposed to be his friends. He would do pieces of work with them and then talk about them. He was the "Great Black Father." Nobody else.

CR: You also said in the essay that you think it is safe to say, at least in fiction of the Twentieth Century in Black America, that we can mark or date everything before and after Richard Wright.

MW: That is a pretty strong statement, and I have been challenged on it. But I think I am still correct. I think that Wright became one of the most honest and brutal of our Black fiction writers. He has had a tremendous influence on both white and Black. I think it is the tough honesty—the power and the passion in the man. Yes, there have been a lot of very fine writers after Wright, and there were some very good ones before Wright, but I think he marks the line where we see this honesty, this toughness, this power and great passion.

CR: Having known Wright very well, you are in an excellent position to evaluate Constance Webb's biography of him.

MW: I think it is a phony book. I just don't understand that book at all. There are some definite errors in it. There are many inaccuracies. The thing that always grates on me is how she speaks of Richard Wright as "Dear Richard." Nobody called him Richard. That's the first thing. Anybody who knew Wright—was friendly with him—either called him Dick Wright or Wright. They didn't call him Richard. I don't know who called him Richard—maybe some of those white people in France did, but I just don't know. All I ever heard was Dick Wright. When I open the book and read "Richard this" and "Richard the other," I get very upset. Then she deliberately said in that book that he was murdered. I didn't know that she had any authority for that because she said she got a great deal of assistance from his widow. She claims to have known him very well, but I doubt she got much of that material from him. She probably saw his diaries, his journals, letters and files. His wife probably made those available to her, but I can't imagine anybody appreciating Webb's book as a great piece of biography.

CR: I have read your essay on Wright about three times, and the more I read it, the more I am convinced that you are, perhaps more than any other writer-scholar in this country, better prepared to write a definitive biography of Wright. Do you have any plans to write a book-length biography of him?

MW: I worked on that all last year on the fellowship from the National Endowment for the Humanities. But every time I would scrape and touch very sensitive sources and places, people would warn me and tell me don't touch it. It is sensitive material. I have a remarkable collection of interviews which I thought had the makings of a very wonderful book. I did about half of it, but everytime I sit down to it somebody tells me, "Don't do it." I have had a lot of encouragement from Black people to do it and a lot of discouragement from white people. It would be a purely Black book.

Notes

1. See Jerry W. Ward's "Southern/Black Poetry/Notes" in *Black World,* 23 (January, 1974): 83–85.

2. "I Want to Write" has been republished in *October Journey* (Detroit: Broadside Press, 1973), p. 30.

3. See Nick A. Ford, "The Negro Author's Use of Propaganda in Imaginative Literature" (Doctoral dissertation, University of Iowa, 1946).

4. See Eugene B. Redmond's "The Black American Epic: Its Roots, Its Writers," *The Black Scholar,* 2 (January, 1971), 15–22.

5. Margaret Walker, "The Humanistic Tradition of Afro-American Literature," *American Libraries,* 1 (October, 1970), 849–54; and "Religion, Poetry, and History: Foundations for a New Educational System," in Floyd B. Barbour's *The Black Seventies* (Boston: Porter Sargent, 1970), pp. 284–95.

6. Reprinted in Addison Gayle's *Black Expression* (New York: Weybright and Talley, 1969), pp. 89–100.

7. Haki Madhubuti.

8. Laila Mannan.

9. Reprinted in David Ray and Robert M. Farnsworth's *Richard Wright: Impressions and Perspectives* (Ann Arbor: University of Michigan Press, 1973), pp. 47–67.

Black Women and Oral History:
Margaret Walker Alexander
Marcia Greenlee / 1977

Excerpt from *Black Women: Oral History Project at the Schlesinger Library, Radcliffe College,* edited by Ruth Edmonds Hill. New Providence, N.J.: K. G. Saur, 1990. Reprinted by permission of the Schlesinger Library, Radcliffe Institute. Edited for publication in this volume.

MG: You mentioned books and music as two very important aspects of your childhood. Were there any other childhood memories that strike you, looking back?

MWA: Yes, my great love of nature. My grandmother and her mother, and I suppose all the members of her family, loved flowers and plants and trees and woods. And near our house, between the house where we lived in Birmingham and the school where my mother and father taught in my very early childhood, there was a stretch of woods. I remember seeing early spring flowers, violets and I remember dogwood in those woods. I remember summertime and my grandmother going in the woods and getting brush brooms to sweep the back yard. It seems to me that the most wonderful thing about that community was that although we were not considered a rural community—and this was on the outskirts of Birmingham, and not really in the country—it had the atmosphere of rural life. Although we had the conveniences, the modern conveniences of city life, running water and hot water and electricity and a telephone and everything else. There were dirt roads in that black community, there was no pavement except the little sidewalk we had in front of our house that my mother and father had put down. We went through woods to school and I remember that.

MG: And you've had occasion to recollect it and use it, haven't you?

MWA: I saw hickory nuts and hickory trees. I remember the pines. Although there was some snow in Birmingham when I was a child, it was not a regular occurrence. The winters were fairly severe, but I remember seeing snow there. I remember the seasons and the seasonal change with great pleasure. It's been one of the things that I'm sure formed a very important part of my life. The childhood games that we played, my sisters and our neighboring friends and all, tie in with that environment. When I was about nine years old I directed a play, a little operetta with neighborhood children, and we went to the woods and gathered flowers and greenery and things to decorate our so-called operetta stage. And I was the director. I was in it and I directed it any my sister Mercedes played all the music. We made Mama bring the piano out on the front porch. We had a big lawn and we used that as part of the stage, but we got saplings and brush and I had that idea even as young as nine years of age.

MG: That's amazing. Did the neighbors come?

MWA: Yes. We didn't think anybody would because there was a fish fry at the church next door at the same time and the people left the fish fry to come—

MG: Your family gave you a strong sense of security.

MWA: They did. To this day I contend that the only real security any individual has is in himself and in God. That if you do not have that sense of security, nothing else can give you security. Nothing else in the world to me offers that same sense of security.

MG: Are all your childhood memories so pleasant?

MWA: I had a difficult time with one of my early teachers who whipped me every day. When my Mama asked what did I do, she said I talked all the time, I talked too much. It wasn't that I was talking, I don't know what it was, but the woman, if there was such a thing as people, school teachers, being very twisted, teaching young children and hating them at the same time. The woman who was the janitor there told my mother that, if she didn't take me out of that school, that woman was going to nearly kill me. She said that woman just lived on me. I would ask to be excused and go to the bathroom and lock myself in just to get away from the woman.

MG: Do you think perhaps she resented a precocious child and didn't know how to handle you?

MWA: That might have been. I never understood what her problem was, why she resented me so. But my mother finally moved me from the school. My father went to the superintendent who told my mother and father to send me back to the school. They wouldn't do it. I remember her name, Minnie Jordan. She was so awful to me.

In any case, I went then to a school downtown in Birmingham and I had to ride the street car. I must have been seven or eight years of age. But when

I was 10, we moved to New Orleans. I can remember, as soon as books were issued I took the books home and read them.

MG: Which must have driven the teachers crazy.

MWA: I don't know. I wasn't aware that was anything unusual. But I didn't do that with the arithmetic books. I didn't like them. Nothing could ever make me like arithmetic and I think it was that I never had a good teacher in arithmetic. The teacher never made it imaginative, never made it interesting, and it never appealed to my imagination. And because of that, I think to this day I have no interest in counting and certainly not in money. Money is tied in my mind with numbers and arithmetic and counting. And even learning the multiplication tables, it didn't make sense to me that two plus two equals four and two times two equals four, when one plus one equals two, and one times one equals one. It didn't. And there was no way anybody could show the reasoning of it. If they could have shown me the logic—and my father said I never had a logical mind. I have never thought in terms of logic; everything is in terms of my imagination.

MG: Well, did your experiences with Mrs. Jordan sour you on education for a while or not?

MWA: No, it had no effect whatsoever. I forgot it as soon as she did it. She hit me and I forgot it. I was that way about whippings at home until I was much older. I seem to have been a child who attracted whippings. My mother whipped me a lot. And I can remember one day in my life when my mother, my grandmother and my father whipped me. And I couldn't understand why they whipped me. I walked home one day from school and it was five miles and it rained and it was muddy and I was late coming. It was almost dark, and my mother couldn't understand why I did it. I gave my car fare to another girl who had lost hers, and I went to my Aunt Rebecca to get the car fare for myself and she said she didn't have it. I knew she had it but she didn't give it to me, but then I decided to walk. I had part of my car fare in my hands, but I had given part of it away. And I couldn't understand why that deserved a whipping. But I was grown before I could understand how worried my mother must have been. I met her in the street. She was standing in the street with a switch in her hands and she was crying. She had alarmed the neighborhood. Imagine worrying about where a little eight-year-old girl could be at five o'clock in the afternoon. And nobody knew.

MG: Were there any teachers you had during this early period, before college, that really provoked you, stimulated your intelligence?

MWA: Well, I think I always had good teachers in terms of preparation. The only teachers who evidently didn't know how to motivate me were math teachers. Even my teacher of physics and chemistry in high school interested me. I was intensely interested in chemistry. Biology I didn't have, but botany, botany-oh, I loved botany. And I studied Latin and algebra and history.

All my life I have been in school. I have either been going to school or teaching school. Very few years of my life that I was not in school or was not teaching school. So that the academic atmosphere is home to me. Now I'm looking toward retirement. I'm tired of teaching. Teaching was never my ambition, but school was second home. My mother and father were always teaching, I was always accustomed to going to commencement exercises from a little girl. I was literally born on a college campus. My father and mother were teaching in a church school in the community where I was born.

I don't know that I always enjoyed school so much. Sometimes school created for me great conflicts and turmoil and problems. I often have had difficulty, since I've been teaching, with my superiors. I've always been de-termined to do a thing the way I wanted it to be done. And nobody, my parents, my teachers, my co-workers, nobody could ever dissuade me from what I set out to do once I made up my mind to do it. That aggravated people. My mother said the reason she whipped me was that I was very impertinent or an impudent child. That I would talk back. That nobody could silence me. and the only way you could silence me was almost to beat me senseless, to the point where I couldn't get my breath, and then I would hush. Even to this day, if somebody makes me angry, I will say what I think.

MG: You were speaking of your difficulty in controlling tongue and temper.

MWA: They've always been my besetting sins. One of my great pleasures is talking. And I used to talk all the time. I found out only recently that talking can be very tiring. I also say that gossip is my favorite indoor pastime, that anything that happens in my neighborhood or on my job, I am very likely to know about it. I don't have to go anywhere, I don't have to be there. Somebody will telephone and tell me.

MG: Does that stimulate your creative imagination too?

MWA: Yes it does. I see stories in so many things and I regret that I can't write all the stories that I know. People interest me. I love people and I'm curious about everything and everybody. I have an insatiable curiosity. I used to think that I had great powers of observation, that I observed things very carefully. If I saw a flower or a leaf, I didn't see just the whole thing, I saw the veins and the color and the texture and everything about the leaf and that flower. At one glance I would see how it was made and what fragrance it had or what color, the shape, everything about it. And to this day, I'm that way.

MG: Your early education, all before college, took place in racially segregated schools. Were there white teachers?

MWA: That's correct. And I think that I was very well prepared in those schools because, with some exceptions, I had teachers who liked me. In racially segregated schools, the average black teacher had a feeling of sympathy and understanding for that black child. Unfortunately this hasn't been true with the average white teacher teaching black children. There are many white teachers who love children and who love children regardless of their race, but that is not always the case, as it was not always my case, in the case of Minnie Jordan. But it is extremely important for a child to have a teacher who cares about him. Yes, I went to school in racially segregated schools until I was 17.

In college, before I went to Northwestern, my freshman college teacher was a white woman who genuinely liked me, who told my mother and father that I was head and shoulders above everybody else in my class and that I should be sent away to a very good school. She recommended Northwestern which was her Alma Mater and where my parents had also been to school, because she felt that I would not develop my potential unless I was sent out of the South into a good university. I'm sure that I got a good background, a good education, preparatory education from black teachers.

Of course, I think I should always remember that I had a lot of help from my parents at home. My mother and father took interest in my lessons and they supplemented my education at school. My mother and father would question me about what went on, what I learned, what was my lesson about, and what did I have to do for the next day. And they explained the things to me. I learned things at home that I didn't learn at school. And I think that is important too.

I regret, in my own case, my children had very little assistance from me in their education when they were in school. But my sisters and my brother, when they were around them, and they were frequently around them, did what my parents had done for me. My sister Gwen especially had all of my children around her for part of their grade school education. The two older children stayed in her school two years, I think. And the two younger children were with her for part of their early schooling and at the time that she knew most about what they should know. I credit her with having gotten them on the right path. My sisters and my brother did what I was physically unable to do. My parents had done for me what I was not able to do for my children. And then, I have never truly been interested in teaching small children. I like the adult mind. I'm not prepared to handle elementary education. And I couldn't do very much with my own children. I did teach them nursery rhymes and stories and sing to them and I did that. I know that's important.

But when it came to their lessons, I was either too busy, too harried or too sick. I was ill all the time. And I was working all the time. I worked right up till the time the children were born and then right after they were born. And I had to work. And when I came home and I was tired, I had to cook. It seemed to me that their health depended upon their food and I was determined to feed them well. I guess I had an obsession with just the business of food and making sure that they were well fed and never wanting them to come in and ask for bread or milk or food and not having that. I wanted them to grow up to be healthy and happy adults. I wanted them to get a good education, a good college education, and I felt if they were healthy and educated they would become useful and then happiness would result from this. I think people are happy when they are busy doing something they like. When their relationships with other people are on an even keel; when you get along with people, in your house and on your job, and you have someone on whom you can shower your affections, then you're a happy person.

MG: You took your A.B. in English at Northwestern, where you received the Alumni Award in May of 1974 and where you were awarded an honorary Doctor of Literature in June of 1974.

MWA: That's an interesting fact. All of that is true. And it's amazing to me because I remember Northwestern as being an extremely racist school. I remember Northwestern in a dual fashion. I remember that although we had no money, and this was an extremely rich school, I was never embarrassed at Northwestern about not having money. My father and mother really were not able to send their children there and yet we received rebates because we were Methodist minister's children.

I made a few life-long friends at Northwestern. One teacher who taught me composition, advanced composition or creative writing, was also the teacher of two other prize-winning writers. He was a fine writer himself and to me, one of the finest people I ever met. I talk of him all the time, he was

my favorite teacher at Northwestern and I had some fine teachers there. But
he was my absolute favorite. Professor Edward Buell Hungerford. And he
taught a young writer named John Gardner who also won the Houghton
Mifflin Literary Award, but died young. And then he was the teacher of the
celebrated Saul Bellow. He taught Bellow at Northwestern.

And you know, the day that it was announced that Bellow had won the
Nobel Prize, I had some strange feelings. I talked to my oldest child, my
daughter in Chicago, and I said, "I have had such a depressed feeling today.
I feel that I haven't been as productive as I should have been. I look and see
where Bellow wrote nine novels, where he has won the Pulitzer Prize, National Book awards, and now the Nobel Prize for Literature." I said, "We are
the same age. We had the same teacher. We went to the same school and
yet," and I said, "when we were there, when Professor Hungerford talked
about him, he said he thought that Bellow was undoubtedly and is undoubtedly the greatest of our young intellectual novelists," but he said to me,
"Margaret, he was no more talented or brilliant than you." He said, "As a
matter of fact, he might have been a little more stodgy that you were." He
said, "You had such a brilliant imagination." He said "I remember a story
you wrote called 'Witches Eyes,'" and he said he thought that I had just as
much promise as Bellow. And I said, "I feel awful about it because, look,
I've barely written five or six books. And I haven't won any of those prizes
and I'm not likely to win any of them." I said, "What is it?"

And my daughter said, "Mama, you know the difference between the two
of you?" I said, "What is the difference? He's male, white, Jewish, rich; I'm
black, female, poor? Is that the difference?" She said, "No, Mama, that's not
the difference. He is at rich, wealthy University of Chicago, prestigious university where they lobby for those prizes. Where they go out and make an
effort to have their professors win those prizes. Where he teaches one course
maybe a year or a semester and makes a huge salary a year and doesn't have
to be worrying and goes on about his business and can do his writing." And
she said, "You have dedicated your life to education for black people in the
South. And you will never make that kind of money teaching. You will never
have that kind of leisure and your university will never lobby for you to win
any kind of prize. That's the difference." She said to me, "You could put in
race and gender if you want to. That does have something to do with it. He's
white and you're black. He's male and you're female. And you aren't going
to be in his shoes. But you have to get your satisfaction from something
else."

I thought she put it very well. We had the same teachers who believed in both of us, who gave both of us A's. I graduated two years before Bellow and we are the same age. I was 20 and he was 22 when he finished. He has had how many wives? Three or four wives. And I have had one husband. But my satisfactions are quite different. We have even a different philosophy of life because, his whole theme is always on the underground man, you know?

MG: This is Bellow?

MWA: Bellow's. Bellow deals with the modern society and his theme is existentialist, almost the secular existentialist, not the religious existentialist. He believes that life is an accident. And that man is the victim of his world, a pawn, who has no freedom of choice, that his future is one of despair and his fate is death. I don't look upon life the same way. And perhaps I should. I remember the man who sold my novel; the Southern salesman for *Jubilee* is the same man who was the salesman for Margaret Mitchell's *Gone With the Wind.* He sold thousands of my books throughout the South. As a matter of fact, the South has been the greatest market for *Jubilee.* And he said he was anxious to meet me because he had met Margaret Mitchell and found out that she was Scarlett O'Hara, that bitter girl shaking her fist at the sky and swearing never to be hungry again. That was Margaret Mitchell he said. He said he read *Jubilee* and he felt that Vyry had far more reason to be bitter than Scarlett O'Hara. And he wanted to see the author and see if I was like Vyry. Of course my philosophy is the same as Vyry's.

It couldn't help but be otherwise, because that's the way I was raised and I was brought up to think the way my grandmother and great grandmother and mother thought. That the world is not the worst place in the world to be. That it's what you make it and, if you look at it through dark colored glasses, it's going to be a dark place to see. If you look at it through rose colored glasses, then it looks rose colored. And if you can see it clearly through clear glasses, it's the world that you make for yourself. What you put out is what you get back.

I had a white friend once, a woman who was over the girls' dormitory when I was a child. The place was called Peck Home and she was called Miss Neil, I think, and she wrote in my memory book, she said, "I shall always expect to hear great things from you, so achieve , achieve, achieve!" You know, I really believe that people expected me to do things so I went out to try to do them. The attitude was that—yes, she said it—"Give to the world the best you have and the best will come back to you." I believe what the

Bible says, "Be not deceived. God is not mocked. Whatsoever man soweth, that shall he also reap." What you put into the ground, what you plant, whether it's corn, wheat, rye or oats, or weeds, that is what you reap. You cannot draw out of the bank of life what you didn't deposit.

MG: Was there someone besides Professor Hungerford that really impressed you at Northwestern?

MWA: Oh, I had a number of marvelous teachers at Northwestern. All of them, with one exception, were men. The woman who taught hygiene. You now, I find it very interesting in the white universities that there are few women professors unless they are in schools that are predominately for women. The home economics teacher and the phys. ed. teacher of course had to be women. Then most of my teachers have been men since I was an adolescent. In college I had a few black women teachers, but very few. The women who taught me in high school and college all influenced me very much. . . . But I had men teachers from the time I was ten or eleven years old. And men have affected my thinking. I sometimes think that I have a tendency to think the way men think because my teachers predominantly were men. And I know the way men think. Sometimes this has bothered me and then again I have said, here I am a strange creature with a woman's body—a man's mind in a woman's body. That is a very peculiar thing to be.

MG: Well, how would you characterize "male thinking"?

MWA: Well, men are far more objective and less emotional in their thinking than women. And I'm an extremely emotional creature so that creates a problem. By that I mean men rationalize, they claim to be more rational, more scientific in their thinking and I am not, but I do say this, that the organization that men have, I have. Most men are highly organized in their thinking when they are good thinkers. My teachers were that way. And what I remember about them was the extremely methodical way they went about everything. The one writer I knew who was both was Richard Wright. He had very effeminate ways and feminine characteristics, but was well organized on paper. And Langston Hughes, Langston was highly efficient and organized in his living. Everything he did every day was planned and he accomplished a great deal because of that.

A man like Benjamin Franklin who was a patriot of this country and an early genius in America; I think Thomas Paine and Benjamin Franklin are the two great minds of the Revolution, not George Washington and Thomas Jefferson. They cannot compare to Franklin and Paine. And those men were extremely well organized. I think that if women lack anything, it is most of the time an organized mind.

MG: Have you encountered any women who have what you describe as "male thinking."

MWA: Yes. They are frequently very masculine in their approach to life and anything. A woman who affects that masculine pose, that woman, even sometimes the lesbian herself, frequently is a highly organized creature. She knows how to get things done because she goes after it that way. It seems to me that men are as emotional as women. Their emotions work in a different way. To understand what is feminine and what is masculine in people is a very, very tenuous, nebulous quality. It isn't physical strength, you see, because women are basically very strong, emotionally and physically. I've discovered that the male animal is frequently very weak and fragile, see. If there's anything that he has that he can put over on women, it is that methodical and systematic, organized way of approaching things.

MG: Do you see that as the kind of pivotal point of difference, male and female?

MWA: I don't know. I don't know, because I know that men depend on women far more than women depend on men, you see? So it's not strength. But when I see men in jobs, they manage even as executives, they have a cruel streak in them that most women, when they affect it, you recognize it again as that masculine quality. They don't care what happens to the next fellow as long as they get what they want.

MG: What were your experiences in Iowa.

MWA: I had marvelous experiences in Iowa. It's like an oasis in my life, like an idyllic stretch, a period in which one moved into a kind of paradise outside the whole existence that you'd had before. All the things that I wanted to do all my life, I was able to do in those three or four years at Iowa. The pieces of my life came together in a creative sense, the wholeness, the organization, the projection. My experiences were marvelous because I found friends there who helped me do what I wanted to do.

I went out to Iowa first because Arna Bontemps said to my favorite librarian, Vivian Harsh, "I hear Margaret is going back to school. If she is, tell her to go out to Iowa, they have a marvelous writing program that has just begun." *Life* magazine had a spread on the program that used creative talent and creative products instead of the usual scholarly thesis. You could get a master's in drama and I had two friends who did that using acting roles or directing or playwright roles, that is, writing plays. And my roommate was Elizabeth Catlett the great sculptor. She did *Mother and Child* as her thesis and she took the Master of Fine Arts degree having spent two years at Iowa. And I don't remember another black person at the same time doing the creative thesis outside the four of us. But these two friends did it in drama. I wrote for my first, for my master's thesis, the book of poetry that became *For My People* and that won the Yale Award. I had already written some of those poems when I went out there and I had published.

I had some bitter experiences at Iowa that first year, some painful memories of Iowa I still have. But I have learned, when I look back upon it all, and put things in perspective, that you take the bitter with the sweet. That you rarely have anything in life that is all good and all perfect and all beautiful.

MG: Are there any of these experiences that you care to discuss?

MWA: Well, I've said them over and over again and I don't know now that there's any point. Paul Engle and I clashed. He was my greatest benefactor. He was my teacher and he and I fussed all the time. But he aggravated me into writing so I began writing what some of my best poems now, folk ballads. I learned and did the first ones at Iowa. But I wasn't satisfied with his criticism, and he got mad because I didn't agree with him on what they should be. I wrote a letter to Stephen Vincent Benét, whom I knew he respected, and that was the beginning of what turned out to be a marvelous experience for me. I have a handful of Stephen Vincent Benét's letters that to this day I cherish. They date back to that time and here is the telegram that my father sent me when I won the Yale Award and that Benét had written the letter saying My father says, "You won the Yale Series Prize. Letter from Benet following. Rev. S. C. Walker"

I've heard from Paul Engle. We have a very good relationship now. He says he's awfully proud of me. He says I'm the only person those 30-odd years who ever came out there to the Iowa School of Writing, to the creative writing workshop, and won prizes and wrote theses that won prizes in two separate forms. I won a poetry prize that was a top national prize and I won a prose prize that was a top national prize. He told my mother at the Library of Congress in 1972, that he always believed in me. He always knew I had great talent and he always believed that I was absolutely perfect.

MG: Well, we've talked about your parents' very intimate involvement in your early education. Were they equally as supportive of higher education for a daughter?

MWA: Oh, we discussed it once, pro and con. I wanted to go off to school when I finished high school and I was only 14 years old. And my father had always wanted me to do whatever I wanted to do so he sent five dollars to Talladega for my room deposit and I was supposed to go to Talladega, where everybody said they had a very fine English department.

But then the pastor of our church, who later became a bishop in the church, said to my father, "Are you crazy? You got a young innocent good girl and you're going to send her off to college to come back smoking and drinking?" And he said, "You're not going to make that kind of mistake with that girl, are you? A nice child like Margaret? You won't get her back." So Daddy and Mama got frightened, and then the white president of the college said what was the binding thing, "You mean you will send your child to another black college and you are working in a college? And you think it's better than the one you're in? If you are going to send her away, you'll have to send her to a white school." In other words, no other black college is any better than. . . .

MG: Than the one you're in.

MWA: But a white one is. That's what he said. I've been winning prizes ever since I can remember. My first prize I won—I must have been about eight years old—for saying the Ten Commandments faster than anybody else, I guess. I won prizes in high school. I was not at the top of my class, I was just the second highest, for grades. But that meant that I won a scholarship to college from the Alpha Phi Alpha Fraternity.

And I also was nominated to go to the Normal school to become a teacher, which I didn't want to be, and didn't want to go because I said, "I don't want to teach in a public school. If I teach at all, I want to teach in a college. And when I finish the Normal I will only be 16 or 17 years old and I would be too young because I wouldn't be 18 and they wouldn't even hire me. So there's no point in my going to the Normal. I want to go to college because I want to be a writer and I want to learn how to write."

When I won the freshman English prize and the teacher told my mother, Daddy tried hard to find out who had won and my family gave a tongue-lashing the morning of commencement because they assumed I hadn't won. My grandmother said, "How can she win everything? She doesn't crack a book at night. All she does is sit down and read and write poetry." But I won the prize. I had made the A and I was the top in the class. And the five dollar gold piece was mine. Matthew Walker, who is a doctor at Meharry, ran home to tell me before Mama and Daddy could come. He said, "You won the prize." But Mama and Daddy had just castigated me that morning for not having won. They told me nobody was supposed to do better than I. I was supposed to be the best. Why? Because I was their child. You see?

MG: And how long did you write in your first journal?

MWA: Until 1936, I guess. No, '33. I took it to Northwestern with me and I guess I finished it off in '36. I was on the Writer's Project when I finished it. And then I had another one. It was green and I got it after I went out to Iowa. "For My People" is in that one. And then, Vivian Harsh sent me one, when I was home ill after I had gone home from Iowa, that I used as a journal.

MG: It looks as though that's really a working journal too, I mean all of your work and fair copies are all in the same place.

MWA: In my adolescence I wrote almost every day. From the time I was 11 or 12. I wrote prose when I was ten; I was composing prose as early as then. I started a novel when I was 12 and I would type that.

MG: What was it about?

MWA: Oh a very sentimental story, a love story and a religious story and no race in it—all these people were white. I didn't know anything. And I was so confused I couldn't figure what they looked like because I was writing about people that were fantasy. I didn't know whether they were black, or white, but they sounded white. And I was writing about religious conversion and love story and beauty and that's all.

And then I started, I guess I must have been 15 or 16, maybe no more than 17 years old, when I began to write articles about the race question. "What Is to Become of Us?" was the title of one. It is amazing to me that I was thinking so seriously at that age about race.

MG: Do you remember the story about Du Bois and that early writing he was doing in Great Barrington? How he offered to help any other members of the black community in buying books for their library. He suggested that they should consult him and he could tell them what they ought to buy.

MWA: I don't remember, but I do know this, that I saw Du Bois for the first time when I was 17 years old and I knew about him. I had read some of his work. I didn't know the poetry but I went up to him and spoke to him. He seemed very stiff and formal and dignified, a little man, not much taller than my father. But he had a Vandyke beard and he was already bald and I told him I wrote poetry and he told me to send him some. This is when I was leaving Chicago. I heard Harriet Monroe read "Is this the face that launched a thousand ships?" while I was at Northwestern. My Chicago years, there's so much stuff there.

Somebody made the remark—I don't remember whether it was my mother or my father or somebody talking to them—when the discussion came up about sending my sister and me off to school, that we weren't going to do anything with our education but get married. And I have thought about that so much afterward. The attitude was that a woman didn't need an education if she was going to get married, when it seems to me that everybody needs an education, whether they get married or do not get married. That a woman who is intelligent has just as much right to her education as a man. And it has been my feeling all along that I would want all my children and now all my grandchildren to have as much education as they want and can take.

I do recognize and I have recognized it over a period of years in teaching that some people are not college material. That they would do better in something else, that they should be allowed to follow their natural bent. But it seems to me that the old ideas we used to have about women with higher education need to be rethought. That people need to think about it more seriously and realize that women today for the most part are working women, and that they have to be prepared not just for careers, but they need to have a college education to be prepared even for marriage. So that was just a comment that was made. I am the only one of my siblings who has married.

MG: Is that right?

MWA: Yes, my two sisters and brother have never married. And all of us are career people. My husband jokes and says that my father remarked to him that they did not prepare their children for marriage. They prepared us for careers. And my father and mother both believed that their children had something to offer in terms of careers. They were not at all included and prone to see their children make marriages feeling that that would necessarily bring happiness. It disturbed me for many years because if there was one thing lacking in my upbringing it was sex education. And I'm not at all sure that I've done a good job with my own children, but I do have three married children. That is, two sons and a daughter, and I would hope that the fourth child would marry, but she has the right not to marry if she doesn't want to marry.

MG: Would you be open to discussing the personal circumstances that led to your marriage to Firnist James Alexander.

MWA: You know, for a number of years when people would ask me this kind of question, I always felt it was my personal business and I was reluctant to discuss it. But I can tell jokes now, now that I have been married 33 years, approaching the 34th year.

I didn't grow up having the normal opportunities to meet eligible fellows and court and get married at an early age. My mother married very young, in her teens and I was born before she was 20. But it seemed her determination that this would not happened to a single daughter of hers, and she seemed very strongly opposed to marriage for any of her children. I don't know why. I never fully understood it. I know that she had two sisters whose marriages to her seemed unfortunate and the older sister married very late and lied about her age, she must have been 40 years old when she married and had a child. The joke in the family was that she really loved my father and thought he was interested in her and to her great dismay he wanted to marry her youngest sister, which he did. My mother's brothers, two of them, died very young and did not marry. The one brother who was married had no children and his marriage did not last. It was an unfortunate marriage. So that I think my mother's family, her siblings, must have colored her attitude toward marriage.

I don't think she ever wanted to admit that she was just as anxious to get married to my father as he was to marry her. But she always said that her mother pushed that marriage. That my grandmother met my father first and was impressed with him and liked him and invited him to the home where he met the oldest daughter first and later my mother. He was pleased on sight and married her. But I think too that this had something to do with the aspirations of the black middle class. The feeling is that if you didn't have money and land, that you needed education. The professional class was going to be the important class in which to move and marry and direct yourself. I think that's been in my family's mind every since my great grandmother. As a slave she was well aware of the difference in social position between Randall Ware and Innis Brown. She liked the idea of a free man with money and education. My grandmother, who was his child, had early in her mind the idea that a minister or a teacher was a desirable companion. She married a preacher who had been trained for teaching and preaching. And she married him in her teens. Her first child was born when she was 20 years old. And that marriage, though, not an ideal marriage by any means, gave my grandmother a feeling of position in the community. And she wanted that for this youngest and dearest daughter. I think that had a great deal to do with the motivation behind my parents' marriage.

When I was first married and for a long time, my mother, and I think more than my father, deeply resented my marriage. She resented the idea of my marrying long before I actually married. And I did not understand it at first. I talked about marrying a young minister when I was about 21. He was in the A.M.E. church and was studying at the University of Chicago Theological Seminary. He represented what my background had been. I know that he liked me a great deal and he asked me on more than one occasion to marry him. Feeling that, oh, I was 21, I wrote home because I thought I would like to have a wedding. I was sure he would have wanted a wedding so I wrote and told my mother, who had already met this man. She wrote back an awful letter, that I was too young, although I was older than she was when she married. She was bitterly opposed to it. When I did marry and she met my husband, she was so annoyed she said she wished now that she had encouraged me to marry that man.

Of course, I'm very glad I didn't marry the first man, that man, because he made the remark one day that if I married him I had to understand that the writing and the speaking and all the career stuff must go, that I was to be his wife and the mother of his children. In other words, as a minister in the church I was to push him as he was bishop material, although I don't think he ever became that. He was one of the first chaplains in the Navy. And that's as far as he ever got. But if he had married me he would have gone a long way. He felt he could go to the top with my assistance. But I had other ideas, I had very definitely in my mind the determination to do something with my own life in my own way. And when he asked me what I wanted to do most, he thought I would say, marry and have a family, and I said, "Oh, I think the thing I want to do most now is publish a book." And he was furious. He said, "Here I've come across the country to ask you to marry me and all you can talk about is a book." And I did like him very much. I thought afterwards maybe I made a mistake. I thought we were compatible. I felt that he was intelligent and sensitive and deeply religious and this would be just what I should do. Now I realize it would have been following the pattern of my family, which did not necessarily mean happiness for me. I guess I had many other-worldly notions and that I was perhaps not as religious as I thought I was. I would have felt very cramped as a minister's wife. I thought I would have made a good minister's wife because that's all I'd ever known and seen. But that was one possibility that didn't work and now I'm very happy that it didn't.

When I married, my husband was a soldier. He was in the service and I met him when I was traveling on an engagement. I didn't want to have anything to do with soldiers. I had vowed and sworn never to bother with them. I was against the war and bitterly opposed soldiers and everybody else, so when he tried to strike up an acquaintance—he made a pass at me from the train I was about to board—I ran. I said, "Oh my God, there's a drunken soldier," and ran two cars away. By the time I got myself settled and got my breath and my luggage—I looked around and he was standing over me smiling. And he was determined never to let me out of his sight. When he told me that same day and asked me to marry him, he said something about just because they had no future a soldier was a person just like anybody else and why should they be treated like scum, you know, like dirt under your feet. And why would I refuse even to let him sit down and speak to me, who was I, some holy sanctified and sanctimonious woman who was going around preaching? My bag, he said, felt like it was either full of books or had gold in it. He didn't say books, he said it felt like iron or gold. He didn't know it had books in it. I told him that "down to Gehenna or up to the throne he travels the fastest who travels alone."

I had had a very bitter rejection at the time from a person whom I had thought a great deal of. This friend had informed me he was going to marry a white woman. This minister friend had told me I was too brown and he wanted a yellow gal with red hair. Richard Wright said he was going to marry white whenever he married. So that was telling me don't look my way because I'm not interested in anybody with your complexion. And both of those were men whom I considered highly eligible and would have been pleased to have married. Now Michel Fabre puts in his book that I was the kind of girl that Richard Wright could have married, but my indiscretions, which I wonder about—he has the very insulting nerve to say that either from indiscretions in my speech or action or something, I was no longer of the standard high enough to be Richard Wright's wife. That is amusing. To say the least. I resented it because first of all it came from a white man talking about a black woman and her friendship for a black man and so I'm just amazed at his colossal nerve. I don't know where he got his ideas.

When I was first married, my husband was in the service. When we first married he seemed to me like the average black fellow I might have met his age. I couldn't have assumed how old he was; I didn't know. I did think this, that he was certainly one of the most striking men I had ever seen. In the early years of our marriage, I never was jealous, but it was always pleasing to me to see women turn around in the streets to look at him. Today, although he is still a handsome man, he doesn't look at all like half the fellow he looked like then. His hair is gone and then it was hanging in his face.

MG: He's still striking, I think.

MWA: And my mother and the woman whose husband was my president at the first job, said that he had just a fine body. He is more than six feet tall. At first, after we were apart so much, I could scarcely ever remember what his eyes looked like, which color they were, because some days they were brown and some days they were hazel and some days they seemed steel coal grey. and I would stop and say, now what color are that man's eyes? And afterwards I realized that he had changeable eyes. We have three children whose eyes are exactly the same—the oldest, the youngest and the third child—my second son, James, has eyes that are light brown nearer my own. But I was fascinated by this man. I had never seen anybody who to me was more physically attractive and more magnetic. But the wonderful thing about my husband was that he has always proved to be a man of very high moral character and great discrimination.

He confessed to me early in our acquaintanceship and in our marriage that he had had no opportunity for education. But that he admired so much people who had had schooling. I think it's been a complex with him. I could not tell at the time that he wasn't as well educated as the young people I had already begun to teach. He spoke and read and wrote as well as the average college student. I would never have dreamed that he had never been even to high school, much less to college. But then I had known Richard Wright and Wright had not finished high school. He'd only had a grade school education and he was certainly one of the most intelligent young people I ever knew. He was an intellectual giant. So that education didn't seem to me to be the most important thing; intelligence was more important than education. But my husband said he wanted to marry a woman who would be an intelligent mother for his children and that he wanted a woman with sense, that he always said if she didn't have money, she'd have to have brains. And he said he always figured that I had potentially both. But then he also said he didn't think too much about the beauty. What a person looked like was not as important as their character and disposition; to me those are ideal things in a marriage. He has always been a very frank and honest person. I don't think I have ever really caught my husband in a lie. What he told me from the day we met to this day turned out to be absolutely the truth. And I believe a marriage can be built on that kind of thing—honesty, frankness, truth. He didn't pretend to be the greatest fellow in the world or any of those things. But he looked like the greatest. And he has worn well. Thirty-odd years and I wish we could have 30 more. I feel that way. He told my mother what he felt about me. He said, "When I first saw her, I thought she was as pretty as a speckled pup." And he thinks dogs are the most wonderful things in the world.

MG: That was high praise. Is there anything you'd like to say regarding your four children?

MWA: Every mother is always proud of her children. I'm proud of my four. They are distinct and different personalities. I sometimes feel sorry for them because, especially in these last 10 or 11 years, they've had to live in the shadow of an unusual amount of success from their mother's point of view. If anybody had ever told me that *Jubilee* would have the tremendous audience that it has received—it's now on its second million copies. And this past year, the price went up from $6.95 to $9.95 for the hardback cover. It has gone through 40 printings and been published in seven foreign countries. People call me all the time to speak. I have more engagements that I can fill and my children have had, in the past 11 years, to finish their development and growth in this. The first two, I think, came through it—they were already finishing college. The oldest girl had finished. And I don't think that it affected them nearly as badly as it did the two younger ones. But I think my children have been very proud of their mother, very happy about the success of *Jubilee,* but I think it changed their lives in a way that I wish it hadn't. My husband always felt that the greatest thing in the world was money. He and I disagreed on that. He talked about making money and having money and he felt that he'd been poor all his days and never had money. Yet his people had land, as much as the average family, and his attitude was a man is worth what he owns. As I think I've said already, my security has never been in money. And I spend it prodigally. I don't worry about where the next dime is coming from.

I feel very unhappy when I think about a person like Zora Neale Hurston who was undoubtedly one of the most talented women, not only of her generation, but in this century. A great story teller, a marvelous raconteur and a great light in the Harlem Renaissance. But the saddest thing about Zora wasn't the failure of her marriage or the fact that she was frustrated and didn't get her doctorate in anthropology, the saddest thing was that she died in abject poverty and filled a pauper's grave. One of the nicest things that Alice

Walker should be remembered for is putting a headstone over Zora's grave. I love Alice for that alone, if she had never become the very successful and fine writer that she is.

I wouldn't like to fill a pauper's grave. I wouldn't like to feel that when I'm dead my family couldn't bury me. I don't crave a headstone. Two or three things give me a great sense of security. I say that emotional security to me is very important. To feel myself loved and respected, you see, was much more important than to feel as if I had a lot of money. But one thing I remember that my husband said to me, when we were married, "Now you know, wherever I am in the world, you're not alone. And as long as I have a dollar, half of that dollar is yours." He didn't say the whole dollar. "Half of that dollar is yours and as long as I have a piece of bread, you have a piece of bread." I thought that was a beautiful thing. And it has proved to be true, that lots of times we had tough times, but he always managed to have a dollar and whatever I had or whatever he had, it belonged to both of us. That's always been true.

I think I have made, and my husband and I together have made, a good marriage, as good as most. I sometimes think that differences in philosophy about money and religion, even about sex and family raising and all of these may be—what do I want to say—not stumbling blocks, not hazards—but may happen sometimes. But my husband and I are very different in every respect. We had different backgrounds, different church denominations, different philosophies about money, but despite those differences, we had always in common two things: our love for each other and then the children, as they came. And no matter what the differences between us were about anything, where the children were concerned, as they were growing up, we were always together. We could be fussing, having the biggest kind of fight and one of the children got sick, and we were together. So to me we made a marriage. I can say the same thing that Vyry said, "We've been together in birth and death and every kind of trouble, every kind of trouble that you can mention, and together with the help of God, we've been able to work it out." I can't conceive of any difference between us that we couldn't work out.

My feeling was, it was up to the woman to make it. For a long time, I figured I had to make all the sacrifices and he didn't have to make any. Only it dawned on me finally that he had made a lot. That he had made many sacrifices that I wasn't aware of at the time. And I said it takes two to make a marriage. That's true. But he says that I was the one who was determined to hold it together because there were times that he was sick, that he was ill and didn't care. But I always cared. I always was determined to make it.

People have said to me many times before, and they said it to my sisters too, "You can do everything but get a man." So I said that getting a man is not the hardest thing in the world; most women have just definite ways that they get a man. And so I got a man. My sisters may feel a little bitter today because they didn't, but I think basically they're happy because they are living the life they chose to live. That if you make up your mind to do something, you can do it. And I always made up my mind to do what I could.

MG: How important have friends and friendship been in your life?

MWA: A great deal. I've always craved friends and from a little girl, I had lots of girl friends, but always one or two that I felt very close to. I felt that my mother didn't encourage us to have friends. If a little girl came to play with us, she wanted to know, "Who is that child? Who is her mother? Where does she live? Where does she come from? Who is she?" And this hurt me on more than one occasion. And then there were those whom she felt their people might not appreciate us enough and she didn't want us to play with them either. Now I look back on it and it was difficult as a child, growing up, for me to make friends.

And I had to discover, since I've been here in Jackson, what true friendship means. I stop and I count on these hands, with fingers left over, the women to whom I feel close in this town, whom I get on the telephone and call and they call me. Or I go to their house and they come to see me. With very few exceptions, I can think of only one or two of these women that I haven't had some altercation or some words or had some difference. But I decided three things. One, that tongue and teeth fall out sometimes. You fall out with your family, you fall out with your mama, your sisters, your brother, and you go and make up and go on again. You have to do the same thing with your friends. There's a saying about when you're old, growing old, you want at least one friend. But I have also believed that friends are worth more than money. And that when you are in trouble and sickness and bereavement, that nothing gives you the consolation of a friend. So you work all your life toward the goal that you set for yourself and among them must be friends.

I remember somebody asked me in an interview a few weeks ago, if I have any childhood friends? "Oh," I said, "yes." "And did I make friends that lasted?" I've had a little gnawing feeling about a girl that I first knew when I was ten years old in New Orleans. We never had really a cross word. But I have felt that in the last few years, that I've gradually grown away from that girl. We had so little in common. The opportunities I had, she didn't have. I loved her and then her life went in so many different directions and now I have no appreciation for it. All we have in common now would be the years. So I feel sad about it. The last time—I don't know whether I called her or she called me—I asked myself, "Have you grown up, are you so big, are you so important that you no longer have any appreciation for this friend?" I used to go to New Orleans and call her and go in to see her and she'd call me. The last time she talked to me, I detected in her voice, some things that sounded to me hypocritical. I think she'd gone to Jehovah's Witnesses or something. And I said, "Oh boy. This is it. This is the final straw." I still like that girl very much, but not as a friendship. And she told me she wanted to come over here to the opera adapted from *Jubilee* because she loved opera, but when the time came and I knew people were coming, I felt very guilty, I didn't call and invite her. I knew I had no special place. My children had turned against her and I feel guilty about it.

MG: But isn't it better to let friendships go than to try and continue them with some past closeness? I mean, it hasn't continued to evolve?

MWA: I suppose two or three friendships really broke my heart. When Richard Wright and I broke up, I didn't want to face the fact that I had probably fallen in love with this man. I couldn't face that. But I felt rejected and I thought I would lose my mind. And that friendship really ended then. And the break was so traumatic that it affected me the rest of my life. Even when he was dead, I still felt the trauma of that indifference. Occasionally I will dream that he is alive. Occasionally I see him and we are laughing together and having fun together. And I cannot understand psychologically what the involvement was. Friends and psychiatrists tried to show me that we were very much psychologically involved with each other. And even in death the involvement has gone on. I cannot understand it.

Langston was a friend like no other friend. Langston was the kind of person that you could just spend the day with or half an evening with and you had lots of fun together. He wrote on a picture once, "For Margaret who is such fun to be with." And I had that feeling about him, he was so much fun. Langston's death really did me harm. I couldn't discuss it for a while because I had no idea that Langston was even ill. I had seen him in October and we didn't see each other often, but I noticed that he looked a little puffy and we had the same big bear hug and sat and talked and all. Then I came home and

I got busy with lots of things. I didn't hear from Langston, didn't think anything about it because we didn't always keep in touch over a weekend. It would just be now and then you'd see him or something. And I don't know whether I heard it over the radio or somebody told me that Langston was dead. And I don't think I could even talk about it first. I think that days and weeks passed before I could even discuss it. And occasionally I will dream about Langston.

The most amazing thing happened here about five or six years ago. It was almost a psychic thing. I was asleep in my bedroom and I dreamed that Langston came and said, "I have just crossed him over. Do you want me to cross you over?" I think I woke up hearing the phone ring. I got up and they told me a man on our campus who was a teacher had just died. And he died at four o'clock that morning. The thing nearly drove me out of my mind. He said, "I have just crossed him over. Do you want me to cross you over?"

MG: That's amazing.

MWA: And I had the same kinds of dreams when my grandmother died. I was not at home when my grandmother died. I was expecting my first child. The word came that my grandmother had passed, and I didn't dream about her until after the child was born. And then I dreamed that she came in the room where I was with the child, sleeping. I was sitting down in front of the fireplace and I had the child in my arms and my grandmother walked in and picked up the baby out of my arms. I knew that she was dead. And I said, "Oh Grandma, you're not going to take my baby, are you?" And she said, "No," and put the baby back in my arms and she said, "I just wanted to see it." The next time I dreamed, my grandmother said, "Tell your father to see about those papers. I can't rest for those papers." And I said I wonder what in the world she's talking about and I called Mama and told her and she said, "There's something around the grave, I'll see about it at once." And I think that same night I dreamed again, I saw my grandmother take off the front porch in New Orleans where she had died and where we had lived and she shot up just like she was going straight up, like you're shooting a rocket. And I never dreamed about her anymore. Have you ever seen anything like that before?

MG: No. What was the paper? Something around the grave?

MWA: Something about the title or something to the grave. My father bought the land and my father was the second one buried there. My grandmother was buried first and my father. There's room for one more. One or two more, I don't know whether Mama said there's room for three or four in that grave. But there was room for her.

We were talking about friendships and got into that. I was thinking about Langston and Wright. I considered these very great friendships. There are half a dozen women in different places. I would say New Orleans, Chicago, maybe here in Jackson, women I have known since I was in my 20s. Margaret Burroughs [founder of the Du Sable Museum of Afro-American History] in Chicago is a woman I knew.

Margaret and I were young women in Chicago together. And we have been to see each other; we consider each other very close friends.

Last year I went to visit Elizabeth [Catlett]. Elizabeth and I have had words and altercations but we still remain friends. She hurt me to my heart when I was in Mexico, but I saw her again in Texas, at Fort Worth, and I was glad to see her. She had made the trip just to be there when I was there. But, friendship for me now, I'm an old woman, past 60 years of age and I have a strange taste in my mouth about friends. I called a girl I went to high school with, when I was on the coast a couple of weeks ago. I got a letter from her after I got back. I tried my best to see her. I hadn't seen her in years and I was on the coast and I kept making an effort to reach her and got friends to reach her and finally they reached her. Well, she sent word she was sick, that was the reason she couldn't come up. And she didn't say, "Come down." It bothered me very much. I was less than 30 miles, less than 25 miles from her, and I hadn't been down that close before. She had been there. I don't know that she had ever been in this house but she'd been on the campus many times. When I had my 25th anniversary, she sent me a half a dozen silver coffee spoons as a gift. But when I got back and got the letter from her, I felt a little better and she said, "Talking to you and your husband made my day." She said, "I had such a bad cold," and she said, "I'm better but I'm still not able to be out." She's older than I am now, she's retired, but I was so disappointed not to see her. And I haven't said any more but I felt she acted so strangely knowing that I was that close and she didn't say, "Margaret, come on down," or "Margaret, I'm coming up there."

But I have had some things happen where friends are concerned, since my so-called success, that people that I was closest to, I don't feel they feel as close to me any more. Two or three times I've thought of something that I remembered with Richard Wright. A number of his friends said he changed so completely after he became so well-known that he broke off with them and left them alone. I have seen two sides of this. No matter how close you feel to someone, and how much you want to remain close to them, if you have had undue success and good fortune, they change toward you and they believe, they say, that you have changed toward them. Somebody said to me the other day, one of my neighbors said a woman asked her, "Where do you live?" She said "Oh, I live on Guynes Street." "Say, you live out there near Miss Walker?" She said, "I live near Dr. Alexander, right across the street." She said, "You live near her? What is she like?" She said, "She is a lovely neighbor and I am very fond of her. She's the same as she was when she moved out there." She said, "I don't see any difference in her. She's concerned about all her neighbors and people as she always was." And she said, "Do you mean that woman that they are talking about, is the same woman? You must be crazy. She can't be." And I thought about what she said. Because if there's anything that I remember, I remember what the Southern salesman says. He says, "I don't think you're going to lose your balance and get your feet off the ground. You got a husband and every time you make a move to fly high, he'll bring you down." That tickled me because I really need that.

I feel sad about friends. I begin to wonder if when you are older things look a little differently to you. I read in a magazine last night a page of poetry about a woman growing old, how she couldn't hear too well, couldn't see, and about her friends and how she looked and what she still valued, with her children, her grandchildren. How folks talked and what they said about you when you were getting old. It was just a very, very interesting page. I've had some of the same feelings, I said, "Oh my, I'm soon going to be in the complete class of the senior citizen. How do you feel?" I talked to my friend here and I talked to a number of friends. "What happens when a woman who has been very active and had a career for 35 or 40 years suddenly finds herself facing retirement? What kind of change?" I discover they say retirement is as traumatic for people as divorce or even death, death of a close relative. That it is very hard for people to adjust to retirement. I keep telling myself, "Well, I've got enough to do. A lot of writing. I won't be getting engagements, because when you don't have a position, people don't call on you the same. When I leave the job, there'll be a difference. I won't be Dr. Alexander, Head of the Institute, Professor of English at Jackson State. I'll just be Margaret Walker Alexander, that old lady who used to go around lecturing and who called herself, as they said, 'a writer,' who almost was, but didn't quite make it."

MG: That's not what's going to happen. That's not it. You know Ingmar Bergman, the film director? He said about growing older, he said, "It's like climbing a mountain. The nearer you get to the top, the more tired you become, but the more extensive your view is."

MWA: Well, that woman said something like that, "I thought it was diabetes." It made me feel so tired. She said, "Well, you feel the lack of energy, so weak and you think, what in the world is happening to me, I don't feel like I used to feel." And I said, "Oh my God, I'm getting old."

MG: But along with that, do you feel that continual evolution and expansion of view?

MWA: Yes. I'll tell you what is true. It's almost tragic, that the truth of it is, by the time you have learned how to live, it is time to die. You look up and you know so much that you wish you knew 30 years ago or 40 years ago. If I'd only known some of this when I was 50 years old, how wonderful it would have been. I would have taken a different attitude. I think about all the difficulties I have gone through.

My son went to war. He was in the Vietnam War and he was so concerned that I would not know that he was in Vietnam, that every time he called me, and he didn't write, he'd call, he'd tell me he was in Okinawa. And he did everything he could to keep me from knowing he was in Vietnam because he knew that that would just almost give me a heart attack. When he came home, he had trouble with the Black Nationalist group and suddenly he was arrested, taken to jail, and for seven weeks I thought I would die. I thought I simply could not live and all I did was follow my faith in God Himself because I figured nobody can get us out of this but God. It kept me from going abroad. It gave me the greatest disappointment in my life because my Fulbright lectureship could not be accepted. And I didn't get to go to Norway and all the wonderful places I had planned to go at a time when I had the energy to go. I thought I was going to Africa. My money, I was going to have the settlement from my book and I figured, well, at least $10,000 of this we can spend and enjoy, you know? And the government took $20,000 and the FBI came and sat in my house, and everything under the sun happened except what we had expected to happen. And yet you live through it.

I was so despondent and asked, "My God, what's the use?" I would remember, every one of your children is alive. This boy was not killed and he is not in jail. Your husband is alive, your children are alive. You still have your job despite the fact that I nearly died. I thought I gave up to die in the

hospital in '74. I had systemic uremic poisoning which most people do not
get over. And I must have had the most marvelous care. Those people were
around the clock. I was in Northwestern's teaching hospital with systemic
uremic poisoning and a temperature of 104°. And I pulled me through. I
really didn't expect to see morning. I was sick enough to die and everything
was getting dark around me. It took them eight days to get the poison out of
me. I had been walking around here with that stuff in me.

And when I think about that, I say every day is a gift. Every morning I
wake up alive is another day that I have a chance to do something that I didn't
do before, that I'm here for a purpose, there's a reason for life. I do not
believe that life is an accident. I believe that it has purpose and meaning. And
I believe that the thing my parents taught me when I was a child, and I used
to hear it every week in chapel when we went to services, about character
and service, the two most important things in the world are your moral character and your service to people. That if you live every day as if that might
be the last day, you know? You never know when it's going to be your last
day, but if you live every day as if this might be the last day, you get a little
something accomplished.

Interview with Margaret Walker

Claudia Tate / 1982

From *Black Women Writers at Work.* New York: Continuum, 1983. Copyright © 1983 by Claudia Tate. Reprinted by permission of Claudia Tate.

Walker began her first novel, *Jubilee,* when she was nineteen and spent thirty years completing it. In an inspiring tale for all black Americans struggling for freedom and equality, Walker in *Jubilee* (1966) incorporated actual historical events into the fictionalized life of her maternal great-grandmother, Margaret Duggans, from slavery to the Reconstruction.

Claudia Tate What was it like to live with *Jubilee* for thirty years?

Walker: You just become part of it, and it becomes part of you. Working, raising a family, all of that becomes part of it. Even though I was preoccupied with everyday things, I used to think about what I wanted to do with *Jubilee.* Part of the problem with the book was the terrible feeling that I wasn't going to be able to get it finished, since I was sick so much of the time. And even if I had the time to work at it, I wasn't sure I would be able to do it the way I wanted. Living with the book over a long period of time was agonizing. Despite all of that, *Jubilee* is the product of a mature person. When I started out with the book, I didn't know half of what I now know about life. That I learned during those thirty years. After all, I started writing *Jubilee* at nineteen, and I couldn't have dealt with, for instance, the childbirth problems. I couldn't have known about them then, not until I had become a mature women who had her own problems. There's a difference between writing about something and living through it. I did both. I think I was meant to write *Jubilee.*

C.T.: *For My People* appeared in 1942, and [Gwendolyn] Brooks's *A Street in Bronzeville* in 1945. Was there any competition between these two works?

Walker: I'll give you some historical background on the two pieces. I wrote the title poem of *For My People* in July of 1937, around my twenty-second birthday. It was published in *Poetry Magazine* in November of that

year. I went out to Iowa in the fall of 1939 and got my master's degree in the
summer of 1940 when I was 25. I then went South to teach, though I actually
didn't begin teaching until 1942. I met Gwendolyn Brooks in 1938, after I
had written the title poem "For My People." Margaret Burroughs, a mutual
friend, introduced us. I don't think Gwen had published in national magazines at that time. I'm two years older than Gwen.

For My People won the Yale award in the summer of '42. Yale had rejected
it three times. Stephen Vincent Benét, the editor at that time, wanted to publish it the first time I sent it to him from the University of Iowa. Anyway, he
kept it from February until July in '39, and he wrote to me telling me he
thought the poems were as near perfect as I could make them. He asked me
to resubmit them the following year, and I did. He said he'd keep them while
he was trying to make up his mind. I didn't really know what was actually
happening at Yale until I won. That year, 1942, was the last year Benét edited
the Yale Younger Poet Series. I think he simply confronted his colleagues
with the fact that if they wouldn't give the award to me, he wasn't going to
name anybody else. In other words, I think he was telling them he was
through with them if they didn't give it to me. After all, he had repeatedly
said the piece was as near perfect as I could make it. I think he felt they were
refusing purely on the basis of race. I didn't know how much the issue had
gone back and forth between them until I went up there. The woman with
whom I'd corresponded said that they had "to come begging" because they
had to ask for the manuscript. I hadn't submitted it that year because I got
tired of sending it.

Three years after *For My People* was published, *A Street in Bronzeville*
appeared in 1945. It was a very good book. I remember saying to Langston
that the poetry was promising, technically and intellectually; the work had
great potential. *Annie Allen* [1949] fulfilled that potential. I think *Annie Allen*
is a superb book. Technically it is stunning. The subtleties come through it
much better than they did in *A Street in Bronzeville.*

Getting back to your question . . . I never felt that I was in competition
with Gwen. But I had this feeling; I may be very wrong, and I've been told I
was wrong. I said in the book with Nikki [*A Poetic Equation: Conversations
Between Nikki Giovanni and Margaret Walker*] that it was ironic that all the
forces that had dealt negatively with my work dealt positively with Gwendolyn Brooks's work. I named them in that book. First, Gwen won a poetry
prize at Northwestern. That never happened to me. Northwestern later gave
me a lot of recognition. But when I was a student there, they didn't. Paul

Engle was my teacher, and he was fighting mad with me for sending *For My People* to Yale. For years he was annoyed about it. I think he helped Gwen. Second, Richard Wright was a man whom I knew very well for three years. We were never intimate, but we were very dear and close friends. After we broke up and our friendship ended, he helped Gwen. I'm certain that Gwen got published at Harper because Wright was there. Nobody ever told me, but I think he interceded for her. Paul Engle, Northwestern, Richard Wright and the Friends of Literature on the North Side, with whom my teachers at Northwestern were involved, all helped Gwen. Paul did do two things for me: he helped me to get a job and helped me find the ways and means to study at Iowa both times, in 1939 and in the sixties. But to answer your question—I never figured for one day I was in competition with Gwen.

I hope the new collection of poems, *This Is My Century,* will be published. I think I've got a good book. I haven't seen anything like it. The power is more sustaining than *For My People.* I've wanted to do it for a long, long time. It's been in me for half a lifetime. What I have here is a complete indictment of our present-day society, our whole world. What's wrong with it is money, honey, money. Inflation blues is what we got. What I have tried to do in this piece is integrate what [Alex] Haley did to me to show that it's just part of the same corrupt scene.

C.T.: What's happening with the Wright biography?

Walker: I sometimes get very frightened because I know so much. I know I've been on the "black list" for a long time. Everytime I pick up the Wright stuff, I get frightened. I realize that I'm dealing with very sensitive material. Sometimes I just turn away from it and wonder will I be signing my death warrant if I do what I know has to be done with that book. You see there are several very sensitive areas. One is communism itself, which concerned the great intellectual debate between black nationalism and the Communist Party: its dictates and policy on Negroes. If you tell the story the way it needs to be told, you're in trouble with both sides—the U.S. Government and the Communist Party. Neither one of them is a friend to black people. When Wright realized that, he got out of the Party.

Do I look like a crazy, foolish, superstitious woman to you? Well, I may be. I've fooled with astrology for forty years. When I first met Wright in 1936, *Horoscope Magazine* was published for the first time. I bought some of the first issues for a dime. I know how to set up charts. When Martin Luther King was killed in Memphis, I was in the Leamington Hotel in Minneapolis, Minnesota. I sat down and made his death chart. The chart shocked me. I didn't understand it at the time because what I saw all over King's chart was not so much death—I saw the gun, the government—as nothing but money—millions and millions of dollars. Money of all kinds, from all countries. Nothing but money.

Getting back to Wright . . . I remember the news flash on television about Wright's death. I was fixing breakfast. It upset me so that I sat down and began to tremble. Wright was just like somebody in my family. I had been that close to him. All that day I kept thinking about it, and I said to Eubanks, "They said he had a heart attack, but I believe it was tied up with his stomach." Because he had a delicate stomach. I know because I had cooked for him, and I knew he had to have simple foods. I didn't think about foul play. I didn't know his death had been kept out of the press for two days. No autopsy was ever performed. *Ebony* came out with an article, "The Mystery Around Richard Wright's Death." And John A. Williams's *The Man Who Cried I Am* suggested in a very symbolic fashion that Wright might have been murdered.

I felt Wright wanted me to write his biography because nobody is going to be more sympathetic and understanding than I. I was in love with him, and he knew it. He could not marry me. I was not what he could marry. That's the whole truth of that. You can't say he didn't love me; I know he did.

People think that Wright helped me and my writing. But I was writing poetry as a child in New Orleans. I had published in *Crisis* even before I ever met Wright. He had a lot of influence on me, but it wasn't on my writing. It concerned social perspective—Marxism and the problems of black people in this country. I helped Wright. He couldn't spell straight; he couldn't write straight. I had just graduated from Northwestern with a major in English literature. Do you believe that I was just being introduced to literature by Wright?

Michel Fabre, Wright's biographer, recognized Wright and I had a literary friendship. He wrote note too long ago on behalf of Yale, asking if I'd donate Wright's letters. Yale wants my letters. Harper & Row called and told me I had a debt to literary posterity. I said, "I'll pay the debt in the way I choose."

They know what I wrote to Wright, but they don't know what he wrote to me. Here's one of Wright's letters. You notice he lived in a different place with every letter: Gates Avenue, Carlton Avenue, Rutledge Place, 136th Street . . . he lived at a dozen different addresses in three years' time.

You know, "Goose Island" was the story that Wright took from me for

Native Son. I had written it for a project, and he read it. It was a slum story. The main character was a girl who went into prostitution. It was very much like Studs Lonigan stuff. I started writing that story in the writer's project, and I took three years. I was supposed to enter my story in the same contest Wright entered *Uncle Tom's Children.*

I remember Wright wrote me a Special Delivery letter, requesting that I send him all the newspaper clippings on Robert Nixon's trial. I sent him enough to cover a nine by twelve foot floor. Then he came to Chicago and asked me to help him for a day or so. We went to the library, and on my card I got that [Clarence] Darrow book, and I took him to the office of [Ulysses] Keys, who had been the lawyer on the case. I asked Keys for the brief. Those were integral parts of *Native Son.* I still didn't know what his story was about. When he did tell me, I said, "Oh, we're writing about the same thing, only your character is a man and mine is a woman." My character was a very talented girl, a musician who became a prostitute. That's what the environment did to her. Of course, I didn't have the violence and murder.

Wright returned to New York. From then on the relationship began to deteriorate. It still hadn't ended until the week he sent the manuscript to the publishers, and then he said that he didn't have any further need of me. He had used me to the fullest extent. He didn't intend to marry me, not ever. I'm glad of that because it wouldn't have worked.

Well, Wright's violence comes out of his anger. I gave a speech at Amherst in which I said the keys to Wright's fiction and personality were: anger, ambivalence and alienation. In the biography I start with him as a child and show how this anger builds up. If you knew him, you would not know how much of that anger was seething inside of him. He was always angry. I didn't understand it. He was like a demon possessed. One of my theses is that Wright was angry as a child. The Farnsworth piece [*Richard Wright: Impressions and Perspectives,* edited by David Ray and Robert Farnsworth] revealed how well I knew him and that I was the one to do the biography. It also revealed the literary content of our friendship. I didn't start out to do a definitive biography. What the editors discovered when I quoted from the letters was that I have a psychoanalytic treatment of Wright. Furthermore, I tied it in with the writing. I did what nobody could do. I dealt with Wright's formative environment: his family background with the broken home, the poverty, the racism, the hunger, and their effects. Horace Cayton was to write the biography. He collected interviews with people who knew Wright, and in '68 was on his way to Paris to complete the research. Vincent Harding suggested

I should do the book, also Charles Rowell. I quit teaching with the full intention of writing full-time. I received a Ford grant in 1979 and completed the
book in the fall of 1980 just two weeks before my husband died.

I organized it into five or six parts. In the introductory statement I state
why I'm writing the book. I have a section on the psychic wound of racism
the first nineteen years of his life. I took a quote from Wendell Berry who
said: "If the white man has inflicted the wound of racism on black men, the
cost has been that he would receive the mirror image of that wound into
himself. I want to know as fully and as exactly as I can what the wound is
and how much I am suffering from it. And I want to be cured." I did the
research. I talk about what's wrong with Constance Webb's book and Fabre's
book. Fabre's book was written in the shadow of the widow. She determined
what should go in that book. He was indebted to her. He wanted to please
her. If he discovered something, he couldn't do anything with it. Then again,
he never knew the man. He never saw him in his life. Constance Webb may
have seen him, but that book is so disorganized. She talks about "Dear Richard," and anybody who knew Wright either called him Dick Wright or
Wright. They didn't call him Richard. She's off-base. In '73 everybody felt
that Fabre wrote the definitive biography. I beg to differ. A definitive biography should recreate the man for you so you see him and you know him.
Neither one of those books did that. I knew the man, and neither book is
Wright.

I went down to Natchez [Mississippi]. I made some contacts with his
father's side of the family. That has never been treated. The Wrights still
exist all over that area, in Mississippi, Louisiana, and in California. They are
just as middle-class as the mother's side. As a matter of fact Blyden Jackson
found out that one of Wright's relatives on the father's side had an advanced
degree and taught at Southern [University, Baton Rouge, Louisiana]. Yet you
are given the impression that his father's side is just a bunch of "dumb niggers."

Wright wasn't really born in Natchez. Fabre found that out, too. Wright
was born twenty-five miles from Natchez on a plantation. I found out that he
was not really born in Roxie. Wright was born before records were kept in
Mississippi. They weren't kept until 1912 on anybody in Mississippi, certainly not on black people before then. All people had then were baptismal
records. When I was born records were being kept in Alabama. I had a birth
certificate, but Wright was seven years older than I. But there are people
down there in Natchez and Roxie who remember the family.

As I said, it was at the Richard Wright symposium at Iowa in '71 that Allison Davis called my attention to Wright's neurotic anger. He talked about the anger that had a realistic basis—the anger that Wright had toward society and toward his family. Then Davis talked about the neurotic anger that Wright could neither understand nor control. He said nobody can tell what the wellsprings of any man's creativity are. You can only guess. The more I thought about it, being a creative person myself, the more I understood. That's why I selected the title, *The Daemonic Genius of Richard Wright.* There are different kinds of geniuses: demonic, intuitive, brooding, and orphic. Perhaps Faulkner had all four. Wright was definitely demonic. It's more than an idea of devils. It's the idea of creativity coming out of anger, madness, out of frustration, rage. Creativity comes out of the madness that borders on lunacy and genius. Allison Davis said that Wright's genius evidently came out of neurotic anger arising from his formative environment, and from the fact that Wright felt his mother didn't really love him. He felt rejected by his mother as well as deserted by his father. This rejection was combined with the cruelty and religious fanaticism within his household.

I talk about the lynchings Wright depicts in his work. There's the poem "Between the World and Me," and the story in *Black Boy* of a man in Memphis being lynched and dismembered. We also know that Aunt Maggie had two husbands killed by white people in Elaine, Arkansas. At the very time and place he's talking about in *Black Boy* there was, in fact, a race riot. One of those uncles [one of Aunt Maggie's husbands] was killed in that riot. Then Wright wrote "Big Boy Leaves Home," which is a story of a lynching. There's another lynching in *Eight Men.* So he's got three substantial pieces dealing with lynching.

When Wright was working on *12,000,000 Black Voices,* he asked where he could find some real, poor, black people in slums. The answer he got was: "Go home, poor nigger, go home."

When I knew Wright he lived at 3836 Indiana Avenue. They have now torn that part of Chicago down. That was a very bad slum when I knew it in the thirties. I was living then in what was considered to be the nice section, Woodlawn—6337 Evans—out there near Cottage Grove and 63rd Street. Now that is a slum. You talk about depravity! The building in which Wright lived had "La Veta" written over the door. Oh, God, what La Veta was like. I went to see Wright and found him in a room that only had one door. I kept trying to figure out what kind of room it was; there was no window; it was not as big as my bathroom. Afterwards, I realized that it was originally built as a closet. He and his brother both were sleeping in it. Don't tell me he wasn't living in abject poverty. I can remember just as clear as I'm sitting here, seeing Wright look in a paper bag and take out a sandwich that was two slices of white bread and a piece of bologna sausage that looked like it was turning green, without mayonnaise, mustard, or anything on it. He would just look at it and throw it over into the wastepaper basket. . . .

The second part of the biography is the period covering the Chicago years, when Wright began to sing his broken song. The Chicago years were ones in which he learnt to write, and his consciousness was raised. Then came the New York years—the Medusa Head. You know Louise Bogan's poem "The Medusa Head?" It's about the whole idea of psychological frustration. Every time you look at the Medusa's head you turn to stone. The psychological analogy is that you freeze and cease to grow. The New York years were the years in which Wright had success: publication, fame and fortune. But it was also the time he broke with everybody. He had started that in Chicago. Now he had no close friends. People like Baldwin weren't the only ones. I wasn't the only one. Neither was Ellison. He broke with the Communist Party. He broke with his family. He spent nineteen years in the South, ten years in Chicago, ten years in New York, and fourteen years in Paris.

He moved from "New York and the Medusa Head" to Paris where we have the "Twisted Torch and the Political Paradox of Black Nationalism v. Internationalism." Wright's marriage and children were just one part of his expatriation. The break with the Communist Party was another. The Communist Party had been the only life he had that was meaningful after he left the South. Now he was outside of that. He had always cultivated black scholars and writers. He always had friendships like the one we had, in Chicago, New York and Paris. No matter what he thought about them, he had them. But they always got to a point when he would cut them off. He could not maintain close, meaningful relationships. It was part of his sense of alienation, his lack of trust. As he had said, it was his protective covering from being hurt because he had been hurt so badly.

The Paris years were the years of the international man; he made an effort to pull together a philosophy that will include black people everywhere: Africa, Asia, America, the Caribbean, and South America—Pan-Africanism. He wanted to be the spokesman for black people all over the world. He also wanted to say, "Workers of the world unite," but he could not reconcile black nationalism with "red" internationalism. During the Presence Africaine conference this dilemma became apparent. He denied what he had said in '37 in

"The Blueprint for Negro Writers." He got up at the conference and said that he hoped that such dictates were no longer necessary. It wasn't that he was saying that we were no longer brothers. As he talked, he alienated his audience by saying that he hoped the black writer was beyond the point of prescriptive writing. The Africans got mad; the West Indians and the black Americans got mad. Every black person there was infuriated, which meant that the very thing he was struggling to accomplish, he had destroyed: the unity of black brotherhood. He was an outsider again. He would not go to the Rome conference.

Wright was a strange person. We could talk all day or all night. I never kissed him in my life, and we spent hours, days and weeks together. I can remember only one time, when he came back to Chicago and we just had a brief embrace. I could feel him freeze.

C.T.: You organized a symposium on black women writers.

Walker: The Phillis Wheatley Symposium. I'm not going to do any of that again. That phase of my life is over. I don't have energy for it anymore. I've got to write for the rest of my life, no matter how short or long it is. I've got to write. Teaching was never what I intended to do. Sometimes it might appear as though I have wasted so much of my life, but the classroom wasn't a waste. I enjoyed teaching; I was a good teacher. When I began to lose interest and enthusiasm for teaching, I quit. I never just sat there and drew the money, though I taught school to make a living. Moreover, I have never prostituted my writing. I toyed with the idea of being a writer-in-residence. But I don't think I will do it. I realized it's late in the day for me to make a list of priorities, but I must.

Writing is the first thing on my list, and I can't live long enough to write all the books I have in me. The sequel to *Jubilee* starts with Minna marrying in 1877, and ends with Vyry's death. Vyry died a month before I was born. Minna's first child was born in 1878, and that's when the family came to Mississippi. The sequel is the story of Minna and Jim. It's the story of the black church and the black school. It's about black benevolent societies, about jazz and blues. It's about Alabama, Mississippi and Florida.

I have another story which concerns a plot that's just recently become sensational. I haven't worked on it in ten years, though I've done over a hundred pages. It's a folk story entitled *Mother Broyer*. It's about a black woman who is a faith healer and a cult leader. Two things have happened that make that story sensational. One is the Jonestown incident; the other concerns Satanic cult activity here in Mississippi. A lot of black people in Mississippi have become involved in it. It breaks up homes, kills people, drives them insane. It's psychosexual stuff, and it frightens me. My mother told me the story about forty years ago. It starts in New Orleans, moves to Los Angeles, Harlem and ends up on the south side of Chicago, involving Jews, Catholics and black people. The main character is a girl who starts out as a Catholic, goes to the Holiness Church and then a Pentecostal church, and then ends up in jail in New York.

I would have done for black people what Faulkner did for the South. Wright wanted to do that, and he didn't. In recent years I've had to decide that nothing is an important as my writing. I've had to look at the effect of the Haley business on my audience, but I know I'm still on top where the audience is concerned. I know that anything I write will have an audience waiting to read it. That's why it's so important for me to do what I started out to do and not to be sidetracked.

About my autobiography . . . I remember something Lawrence Reddick said to me. He asked whether I was going to tell the whole truth. I said I'm not writing a confession. I don't have to tell anything I don't want to tell. I respect people being honest. Nikki is a very honest person; I don't think I have that kind of honesty. I don't believe in flouting what is contrary to the conventional. In "On Being Black, Female and Free," I said I have never felt like I could just defy convention to the point that I went out there all alone. That's a kind of brazen honesty I don't have.

America has a tendency to praise the rags-to-riches phenomenon, the self-made man image. When you talk about being self-made, that's a bubble I intend to burst with the Richard Wright story. The white man in America, the white world, caters to the black person who didn't go to school. I represent education, family, and background. I represent scholarship. I don't see why I must go out and be an entrepreneur. Everybody has help. Richard Wright didn't just learn all by himself. There's no such thing as Topsy just grows.

Being classified as a middle-class black woman has been my undoing. I'm considered a black snob. I have to face the fact that I inherited a tradition—I'm a third-generation college graduate. Society doesn't want to recognize that there's this kind of black writer. I'm the Ph.D. black woman. That's horrible. That is to be despised. I didn't know how bad it was until I went back to school [to teaching] and found out.

C.T.: Has the image of black women in American literature changed in Recent years?

Walker: I got this unpublished manuscript out for you because it addresses your question on images of black women in black American literature. Let me read some of it for you:

The image of black women in American literature has rarely been a positive and constructive one. White American literature has portrayed the black woman as she is seen in society, exploited because of her sex, her race, and her poverty. The black male writer has largely imitated his white counterparts, seeing all black characters and particularly females as lowest on the socioeconomic scale: as slaves or servants, as menial, marginal persons, evil, disreputable and power- less. The status of women throughout the world is probably higher now than ever before in the history of civilization. Black women have as much status in this regard as white women (who really don't have much either).

All black characters fall into typical and stereotypical patterns. Black people were portrayed in slavery and in segregated situations, equated with animals and having subhuman status: wild, savage, and uncivilized. This, in the face of great African civilizations and cultures, is shocking only if we do not under- stand why demeaning and dehumanizing roles have been assigned to blacks by whites in the first place. If we understand the underlying philosophy of white racism, and its development as a buttressing agent of slavery and segregation and if we see these social institutions as necessary for the development of West- ern world capitalism, then we would know why these subhuman roles have been assigned to blacks. But why blacks feel they should imitate such castigation of black characters is harder to answer.

It is necessary as always when approaching Afro-American literature in any form—poetry, prose, fiction, or drama—to give a background of the socioeco- nomic and political forces and the historical context before proceeding to a literary analysis or synthesis. Then we will have the necessary tools with which to examine the strange phenomena found in American and Afro-American liter- ature. Race is the subject of much of American literature, but race is almost the entire subject of Afro-American literature. Character, setting, action, event, tone, and philosophy all partake of the American myth and ethos of race. This focus may seem particular to the Southern literature of whites, but is also char- acteristic of black literature wherever it is found. There are some blacks who debate this issue, who beg the question of black humanity by seeking to avoid racial subjects and claiming a broader theme of universal subjects. I do not wish to avoid the subject. I think it is a natural point of departure for a black writer.

I do not, however, feel comfortable with the kind of treatment black women have received.

The plantation tradition is the source of female characters as the mammy, the faithful retainer, the pickaninny, Little Eva and Topsy, the tragic mulatto, conjure-woman or witch, the sex object, the bitch goddess, the harlot and prostitute and, last but not least, the matriarch. These are typical and stereotypical roles of black women in American fiction, poetry, and drama. Furthermore, black as well as white writers have worked within this tradition. It was on the plantation that the brutalizing of black women was at its greatest. Cooks, maids, wet nurses, forced mistresses and concubines were the most "refined" roles of black slave women. In that system it was "tit for tat and butter for fat." There were a lot of critics who tried to show that the field hand was the real black person, while the one in the house was treated more favorably. (They tried to do that with Vyry in *Jubilee*.) Miscegenation became a trite and hackneyed theme. . . .

Leslie Fiedler in *Love and Death in the American Novel* has made a brilliant study of the equating of black with evil and the black woman as portraying the loose, amoral, immoral harlot or slut, while the white, blue-eyed, blond woman was put on a pedestal and worshipped for her virtue and virginal purity. White was not only all right, but perfectly pure, while blackness and darkness meant evil. . . . John Pendleton Kennedy's *Swallow Barn* and Faulkner's *The Sound and the Fury* certainly had great influence on black writers. W. E. B. Du Bois in his *Dark Princess*—and even Sam Greenlee's *Spook Who Sat by the Door*— tried hard to portray black women with sympathy. James Weldon Johnson wrote one famous novel during the span between Dunbar/Du Bois and the Harlem Renaissance, but in it we see the white woman is again favored over the black woman. Langston Hughes and Arna Bontemps did a little better. . . .

Black men seem better when portraying old women. Ernest Gaines does this exceptionally well. No one can deny that a strong theme in Chester Himes is hatred for the middle-class black woman, whom he believes castrates and destroys her black male lover. Richard Wright does a bad job on women, period; but his black women fare even worse than his white women. Violence in his novels is a pattern, and this violence is frequently wreaked on women. The black woman is, therefore, a stereotype in fiction. Rarely does she achieve humanity, at least in the hands of male writers.

Of course, the positive view of women in Afro-American literature is only portrayed by black women. The earliest novel—*Iola Leroy* by Frances Harper— created a woman who is intelligent, attractive, human, and forceful in her personality. Harper sees black women as she sees herself—having strength of moral character, an indomitable will, perseverance, and a determination to overcome all handicaps and obstacles in her path. Zora Neale Hurston created an immortal love story in *Their Eyes Were Watching God,* and her portrayal of

Janie and her love for Tea Cake is recognized by black women as typical of their love for black men. . . . Black women have received such cruel treatment in the literature. Only when the author is a black woman does she have half a chance. With poetry it is slightly different. The brown girl was a beautiful subject during the Harlem Renaissance.*

I was distracted with *Roots.* I'm not distracted anymore. There's nothing that's going to happen, short of my health, that's going to keep me from my work.

You asked what advice I had to offer young writers. Well, I avoid giving advice because people don't want advice; they want sympathy. They want somebody to bolster and buttress them and say what they're doing is right. And I've found folks will not take your advice if you give it. They have to learn their own way.

I had a lot of people tell me I couldn't write. In fact, very few of my teachers encouraged me to believe that I could write. If I had believed them, I wouldn't still be trying.

---

*This excerpt is from a talk Margaret Walker gave at Purdue and at Texas Southern Universities in the late seventies, and is unpublished.

A Mississippi Writer Talks

John Griffin Jones / 1982

From *Mississippi Writers Talking*. Vol. 2. Jackson: University Press of Mississippi, 1983. Reprinted by permission of University Press of Mississippi.

March 13, 1982

She lives in a house at the end of Margaret Walker Alexander Drive in Jackson. Earlier on the day I came to call she'd attended a neighbor's wedding, and when the squad of young children who met me at the door brought me into the den to meet her, she was resting on the couch. She apologized, got to her feet and shooed away the kids, and suggested that we move to her study for the interview. As soon as I set up my equipment among her books, scattered papers and memorabilia, we began. She does not appear to be a woman in her seventies. There is nothing frail about her. It quickly became clear that ideas are her stimulant. When the issues we were discussing reached some level of complexity, she became animated. I realized in talking with her that, although she has behind her a distinguished literary career reaching back to the 1930s, her work is not done. She knows too many of the questions about black American experience to stop attempting to find answers in her work.

Jones: What I wanted to do, Dr. Alexander, to begin with, is just ask you to give me something about your early background and your early education, something about your parents, where they were from, and things of that nature.

Alexander: I was born two hundred fifty miles from here in Birmingham, Alabama, and I grew up two hundred miles from here, southwest of Jackson, in New Orleans, Louisiana. My father was born in the West Indies. He came from Jamaica Bluff Bay, Jamaica, British West Indies. At the time it was a British possession. He came to this country about seventy-four years ago, in 1908. He came to study and to become a minister, a Methodist minister. He went for a while to Tuskegee Institute, where Booker T. Washington and George Washington Carver and Emmett J. Scott were at the time. He did not like Tuskegee. It was not the school that he wanted to go to and that he thought about; and a friend of his came there and told him that where he wanted to go was Atlanta. He left Tuskegee and in 1910 he entered the divinity school called Gammon Theological Seminary in Atlanta. He graduated in 1913, and even before he had taken his degree he was selected to be an interim supply pastor in Pensacola, Florida. On the way there he met my maternal grandmother on the train, and she told him that her daughter played for the church where he was going. Her daughter was her oldest child, and my aunt. My mother was away in school at the time, in Washington, and when she came home that summer, my father saw her for the first time and fell in love at first sight. They were married the next year; and the night they were married they went to Birmingham, Alabama, where my father pastored the Second Church, as they called it then, in Enon Ridge, where all four of their children were born. I'm the oldest of four, and I was born in Birmingham—possibly, I guess, the next year after they were married. My sister is almost two years younger, and then another sister is two years younger than she; and we have a brother. The four of us are still alive and kicking, I guess. All of us teach school, at last I did until I retired. My two sisters teach. My mother is a music teacher—at least she taught music for twenty years—is now, of course, retired and almost bedridden. She's well up in age, still lives in New Orleans in the house where my father put us when we moved there in 1925. Two weeks after we went to New Orleans we moved into this house, where my family still lives. It's uptown in the University section of New Orleans, in walking distance from Tulane and Loyola and Newcomb, five blocks from the school on St. Charles Avenue where my mother and father taught, which later became Dillard University. I grew up in a home surrounded by books and music. As you can see, I like books.

Jones: You're surrounded by books here.

Alexander: Yes, my father's books were his most prized possession; and he had a room full of books. My mother had a very good piano. At the time it didn't seem like much, but now, looking back, they realize it was a very good piano. They began housekeeping with books and a piano. A typewriter and their books and the piano were all their worldly possessions, besides their clothes. They had no furniture. At first they rented a room, when they were first married, to live in. I was born not in a parsonage, but in one of those rented places, the old Boulware house, where they lived when they first lived in Birmingham; but by the time I was six years old, my father had bought a house in Birmingham. We went to New Orleans when I was ten, and he bought another house. So I have grown up under the roof that my parents owned. It's always been a feeling of pride that I can't remember when we rented.

Jones: Yes, ma'am.

Alexander: I think that's typical of a certain type of people in the South, always feeling that you should have your own house and land.

Jones: Yes, right.

Alexander: It goes as far back as the first years after slavery when my great-grandmother, who's in *Jubilee,* sought and succeeded finally in getting a home of her own.

Jones: I remember.

Alexander: It's part of a Southern tradition, I think. I went to school first here in Mississippi. My very first day of school was in Meridian, Mississippi. My father and mother were teaching that year in a church school in Meridian called Haven. They stayed there the year that I was five years old; then they moved back to Birmingham. And when they moved back to Birmingham, I went to public school for a while, oh, two or three years. The school where they were teaching in Birmingham burned, and that's the reason my father sought employment in New Orleans. He taught for a while there in the public schools, taught at Miles College and at the public high school, which was known then as Industrial High and became later Parker High. In New Orleans, I attended the Model grade school, which was part of the old New Orleans University, where my parents were working. My father taught Bible and philosophy, religion and philosophy; and my mother taught music. My two sisters and my brother are all musical. I wish I were! I always wanted to play the piano—I took some lessons—I tried to learn to play the violin, and I tried to learn to sing, but I am literally tone-deaf and can't even pitch myself on key. I think those are the important things about my early education. I finished grade school and high school in New Orleans. I went to Gilbert Academy, and I had two years of college in a black college where my mother and father were teaching, before I transferred to Northwestern in Evanston, Illinois. I was seventeen when I went there, and I was a junior in college. It seems as if I might have been precocious; maybe I was just pushed along, because I went to school when I was four or five years old. I could read when I was four. I finished grade school when I was eleven, and I finished high school when I was fourteen—in three years I finished high school; and I would have finished college at eighteen, but I was out my senior year because we had no money to send me back to Northwestern, and I was a nervous wreck anyway! But I went back following my nineteenth birthday, and I graduated that next summer. I was nineteen as a senior, but about six weeks after my twentieth birthday I graduated from Northwestern. I started working seven months later on the WPA writers' project in Chicago. It was a wonderful place to work, because many very famous and illustrious writers were on that project. Some of them I knew. Richard Wright was on that project. Nelson Algren was on that project. James Farrell's wife was there when I went there; I don't know that James Farrell ever really was on the project, but he was around, and he had written his Studs Lonigan stories then.

Jones: Right!

Alexander: Arna Bontemps was a special person on that project. Katherine Dunham, the dancer, was on that project. John T. Frederick, who was editor of the *Midland Magazine,* was project director for a while. It started with Louis Wirth, who was a professor in sociology from University of Chicago and before I had gotten on it, I had worked for the Institute for Juvenile Research, which was directed by Clifford Shaw; and he had two men under him who went on to fame in the area of sociology—Eustace Hayden, Jr., and Joseph Lohmann, who went out to California and became sheriff of Orange County. The people on that project were just amazing. Willard Motley and Frank Yerby were on that project, and Fenton Johnson. They tell me Studs Terkel was there. I vaguely remember Studs Terkel, but I don't think that I remember him from the project. And Saul Bellow had been at Northwestern with the same teacher in creative writing that I had, but he graduated two years later, so that if he came on the project I didn't know him.

Jones: Now, who was the teacher?

Alexander: The teacher was Edward Buell Hungerford, a wonderful scholar, and great man. I think there's a card right there on the desk from him just recently.

Jones: There it is.

Alexander: He was my favorite teacher; he's up in age now.

Jones: That's right. Let me reach back. We've covered a lot of ground, so let me reach back and set up something here. You say your father was at Tuskegee before you were born? You were born in 1915?

Alexander: Yes. My father was at Tuskegee around 1908. Booker T. Wash-

ington died, I think, the year I was born. It's interesting, because Frederick
Douglass died the year my mother was born; and my mother remembered
hearing and reading of Paul Laurence Dunbar, but he was dead about nine or
ten years before I was born.

Jones: That's what I was wondering, because you said your father didn't
like Tuskegee, and I was wondering if it was . . .

Alexander: He didn't want that kind of education. My father said that
when he went to Tuskegee, they put him in the kitchen washing dishes, and
he broke all the dishes. Then they put him in the fields, and he was no good
there. So they said, "What can you do? What do you know how to do?"
Everybody at Tuskegee worked. And he said, "Well, I keep books and I can
take shorthand and I type." "Oh," they said, "you belong in the office." So
he went into Emmett J. Scott's office, who was assistant to Booker T. Washington at the time, and my father worked there until he left Tuskegee. But he
said it was a school basically for vocational and industrial education; and
even though Tuskegee became in a way a great university, it did not emphasize classical education.

Jones: Right.

Alexander: That's right; and my father wanted to study for the ministry,
which was a professional, graduate type of education. He had already completed what was the equivalent of college work before he came over. He did
later take a degree from a college in this country. He got his divinity degree
at Gammon and then went to Northwestern and took a master's in Biblical
literature. After that, my mother could not persuade him to go further. He
said he didn't have any use for a doctorate and would go no longer to school.
By the time he had gotten that master's he was nearly forty years old, and he
said he didn't want to go to school anymore.

Jones: I was wondering if in leaving Tuskegee he was rejecting Booker T.
Washington's philosophy.

Alexander: I think he was. My father had no great admiration and respect
for either Booker T. Washington or George Washington Carver, or any of the
other people at Tuskegee. He felt they were flunkies and toadies to the white
man, you see; they were the great compromisers. He liked *Souls of Black
Folk*. Du Bois was in Atlanta at the time my father was at Tuskegee; and by
the time Daddy went, in 1910, to Atlanta, Du Bois was just leaving Atlanta.
He was going then to New York, to the NAACP and the *Crisis Magazine*. But

my father greatly admired Du Bois and everything he stood for. He did not admire Booker T. Washington or Carver at all. My mother did; and the strange thing was that my father had had enough training to be able to use his hands. He was a good tailor, and I don't know whether he learned something about it at Tuskegee or not, but I think he already knew it, because he practiced that trade even after he was married. My father was a good tailor, a bookkeeper, as he said, and he knew shorthand and typing. He taught my mother some shorthand, and she was a good typist, too. But Daddy was a man interested very much in higher education, in book learning. My father was a scholar of the classical order. He even knew Latin, Greek, and Hebrew. And he was interested in languages. He spoke Spanish, and he read and spoke French; and he knew Hindustani. He could even converse with the Jewish merchants in Yiddish. That was the kind of education he admired.

Jones: Did he instill this in his family?

Alexander: Yes. As I look back upon it with my own children and my siblings, we were a family who were expected to pursue goals in higher education, always. My sisters and brother went to graduate school. The sister in New York has completed most of the work for the doctorate in music; the sister in New Orleans took two master's degrees, one from the University of Chicago in child psychology and another at Loyola at New Orleans in the teaching of science and math to little children. My brother pursued the master's in mathematics. My mother went to graduate school; so you see, we tended to look up to a professional graduate education. I have four children. All of them have had a college education. One is a lawyer, so he went to law school, beyond college years. The others still aspire to go to school. It just follows a kind of pattern in the family.

Jones: Yes. Was it your father's idea that book learning was the fastest way to racial equality?

Alexander: I don't think that was ever in my mind. I really think now, as I look back, that my father believed in learning for learning's sake, for the sake of knowledge.

Jones: Yes.

Alexander: That was the much bigger idea. My grandmother and her family aspired to middle-class citizenship and considered education a means toward it. That was the American Negro attitude. But my father was not an American Negro. He had come from out of the islands, and knowledge for the sake of knowledge was something they knew in those islands. There's a difference.

Jones: Did your father—did you ever see that he was chafing under the atmosphere that was in the South at the time that you were growing up?

Alexander: Well, I think so, yes. Once in Birmingham he was chased by a policeman who saw him with books and a fountain pen; my father had been teaching night school. He couldn't conceive of a black man as a professional man. I wrote a poem once about my father, and I said that he was always puzzled, bewildered, disturbed about race prejudice in the South. He was never prepared for it. But I don't think black people as a whole, no matter how many years we have lived here, are ever prepared for sudden racial frontal attacks. Nobody ever gets complacent about it. It's always a feeling of what could be more stupid than this, and why did people take this attitude, and when will they cease to think this way? You see, I think that's true with the average black person. The feeling of slavery and previous condition of servitude, I think it's more in the white mind than in the black mind. I don't think black people—now that we say we are a hundred and fifteen, nearly a hundred and twenty years away from slavery—I don't think the average [black person], and certainly not the black child or the young black person, slavery never enters his mind as a reason or cause for this. In writing abut Richard Wright, I came upon some interesting deductions and conclusions of this man who was badly scarred by racism.

Jones: That's very interesting. You deal with this problem in your new book on Wright? [*The Daemonic Genius of Richard Wright,* to be published by Howard University Press.]

Alexander: Certain conclusions that he made, in which he seemed to feel that the only explanation for the kind of suffering and racism and racial pain the black man suffers in America, not just in the South, is an existentialist one. He says that we suffer for no reason at all, that the idea of black people suffering simply because they are black is not a reason for human suffering. It's absurd.

Jones: It is.

Alexander: An absurdity is explained best by the existentialist, you see, and he thinks that there is no justifiable reason for racial suffering in America. I think earlier he might have felt as the Marxists felt, that it was an economic determinism, that it was because of the use of slavery—to buttress rising capitalism and industrialism—that this is the reason for slavery; and that the slave-holding people, the slavers, slave masters, had to develop some kind of rationale to justify their keeping other human beings in bondage. I talk about it a great deal in *Jubilee.* I think it's a theme, a thesis, that runs through much of Afro-American literature. Do you have another question now? Are you ready to go on to something else?

Jones: I really did want to ask you some more questions about slavery and the way you use it in *Jubilee,* the way you came to conceive of it as a young writer. You know, taking graduate school history courses—I'm not so sure that that's the real correct and best image of slavery that one can get, just discussing it from a scholarly standpoint.

Alexander: Well, fiction, I think I say in a little book that I wrote called "How I Wrote *Jubilee,*" I say that more people will read a story than will read the actual history books.

Jones: That's true.

Alexander: And, therefore, the novelist as a social historian, has a job to do that the historian cannot do.

Jones: Yes, ma'am, I agree.

Alexander: *Jubilee* took a long time in the writing, because I guess I had to live a lot of things before I could do the authentic writing. I didn't know how to write a novel, and I had to learn. But then I had to become saturated in the period, and I had to do a lot of research. I spent ten years in actual research, thirty years from the time I started writing that book at Northwestern until the conclusion in Iowa. Meanwhile, it had grown out of my childhood.

Jones: Yes, ma'am.

Alexander: My grandmother told the story to me when I was just a little girl sitting around at night before bedtime, or at bedtime. When I was nineteen and a senior at Northwestern, I thought I was mature enough and ready to write the novel. I had already tried to write a novel when I was about twelve, and it didn't do very well. I started this one and it didn't do very well; but I wrote about three hundred pages and then realized that I didn't know how to do it. It didn't sound right and I put it down. I had an ideal for *Jubilee.* I don't know why even—I guess it's amazing that I actually finally got through it, because I wanted it to be perfect; and I think that is a great mistake many writers make, that they want their books to be perfect—their first book or their next book or whatever; and they do as much as possible to be perfectionists. That's all very good, provided you eventually let go of the thing.

Jones: Get it down. . . .

Alexander: And leave it alone! I think Ralph Ellison's *Invisible Man* did that to him.

Jones: Yes, ma'am.

Alexander: And I really believe that is the reason that Ralph hasn't been able to finish another book, that perfectionist business.

Jones: That's right.

Alexander: I don't think Wright was as much of a perfectionist . . . he might have been a perfectionist because he was highly critical; but he wasn't too introspective; otherwise he would not have written over and over again the same plot.

Jones: That's right. But it was something that you always had to grapple with as a writer, and the poem "For My People" came from other places in your mind than did the story of *Jubilee?*

Alexander: I don't know. You see, that's an interesting comment on the creative process. I started writing poetry when I was about twelve or thirteen, but I had already tried to compose prose when I was ten. I never thought it was going to be as hard to write prose as it was to write poetry, but as I grew older I realized that it might sometimes be harder. Most young people, and I think I was no exception, have the notion that poetry is rhymed and metered writing, whereas prose is not. And that is not really a good definition of either poetry or prose. Good prose has as much rhythm as good poetry, and it has its own imagery, and it has all the same things, but the structure is different. The use of metaphor and simile for the poet is much more necessary and involves poetic patterns that come from the same thinking creatively as the prose patterns. It isn't in one corner of the mind and then another corner; it's all from the same creative thinking. And creative thinking, all of it, begins the same way. And the artist, whether he is visual or graphic or plastic, whether he's a writer, a musician, an architect, or a sculptor, or painter, regardless, he simply learns to conceive things in terms of the unit of his work. If he's an architect, he sees space and design; he's confronted with a certain creative use of space. The musician has a motif, and he hears the certain musical sounds and patterns together. The painter sees color, line, and movement in building a composition. And the writer has nothing but words, you see, but he gets an idea; he has a concept first and then a thought and then an idea, and then figurations and configurations, and he's off to the races.

Jones: Yes, ma'am. It seems to me, though, that with *Jubilee* you had the great pressure of not only making sure that your work had historical integrity, getting down the slavery and events of the Civil War and Reconstruction accurately, but you also had the pressure of making it worthy to your family.

Alexander: Well, I think I'm faced with more problems with the sequel than I was with that; because people now have a certain conception and a way that they want things done, and maybe things won't always fall into those patterns. How a family feels could be very, very opposite to what you're going to do. Then they would feel that you had been unfair and un-faithful to your family heritage and maybe something there was detrimental. I don't know. I've got it in my mind and I hope I'm going to live to get it down, but it better be soon!

Jones: Right! But your poem "For My People" came out in 1942.

Alexander: No, I wrote that poem in 1937; and the book—as a thesis, I composed a thesis for my master's degree in English at Iowa in 1940, I did that book; and I won the Yale award in 1942, and that's when the book was published. [*For My People,* Yale University Press.] But the poem was five years old when the book was published. And I had written that poem some-time around my twenty-second birthday. It was written in fifteen minutes on a typewriter, with the exception of the last stanza of strophe, and then I took that to the project [WPA] and showed it to Nelson Algren, who told me that I ought to say what I wanted for my people, and then I'd have a poem; and of course I knew what I wanted to say there—another world, another whole earth to come into being. And I never changed in the ideas of that last stanza. I wrote a number of poems at the time in the same vein, with the same kind of long line. My most recent book of poetry has one or two poems in it like that, but for the most part, the verse, my pattern of free verse, has changed greatly since I wrote "For My People."

Jones: At the time that you sat down at the typewriter to write "For My People" and you were twenty-two years old, were you angry, did you feel like . . .

Alexander: No, I don't think it was anger that that poem came out of . . . I don't think I write out of anger. I say that is the way that Richard Wright writes; and there's a lot of protest. I don't think my writing has grown out of anger or hostility. I think it's grown a great deal out of a kind of brooding, intuitive, internal questioning and seeking answers. I don't think that ever I was writing out of anger. I don't think so. When I look at Wright's work and see what you produce out of anger. I know that we were thinking differently. He writes violently.

Jones: Yes, he does.

Alexander: And I never have done that. Both of us have sometimes ex-pressed revolutionary ideas, but mine didn't come out of anger. They came out of deep consideration and contemplation of problems. I think it's been more intuitive than demonic.

Jones: Right. When you say "let a new race of men rise and take control," it's revolutionary . . . especially for 1937, and for a Southerner.

Alexander: The thirties . . . well, black people, black literature, Afro-American literature was very revolutionary. It was protest literature, and Wright was the leader of that. I knew Wright, and I think he influenced my thinking in that respect. Langston had come through the twenties writing a very different kind of stuff, and then in the thirties and forties he was writing more in terms of the mood of black literature. In the thirties it was protest. In the forties we were getting into the war years, and the cold war years in the fifties. And of course the forties, the fifties don't sound like the thirties and the twenties any more than the sixties and the seventies sound like the eighties. They're very different. Each decade is different.

Jones: That's right. What about Richard Wright? Tell me about meeting him. We just got through reading *Black Boy* for a graduate history course that I took.

Alexander: Did you like the book?

Jones: I did, personally. It affected me personally and made my heart bleed. It was interesting to see the reaction that young whites have to it today, because most of the class is made up of young whites.

Alexander: Some of them did not like it.

Jones: Some of them felt that he lacked objectivity and that all of the white people that he encountered growing up in Mississippi in the twenties and thirties could not have been that purely evil.

Alexander: They weren't the twenties and thirties. He left here in '25. He was a very angry man. I don't know why people would expect a biography to be objective.

Jones: He's not pretending to be objective.

Alexander: Not there. But I talk about *Black Boy* in the book. And two black writers, two Afro-Americans, have done an excellent job of criticizing the book. The book is a social document. Today it's more than a literary work of art and a legend, it's a social document. *Black Boy* is Richard Wright's youth, and he is an angry young man. He's ambivalent and angry and alienated and aberrated—all of those things. I think you can see most of that in *Black Boy.*

Jones: Certainly. A great deal of the book is about stereotypes. Most of the people that he runs into represent a stereotype of the Southerner, white or black.

Alexander: I think that's the very first thing I talk about when—I have an essay in there that I took over from something I did for the Mississippi Arts Festival, and they printed it, and I'm using it in the book because I think it's a very good introduction to a side of black, Southern literature that we haven't thought about. That's the black side of it. We've studied the white. Wright is very Southern, he's very Southern; and he belongs to a definite tradition in Southern literature, which is called Southern gothic, gothicism. A man like Faulkner belongs in it; even Miss Welty belongs in it.

Jones: Erskine Caldwell?

Alexander: Yes They're all very much Southern gothic. And Wright is more than that. Wright belongs in four great traditions. He's Southern gothic; he's American naturalist of the Middlewestern brand, naturalistic writer; he's an Afro-American who's interested in humanism, and the humanism runs through two hundred years of Afro-American literature; and then he's a realist. Wright is a great intellect. His intellect was so great that his own world view incorporates five great ideas of the twentieth century. And I don't think even Faulkner could top that. Wright is Marxist—everybody knows that, but Wright is Freudian; Wright is existentialist; Wright is a pan-Africanist; and Wright understood a great deal about industrialization, but he didn't understand too much of the technological nature of society, but he was trying to. So you see, those five ideas are in his works. And that's a great intellectual synthesis.

Jones: What about the danger—I wanted to ask you about this later but now's fine—what about the danger of combining? As you say, he's combined so many ideas, the biggest ideas. Most novelists say that the most dangerous thing and the most threatening and harmful thing to the novel itself is didacticism and preaching and that type of thing. Do you . . .

Alexander: Wright is not always didactic. He is sometimes, the didacticism is there sometimes; but I think what I thought about when I was writing *Jubilee* was how much burden of history can fiction bear? You see, a lot of people think of Wright's protest novels as being thinly veiled sociology and that a novel is not that. All I ever heard people say is that a novel is not sociology, and a novel is not psychology, and a novel is not philosophy, and a novel is not history, and a novel is not all these things. But a novel is all of those; a novel has all that in it.

Jones: Did Wright influence you as a writer?

Alexander: Yes, I think he influenced me. I think I have to say he did. He didn't, as Fabre [Michel Fabre, *The Unfinished Quest of Richard Wright*] very tritely and very glibly says, "introduce me to literature." It's obvious if I had graduated from Northwestern when I met Wright, and I was a major in English literature, that he didn't introduce me to literature.

Jones: Right.

Alexander: But he did influence me because I learned not to accept dialectical materialism. I'm not a materialist—I consider myself still grounded in Christianity and the idealistic philosophy of my father and my forefathers; but I did get a different social perspective. I did begin to think more seriously about racial affairs in America, and I did get a pole of meaning around which I could integrate ideas from Wright. He and I read many of the same books. I think three black writers outside of my own family influenced me, and Wright was one of them. Langston Hughes was one and W. E. B. Du Bois was another. Those three men, I think their ideas took hold of me. I saw Langston when I was sixteen, I saw Du Bois when I was seventeen, and I saw Wright when I was twenty.

Jones: They all came to Northwestern?

Alexander: No, no. Langston came to the South and told my parents to get me out of the South so that I would develop. He came to New Orleans where they were teaching, and I guess I was instrumental in their bringing him because I wanted to see what a "real, live poet" looked like. I'd never seen one. I saw James Weldon Johnson in New Orleans, heard him read his poetry. I heard Marian Anderson and Roland Hayes. I don't think I heard

Paul Robeson in the South, I think I heard him first in the North. But these were just magnificent voices. Langston—I knew him for thirty-five years, and I think I was influenced by Langston. I don't write like him, no. But we spent a lot of time together, and I have a number of books that he autographed to me. I was looking at one today that says "This is with the hope that you will continue to grow in the wonder of poetry," something like that. I believe it's right there. "For Margaret, your health, salud. Spanish Revolution."

Jones: And it goes on. "March 30, 1938, Chicago, Langston."

Alexander: And "For Margaret, with high hopes for your continued growth in the wonderland of poetry. Sincerely, Langston." That was at Atlanta University.

Jones: 1947.

Alexander: Yes. I have another little one here. It was a Christmas greeting to me and my husband, and I thought I had another one here. I had at one time sixteen books by Langston. Most of them had been autographed for me. I didn't know Du Bois nearly as intimately, or closely, as I did Langston and Wright. I saw Du Bois at Northwestern. He came there to speak. I saw Harriet Monroe at Northwestern . . . I don't have nearly as many of Du Bois's book. I'm getting ready to do a speech for the behavioral scientists' convention here, and I'm going to talk about the seminal mind of Du Bois. He's father of sociology or behavioral science; and in my estimation there are five men who are the giants of the century. Wright, of course, is taken with all of them, and I realized as I wrote a book of poetry about three years ago when I came into retirement that Marx and Freud, Kierkegaard, Einstein, and Du Bois are the five great thinkers of the century. Du Bois—everything that deals with the race, the sociology of the Negro, the history of the Negro in this country, the problems of world Negroes, the black world problems, pan-Africanism, and freedom and unity in the black world, all of that is out of Du Bois, those very great ideas there. Then Marx, of course, is the man the revolutions have all been patterned after. Socialism, there's no question, is the politics of the twentieth century. All revolutions have been based on it. Whether we like it or not, that's the way it is. Freud is the person who dug the groundwork for the understanding of self and psychology, and we've gone a long way from him; and I'm not a Freudian. I don't hold to him: Freud is no good for women. I like what Karen Horney says about psychoanalysis and about the neurotic personality of our time, and about personality, period. Wright and I believed very differently about personality; he believed the Freudian ideas of

creativity, of art, of sex, of everything, you see, whereas I think the best of
Freud is his groundwork for psychoanalysis. That's it. I don't think he understood women at all.

Jones: You were going on to define how you differ from Wright.

Alexander: Well, I differ from Wright in psychology and philosophy. I'm
not a materialist. All of his life, from Marxism on, Wright was interested in
the materialist stance in philosophy. But I am not a materialist at all. I think
that in economics Marx is sound, but I think he is spiritually bankrupt and he
can't work a philosophy in the same way that I would not branch off with
Hegel as Marx does. You see, Hegel goes two ways. I would rather go along
with Immanuel Kant than Hegel. That's a way that we differ, very, very much
so. Our perspectives differ, too, in that I'm a woman and he was a man,
though I think he was as ambivalent sexually as he was racially, socially, or
politically. And that's saying a lot, but I think I've come up with that. I think
that what happens to black and white men in the South is a very, very serious
psychological problem. I think that there is an aberration that comes out of
the aberrational South, in that there's a mirror image of racism in the South,
that what white men see in black men, black men see in white men. Have
you ever thought about that?

Jones: I've never thought about it, no.

Alexander: What happens is that there is a kind of sexual warfare in the
South between black and white men over their women. Everybody understands that.

Jones: Yes, ma'am. Certainly. The cult of Southern womanhood and all of
that.

Alexander: Yes, all of that. And the black man in Mississippi particularly,
is eaten up with the same kind of racism that the white man is. He, and
Wright was—they suffer from all the problems of the racist sexual warfare,
and race and sex become corollaries in the South. And I don't know why it
hasn't—it dawns on me, I haven't read it anywhere, I haven't seen it, but the
more I read Wright the more I realize what had happened to him; and of
course, I have Wendell Berry, *The Hidden Wound,* in which he says if the
white man inflicted racism on the black man he got it in himself at the same
time, because there's a mirror image; and he couldn't hate this man without
bringing some of that . . .

Jones: Hatred into his own life. Is that what you mean?

Alexander: That's part of it. But that mirror image of racism—the worst thing for the white man in the Deep South, the Southern white man, the worst thing in the world was a black man with a white woman.

Jones: Sure.

Alexander: For the black man, the worst thing in the world was a black woman with a white man. Same thing. See, same thing, isn't it?

Jones: But the black man, in his entire experience in America, had been used to seeing his black woman with a white man all through slavery.

Alexander: Yes, but wait a minute, wait a minute. It's not that he got accustomed to it; he never did. He was mad about it all the time. It was a part of his anger, part of black rage, you see, and he was living with the white man. That's part of his black rage. And for the white man, he said any day he catches that black man with a white woman, he will lynch him. So he's got the rage, too, hasn't he?

Jones: Yes, ma'am, I understand what you mean.

Alexander: It's there, and it's been there a long time. The problem won't be suppressed. You have a philosophy of race that says there's superiority and inferiority; an oppressed people who develop a sense of inferiority, because they are told that so long. This is denigrating and denying humanity; and it affects the psyche of the black male. It hurts him worse than it does the black woman, though she's affected too. The white woman is affected in a different way from the black woman; therefore, you have in the women's liberation movement two strains. That Southern white woman's quest for liberation is very different from that Northern or that Southern black woman's quest for liberation. They're not moving down the same path. They don't have the same goals; they're not of the same mind.

Jones: Yes. Perhaps that accounts for the way the women's movement is fragmented and hasn't been successful in a lot of areas.

Alexander: As long as it went along in a universal way with the civil rights movement and the movement for black liberation and the movement of all people, the gay business and all of that, it's all right, as long as everybody wants to be free. But when you come to certain segmented sections of it. . . .

Jones: And you said that the kind of bitterness and outrage that grew within Wright about the problems of sex and the South and the other problems. . . .

Alexander: They aberrate him, they make him aberrant. For example, take that child, that black boy in Atlanta. The white papers scream out right away that this is a homosexual, but I don't think anybody understands that that's deep in the Southern culture, to say that any time you have a very brilliant, smart, intellectual black, that he's gay.

Jones: Yes, gay.

Alexander: And as Leroi Jones said, "White man called us faggots until the end of our lives." I remember the very first time that anybody approached me with the idea of—a white fellow in Iowa who was married to a black woman, at least they were living together whether they were married or not, said to me, "Why is it that all black intellectual men are so emasculated?" I said, "Are they?" My father was intellectual, a scholar, and I didn't think of him as emasculated at all. Do you see? It's deep in the culture.

Jones: Yes, ma'am. I did want to ask you—I know that all during the early 1960s you were in the process of writing *Jubilee* in the final form, but what about what took place here in Mississippi in the sixties, the early sixties, with the violence and the civil rights workers coming in, how did that affect you? I know you were at Jackson State.

Alexander: Well, I wasn't here. I found myself in an untenable position in the early sixties. My students were in revolt, and the administration was holding the line for segregation on orders of the powers that be—shall we say, the establishment. And like most of the teachers, I was called in and asked whether I was on the side of the students or on the side of the administration. And I said I couldn't take either side. If I sided with my students against the administration, I wouldn't have a job; and if I sided with the administration against the students, I wouldn't have anybody to teach, and I wouldn't be able to do that either. So I went to school. I was ill in the summer of '60, in the hospital, so in '61 I went out to Iowa, and I came back in the state through a hellish year, '61 and '62, but the fall of '62 I was in Iowa and I stayed there three years. And I came back, and it was still going on. But I was gone the most violent year of all. 1963 was the most violent year.

Jones: The death of Medgar Evers.

Alexander: Yes. Kennedy was killed, the march on Washington, the children bombed in the church in Birmingham—it was a violent year, it was a horrible year. Then in '65 they killed Malcolm X; and in '68 both King and Bobby Kennedy. All of the sixties were violent. But '63 was the worst year of all.

Jones: Do you remember it as a time of great excitement? Were you excited about what black people were finally doing?

Alexander: I think it was a time of sheer terror and, well, there were some things you liked, and some things you were afraid of. There were times you were just plain fearful of what was going to happen. I was here in the summer of '64. We hadn't remodeled the house; we didn't have this part of the house. And I would sit out under the tree and read for my comprehensives. That was the summer that the civil rights workers were murdered.

Jones: Goodman and Schwerner [and Chaney].

Alexander: Goodman and Schwerner and Chaney were killed over there out from Philadelphia, and everybody said they were going to find out that . . . and, of course, Dulles [Allen Dulles] came down here and said it. It was clandestine. . . .

Jones: Civil rights activities.

Alexander: Civil rights activities. Subversive activities of the Klan; the Ku Klux Klan did that.

Jones: Yes. Right.

Alexander: That wasn't the civil rights workers. I lived in a neighborhood here where a lot of civil rights workers from out of the state came and stayed in here. One night I kept the daughter of a Tufts professor and doctor, and I was afraid. I told her, "Oh, you can't get out on the road now and go." You know, coming out of a black community and going back there. I said, "You'll have to wait till morning." And I kept her overnight. But nobody knew when people were in here.

Jones: Yes, that's right.

Alexander: I don't think I had nearly the problems in the sixties that I had in the seventies. My problems were very great in the seventies. The whole decade of the seventies was personally traumatic for me. My son was caught up in the RNA [Republic of New Africa] stuff, and two students were killed at Jackson State.

Jones: May of '70.

Alexander: That's right. My son was in Vietnam and came home in '70; another son in law school came very nearly being killed. His car was totally wrecked; people had deliberately run into him. Oh, I just went . . . I had it in the seventies—ending up with *Roots* [the controversy over *Roots* and its alleged plagiarism from *Jubilee*].

Jones: Yes, ma'am.

Alexander: I was supposed to go abroad on a Fulbright, and I couldn't leave home. I don't think the decade of the sixties was nearly as traumatic for me as the decade of the seventies.

Jones: I read a book, conversations between you and Nikki Giovanni.

Alexander: Did you like that?

Jones: I enjoyed that very much, but I was—I know what you mean when you say that it was a traumatic time for you because of the conflicts between a young black writer who was the product of the sixties and all the turmoil at that time.

Alexander: I heard from Nikki last week, and I was surprised because I hadn't heard from her in almost a year. Everybody says she's mellowing. I don't think I'm mellowing at all!

Jones: The conflict between your traditional Christian values, the Christian tradition that you grew out of, and the tradition of the sixties that produced Nikki Giovanni and her generation of poets—it was a fascinating kind of confrontation between the two of you. Black culture, the whole face of black existence, was changing at that time. Wasn't it?

Alexander: Well, in a way yes and in a way not. What was it, the saying—the more things change the more they seem to remain the same. Change, yes, but not enough change. Perhaps the eighties will be even more difficult than any of those decades, because we are in such an economic pit. I don't see us getting out of that economic pit; and the political reins are pulling tighter into neo-conservatism. What Reagan is setting up can last an awful long time. Of course, black people are not going to be able to change it by themselves. It will take thinking white people to change it, too.

Jones: Yes, ma'am. What does it mean for the black artist?

Alexander: Well, for me, I don't know what's going to happen when the book on Richard Wright comes out. I don't know. I wondered what would happen when *Jubilee* came out. I didn't expect it to be as well received as it was. It sold into the millions of copies. People used to say to me, "If you have trouble in Mississippi, you'd just leave, wouldn't you?" I'd say, "Yes." But then I had trouble and I didn't leave, because I contended there was no place to go where it was any better. Might be terribly bad here, but show me where it's better!

Jones: Are you glad you made that choice?

Alexander: Oh, I think Mississippi has been good for me all along. I'm glad I made the decision to come to Mississippi, and I'm glad I've stayed here. It's given me the pace I needed. I couldn't take the pace of New York. I don't like New England. I don't like cold weather for one thing. But that's not all of it. Climate of opinion. You hardly have anybody to talk to. There's nobody to raise an intellectual issue with you. That's the truth.

Jones: Is it?

Alexander: That's the truth. The few black and white people I know who are intellectually of some size or some stature are too busy to be bothered most of the time. Of course, the condition of the country is the same everywhere. You pick up the newspaper, and you're just about as well off—I don't see the New York papers and I don't see the Washington papers, almost never anymore. It used to be that if you didn't see those papers, you didn't know what was going on. "There ain't nothing going on, see?" And I'd just as soon be in Jackson, Mississippi, as Podunk, New York. But it is a sad state of affairs. And education in the country is a disaster area. We're certainly not going forward. If we're not going backward, we must be standing still.

Jones: We could talk for a lot longer, if we had time.

Alexander: I have been known to go on for a twenty-four-hour stretch, but I'm tired now.

Jones: I know you're tired. I'm sorry to have kept you so long. And thank you.

Interview with Margaret Walker

Ruth Campbell / 1983

Transcribed from an interview aired on Mississippi Educational Television, August 4, 1983. Reprinted by permission of the Mississippi Authority for Educational Television.

RC: Alexander, when did you first begin to write?

MW: Well, as nearly as I can figure, I was writing prose before I wrote poetry. I was composing little pieces when I was ten years old—that's the earliest prose. But I began writing poetry at age—oh, I'm not sure whether it was 11 or 12—but I have poetry that dates back to age thirteen. I know I was writing before then. My father said it was a puberty urge. I began writing about the time I entered puberty. I don't remember when I learned to read, and I finished grade school at age eleven, and I finished high school at age fourteen. So I had a problem of social adjustment, yes. The older girls and boys in my class were always using me to help them get their work. And I thought that it was because they wanted to be friendly with me; they were really using me. And I really had no peers my age. Even in college that was true. I understand that college is the age when young people are courting and looking toward marriage or careers—and I was too young for anything. Courting was out of the question. I didn't know what it was all about until I was out of college.

RC: You must have been a little lonely then.

MW: I don't think so. I always had a world within. And that world was a very satisfactory world. I look back now in journals that I kept—I kept diaries and journals—and when I had nobody to talk to, I wrote to myself. And I was not aware of extreme loneliness. I realize now that I did not talk to people around me; I was in conflict with those around me.

RC: When you were young, did you have imaginary playmates? Did that influence your writing?

MW: As a very young child, my mother said I would come in from school and if it, even in the wintertime, I would put on a hat and go out in the backyard in my coat and hat and talk to all my imaginary playmates. My sister didn't want to play [outside]. She wanted to play the piano all the time.

And so I, yes, I invented playmates. Miss Choomby is one of our invented playmates. We played Miss Anne and Miss Choomby. Miss Ann was the white lady, and Miss Choomby was the black lady, and we took turns being Miss Ann and Miss Choomby.

RC: That's marvelous. What has influenced your writing most—family, commitment to the Southern sense of place, race?

MW: Well, I think it's all of those. I think it begins with my family, my mother's music, the Southern landscape, the woods and the world around me, and the problems of race in America. I think all of those have been grist in my mill. It's more than family, it's more than the Southern environment. But that Southern climate, that southern landscape, both social and physical—that environment has been of tremendous influence. If you look at the poetry, you will see that the images have come out of the Southern landscape. You will find the rhythms of black music in much of my work and of course my mother, grandmother and my father, who made indelible impressions upon me as a child. The whole sense of morality, which I think is fundamental for me. I read somewhere in *Newsweek* where Margaret Walker is one of those moral writers and that is supposed to be a form of derision, but to me, I could not have a greater compliment, since my morality is obviously in conflict with the new morality.

RC: How does a writer like you approach writing? How do you begin? What do you do first?

MW: Well, the first thing you do in any creative task is think about it. The idea comes first. The concept and the thought and the idea are there before you have the word and the sentence and the paragraph, or before you have a figuration of ideas or a configuration. And writing grows out of creative thinking, which is nothing more than what perceptive and apperceptive are —conceptualization. So that's the first thing. The first step is conceptualization. Sometimes you are conscious of that conceptualization, sometimes you are not. You perceive a thing outside yourself and the idea or the concept or the thought and the idea grow from that. Whenever society is in ferment, wherever the trouble spots are, you can look for extraordinary and fine writing. There's an explosion of the imagination out of social ferment.

RC: Is it best, do you think, to follow a daily schedule in writing, or to write when you have a flash or inspiration?

MW: It depends upon what you're writing. When I was an adolescent—

the time I began writing until I was early twenties—I wrote every day. I wrote diaries and journals, I wrote poetry almost every day. I wrote papers or vignettes, little characters sketches. I wrote because that was my only outlet, so I wrote all the time. But after I had graduated from college and after I'd had some very bitter experiences with other writers that every day pace slacked. I became more conscious and self-conscious. And when you are extremely self-conscious, you do not write as much. I've written three novels. I started a novel when I was twelve, and I never finished that novel. But I wrote hundreds of pages; I'd just sit at the typewriter and write. It was a very sentimental, religious, non-racial thing, I guess more white than black, and I didn't know what I was doing. But I was learning to type, so I was using that to write this novel. When I was an adult and looked at it, I said, "Oh, my goodness, what drivel, what trash." Then I wrote a novel when I was on the Writer's Project in Chicago called *Goose Island.* I completed it, but it has never been published. It was not a very good novel, either. I had excellent characters and some of the dialogue was very good. The plot was all right, but basically it's the reverse of the *Native Son* plot. The third novel, of course, was a novel I began when I was a senior at Northwestern. It was my family story, the Civil War novel *Jubilee.* I spent thirty years learning how to write that book—ten years in research, and all kinds of research, but then I had the job of transforming fact into fiction. And I didn't learn how to do that until after twenty or twenty-five years. I went out to Iowa the second time and learned how to do it. The main thing I didn't know how to do was to create scene, or to dramatize the material. And anyone who doesn't know how to draft a scene doesn't know how to write fiction. Fiction is never pure reality. Fiction is a blend of fantasy and reality. To write reality is not to write fiction. And to deal with all the evils of the world without any mitigating influences is not my idea of good fiction.

   RC: Could you talk about style?

   MW: Style, in my estimation, is nothing more than the impression of personality on the piece of writing. Style is a very individual matter. It is absolutely personal. No matter whether you call it a simple style or a sublime style, style is absolutely individual. My style is me, it's my voice, it's the way I express myself. I write a certain way because I am me. And no matter how you would describe that style, or define it, style is the personality impressed on the piece of writing. The form in which a thing is written will frequently [work] against the style. Content has almost nothing to do with style. The form and the content need to be wedded, yes, but when you talk about style and the stylistic elements in the writing, you are talking about the method that [a writer uses].

RC: Are any of your characters based on real people?

MW: I think I do some things with character, other than to base them on real people. I have a rule of thumb for character that was taught to me when I was out at Iowa and living with Miss Hoovey.[1] And she taught me there are only five things you can do with any character, and given those five things, every time that they appear, the character appears, there must be consistency. You can only describe the character and tell how he looks. And you have the character talking and hear him talking. And you go behind the mind of the character and experience him thinking. Then you see him in action and you see him reacting to others. That's all you can do with a character, those five things.

RC: How important are revisions to a writer?

MW: I think writing is nine-tenths rewriting. Even with poetry. Sometimes the poem comes out whole because you've thought about it a long time and it's been in the unconscious or in that secondary imagination a long time, and you put it down as it should be, and there's been this long period of gestation. But if you get a flash and you think you've got a sudden idea, you sit down and you attempt to do it right away—frequently, that is not going to come out right the first time. You have to think about it and rework it. I have one poem in *For My People* that I reworked at least twelve times, and worked on it about five years. That's a poem called "Delta." On the other hand, "For My People" was written in fifteen minutes, with the last stanza not there. I had to think about that a long time before I could write that final stanza.

RC: What makes the difference between whether something rolls off your pen, or whether you have to take this time of gestation?

MW: I think it is again a question of the conceptualization. How complete is that at the very beginning? You cannot organize and realize the work, compose it, when the concept is half-baked. When you conceive the thing, when you have the complete idea or configuration in the first conceptualization, it doesn't take a long time. But if you do not have that all together in

---

[1] Walker lived with Alma Hoovey, a former English professor at Iowa, from 1962–65.

that earliest intuitive moment, then you have to rework and rewrite. When you type very fast and use the touch system, and I think rapidly and I write rapidly; I write as I talk—too much, too easily, too much, too soon, too fast. And when it comes out, you get a lot. But, you know, everything you think is not what you want on paper.

RC: What are your views on modern life today, the permissive attitude, et cetera?

MW: I think it's like the last days of Pompeii, or the last days of the Roman Empire. I think that we have lived through a century of war and revolution, and that we have not been able to implement the positive elements of the Einsteinian Revolution so that high technology—in terms of the sciences and math—and we are completely adrift in terms of the humanities and the social sciences. I think something that people were talking about at the end of the nineteenth and early twentieth century has had a terribly demoralizing effect on people today. Since I believe that—I consider myself more a Christian humanist—I am not inclined to believe that God is dead. But people like the Marxists and the atheistic existentialists say that the reason we are so morally adrift is that we have lost God, that for modern man, God no longer exists. And when God does not exist, then the people have no vision. They perish because they are without substance, without balance, without anything to believe or hold on to. And so in our secular society, we have lost all our God. We have no ideals left. Our world is a world of chaos, crime, corruption, and that's it.

RC: Do you think too much of that crops up in today's writing?

MW: Yes, I think that one of our brilliant young black women writers—in fact, I could name three or four of these black women writers who are selling hot stuff everywhere—they are on the border of, if not including, soft-core pornography.

RC: Then how should a love scene be handled?

MW: I think that subtlety is more effective than blatancy. I think that when women or men decide that everything has to be sexually explicit, that there's something kind of twisted with their sexual natures. That's what I really believe. That when sex has ceased to be anything sacred—when it ceases to have anything sacrosanct or private about it, then it has lost its true, basic meaning. Sexuality is a part of humanity. But then humanity strives towards divinity, you see. And if sex is not tempered with genuine spiritual love, then something pretty ugly comes out.

RC: Some years ago, you wrote a poem "For My People." It still has application today.

MW: I wrote that poem when I was twenty-two. And I hope it has significance today. I was told already—I've been told many things about the poem—but during the sixties, when we were at the height of the Civil Rights Movement, friends came to see me from California. And they said when young men and women were thrown into the jails in California, one of the civil rights leaders would go in there and read poetry to them, and they always read "For My People." That was one of the crowning glories for me. They were saying that this poetry helped to spawn a kind of revolution. That's precisely what it was intended to do. And that was a compliment.

I'm not a native Mississippian, but I've lived here a great part of my life, and my family has been here, members of my family, for a hundred years. And I think Mississippi is one of the most interesting places and certainly a climate for genius. I think it's a great place for writing. The social ferment has been so horrible that out of it, you were bound to get great writers like Faulkner and Wright. You were bound to get very great writers like Tennessee Williams. Those are great, great writers. And their genius, their genius really came out of Mississippi.

Southern Song: An Interview with Margaret Walker

Lucy M. Freibert / 1986

Reprinted from *Frontiers* 9:3 (1987): 50–56, by permission of the University of Nebraska Press. Copyright © 1987.

Freibert: You have been a writer, teacher, activist, homemaker, and cultural analyst. What is the unifying role in your life?

Walker: Well, I think that the feminine principle of being a daughter, a sister, a mother, and now a grandmother has been the motivating and inspiring agency. I think I said that first in a piece I wrote called "On Being Female, Black, and Free"—that being a woman is first, that when the doctor says "It's a she," that's the first thing.

Freibert: Would you talk about some of the people who have influenced you the most?

Walker: Well, my parents had the first influence on me. They were teachers. My mother taught music, and my father taught religion and philosophy. My father had taught in high schools before he taught in college; he had taught many different subjects. He was a fine English scholar, but he was first and foremost a theologian. Hearing my father give his sermons, watching him prepare them, and seeing him exemplify in his daily life what he preached had an effect on me. My mother was a musician—just hearing her play and hearing that music every day had a real influence on me. But equally important was my grandmother. When I think of how I grew up, I think of the three of them.

My teachers until I was almost college age were mostly women. I had only one male teacher in grade school, and then in high school I had three or four male teachers. When I was in college, my freshman English teacher was a woman, a very fine teacher who had graduated from Northwestern. She told my parents they should send me to Northwestern, where they had gone to school. And then when I was sixteen, I saw Langston Hughes for the first time. He was one of the first black male writers influential on me. . . . Then I went to Northwestern when I was seventeen, and I had no more women teachers. The only woman who taught me at Northwestern taught hygiene. I was surprised to discover that black women teaching in black colleges in the South had far more position, prestige, and status than white women teaching in northern coed universities. The black woman on the black college campus can be anything she wants to be, but the faculties of Northwestern and Iowa showed me the lower status of white women teachers.

Freibert: Three black men influenced you?

Walker: My three black writer friends didn't teach me formally in school but influenced my work very much. I read Langston Hughes first when I was eleven years old, and I saw him when I was sixteen. I knew him for thirty-five years. He was a close friend and a real influence. W. E. B. Du Bois, whom I also saw for the first time when I was about seventeen at Northwestern, published my first poem in a national magazine, *Crisis*. It was called "Daydream," but it's now called "I Want to Write." That was my dream—to write. And the third black man was Richard Wright, whom I met after I was out of college.

Freibert: Did your parents directly encourage you to write?

Walker: Yes, they did. When I was twelve years old, my father gave me a daybook in which I could keep my poems, and told me to keep everything I wrote together, not to scatter my work. That motivated me to fill the book.

Freibert: That became your journal, then?

Walker: Well, it wasn't really a journal. I started a journal when I was thirteen. My journals were kept in composition books. I think that I may be able to go back to them and use them for the autobiography. I have been blocking it out in my head and looking for a theme. I am sure that there will be passages from those journals that I will want to go back and remember and include in the autobiography.

Freibert: Do you normally use materials from your journals in your literary works?

Walker: I think so, but it has been an unconscious thing. I was consciously writing journals. I wasn't consciously taking material from them to use in the books, except when I was working with the Richard Wright book. For that I went back to entries in my journals deliberately. I read his journals but wasn't allowed to quote directly from them. But I could quote from my own. The episode in which our friendship ended is recorded in the book in its entirety. I was a very young woman, in my very early twenties. As I look back on it now, the experience is as clear and concise and direct as I recorded it then. I have not changed a word in that journal entry. . . .

Freibert: I am sure you are pleased to have the Wright book finished and to know that it will be coming out soon. Would you comment on the title you gave the book: *Richard Wright: A Daemonic Genius.*

Walker: I am using the Greek term "daemonic," and using it in an aesthetic sense. The creative genius of Wright was not orphic, and it was not, shall I say, visionary like that of Blake. It was daemonic in the way that we speak of the shield of Achilles made by Haiphaestus as being daemonic. Daemonic genius is genius driven by devils or demons but not purely Satanic. Wright was also like the god maker, the person of character and personality like Pygmalion. It's that kind of daemonic. I am not calling him a devil, although I think his widow must believe that's what I'm up to.

Freibert: Your relationship with Wright ended rather abruptly. According to one report, you said that Wright picked your brains and then dismissed you.

Walker: [laughing] Well, I think feminists will grab that, but wait a minute, let's stop there. People have made a great deal over the friendship and the breaking up, and I don't look back now with any regret. I have written the book with a great deal of hard work and some pleasure, and I hope that it is going to be available soon. I suppose that I may have gotten a great deal from the Wright friendship. I know he got a lot from me. Whether he picked my brain—he may have tried to—I doubt that he could have thoroughly picked my brain.

Freibert: Would you discuss the other works that you have in progress? I saw a rather lengthy list in your file over at the Jackson State library. It starts with *Minna and Jim.*

Walker: That's the sequel to *Jubilee.* I have only blocked that out. I haven't done any work on it.

Freibert: And *Mother Broyer?*

Walker: I'm working on that now. I've done a hundred pages, and I'm in the second section of that. It is laid in four cities: it starts in Algiers, across the river from New Orleans, moves to Los Angeles, California, and then to Harlem, New York, and ends on the West Side of Chicago. Mother Broyer spends the first twenty-two or three or maybe twenty-five years in New Orleans, then about ten or twelve years in Los Angeles, about a year, six to eight or ten, maybe twelve to eighteen months in New York, and then spends the rest of her life in Chicago.

Freibert: Then there's *This Is My Century.*

Walker: *This Is My Century* is a book of my poetry. It is going to be the collected poetry. It will include five books: *For My People, Prophets for a New Day, October Journey, This Is My Century,* and *A Poem for Farish Street.*

Freibert: And then you are working on the autobiography.

Walker: Yes, I have done a hundred pages on the autobiography, but I am going to have to rearrange and reorganize it in terms of the themes that I have in mind. . . .

Freibert: Do you write on schedule, or do you just wait until the spirit moves you?

Walker: Well, I can write any time that I sit down to the typewriter or with my notebook. It depends on what I am writing. I really had a schedule that last year with *Jubilee,* in the last few months especially, but never before or since have I been able to get back to a schedule.

Freibert: When you write poetry, do you carry the poem around in your head first, or do you start right out putting things on paper?

Walker: Regardless of the medium, whether you are a musician, a painter, a graphic artist, a plastic artist, or a sculptor, whether you are a writer or an architect, you begin the same way. Creative writing grows out of creative thinking, and nothing begins a work before the idea as a conceptualization; that is the beginning. All writers, all artists, all musicians, all people with creative talent begin with that creative thinking. They begin with conceptualization. You get an idea, and sometimes the whole process moves on mentally and unconsciously before it is given conscious artistic form, but the process begins with the idea.

Everything begins in the mind. You have an idea, and you may not know for a long time what form this idea is going to take or what you are going to say or how you are going to say it, but you have that first. For me it is intuitive. Some people are not intuitive. I'm intuitive. I in-tu-it. For me it begins with a concept, maybe before it is even an idea—a concept before it becomes thought or idea. It may begin with a picture. For the musician, I am sure it begins with a musical motif or a sound that the musician hears or senses. It is a process using the sensory perceptions, I guess you would say. You perceive or conceive. You perceive what is outside. You conceive what is inside. And you move from the perception of a concept or thought or idea to a figuration and a configuration.

The poet has nothing but words and language to be used as tools. And the poet—I think my father taught me this—the poet in my instance uses rhetorical devices. I have been told by some poets and even by some teachers that I am too rhetorical. I cannot conceive of writing poetry without metaphor and simile, synecdoche, metonymy, hyperbole. I grew up with that, and my work is rhetorical, but I think it is rhetorical in the best sense of the word. I had teachers who tried to break me of the habit. My father taught me my first lessons in rhetoric from an old English book that he had brought to this country. It gave all the rhetorical forms. I don't think a poet writes simply in grammatically correct language. I think all the greatest poets in the world were rhetoricians, and I believe in the rhetoric. Paul Engle has criticized me for it. He said, "Margaret was just too rhetorical." I laughed, because I am still rhetorical, and I always will be.

Freibert: That's what makes your voice so distinctive. What or who helped you to find your voice?

Walker: My father, really. I think Stephen Benét tells it in the introduction to *For My People*. It was not just that I heard the sermons my grandfather and my father preached, but it was that training my father gave me in the use of rhetoric. And I really didn't believe when I was a teenaged youngster growing up that you could write poetry without the use of simile and metaphor. I thought you had to use them. After I was older and had gained my own voice, I realized that I had read the Bible all my life and that the use of parallelism was what I had learned from the Bible: cataloguing and repetition and internal rhyme—not so much end rhyme, because that was what I had learned from ordinary poetry. I didn't think of the poetry in the Bible as ordinary. I thought it was extraordinary. And when Benét says you can feel these Biblical rhythms in my poetry, that is the greatest compliment he could give me. I think most of us in the South grew up on that Bible, the King James version of the Bible, as much as on reading Dickens and Sir Walter Scott. Because if you were a student in the South, you have read Scott, Dickens, the Bible, and Shakespeare, and you may have read Milton, because we are very Miltonic in the South. And these are the great influences in English and American literature. And just because we have learned to speak in cryptic language and monosyllabic sentences, making sentences out of monosyllabic words, that is no reason to drop rhetoric from poetry. I'm very certain that I am one of the few black writers who believes that strongly in rhetoric. But I can't help it. It's a part of my background.

I think the voices I have heard in the classics, whether it was the great English, American, or Continental poetry, carry with them not only the surge, the melody, and the rhythm of Biblical poetry, they also have power. And I have had people tell me that my words have power, the power that comes out of that Biblical background, that religious background that makes you aware that words are not just some idle spoken things but they should carry great meaning with them. My father taught me that poetry must have three qualities. It must have rhythm or music, but first it must have pictures or images, and third it must have meaning. And everything I write I test by those three standards. Are there any pictures here in the poetry? Do you see images? Do you feel the rhythms? Do you sense the power behind the meaning? Those are my three major standards. I was a long time coming to this in prose. I thought that prose was completely disconnected from poetry. I didn't grow up realizing that stories and novels and biography and autobiography had sometimes the same rhythms, the same images that poetry has. I was taught versification and scansion by masters. When I was at Northwestern, my teacher, Professor Hungerford, rigidly schooled me in versification and scansion. He has written a little book, *On Remembering the Rhythms.* He believed in that sweep, and he liked my poems. He said that in "JEAN LAFITTE, the Baratarian" I was writing like Keats, that I had that sensuousness that Keats had, that it came from my descriptive power in the pictures, the images, but it was also in the rhythm, because I wrote in couplets. But they were not heroic couplets; they were run-on Keatsian couplets. I was always determined to have meaning or power in these things.

Freibert: The connection you made between poetry and prose shows up so well in *Jubilee.* Almost every chapter is like a poem in itself.

Walker: I appreciate your saying that because one critic said that my style was atrocious and that I had no poetry in *Jubilee.* I was amused at that. He said that the book wasn't interesting, was dull, and didn't have any sex in it. When I read that, I laughed because I said, "Millions of people do not agree with you."

Freibert: *Jubilee* was probably the earliest book to focus on the complexity of the relationship between black and white women.

Walker: Well, I think that's what Minrose Gwin is talking about in *Black and White Women of the Old South.* She says that I do express that connection, that relationship. And I am sure they must be there because my audience consists of both black and white. And I have had many, many white people in the South tell me they relate to the book. They feel with the characters in there. They recognize people. And, of course, black folks tell me, "Oh, Vyry is everybody's grandmother." They love Vyry because they say, "She's just like my grandmother. She was like my grandmother was. Where does she come from?" They know her. They recognize her. It wasn't a simple, easy, quick task to bring her to life.

Freibert: Was that perception of the black and white women's dilemma in your grandmother's story, or is that where your artistry comes in?

Walker: I think it was both. Of course, you know, I never saw Vyry. Vyry was really Margaret, my great-grandmother, and Minna, who told me the story, was really Vyry. Her name was Elvira. My grandmother was a part of my raising, my rearing. She told me the story. The story, as she told it, reflected the relationship of my great-grandmother to all people around her, black and white. I think you recognize the humanistic value of Vyry because whether it's Aunt Sally or Mammy Sukey, whether it is Miss Lillian or Miss Lucy, you see the kinship of women. When the poor white woman in the house with the children has not been fed, Vyry feeds her, and she tells Randall Ware and Innes—the night that they talk and she shows her back—she says, "If any of those people came to my door in the mornin', no matter how bad they treated me, I would feed 'em."

One of the reviewers said that *Jubilee* is a powerful testament to Christianity, to Christian love, because that thing that we get from Vyry—and people don't want to believe it—is that out of outrage and violence and bitterness, she comes up with this Christian love and forgiveness. And you know, I was raised that way. My grandmother was that way. And she was Vyry's child. And I realized when I finished the book that I had never known Vyry, but I knew her daughter, and she was like Vyry. My mother said, "Oh, you've got my grandmother down. She was just like that." I said, "But you know I was really using grandma." Then she said, "Well Mamma was like grandma." And I said, "And my mother was like her mother." I'm like my mother. The older I get, the more I look like my mother and I think like my mother. My grandmother was just like her mother. Women are like their mothers.

And childbearing women—I have a daughter expecting—and I told her, "Women have their children the way their mothers had them." That's part of being a woman—in the difficulty of going into puberty, the problems of early marriage, or even when marriages don't last (because all marriages are not made in heaven), and divorce, which is perhaps the worst thing a woman can go through short of death itself, and the whole business of estrangement—in all these instances women follow the pattern of women who have gone before them.

But then we have an interesting thing happening, which has happened with the sexual revolution. We have women who look at the pain they have suffered and who have been through some excruciating sexual pain, that is, in their relationships with men and other women so that they determine to break the shackles, to do away with the icons, and to avoid the stereotypes. And these women are speaking out more and more, but this is what the women's movement has meant. At first it was simply to break the terrible slavery of domestic bondage, where they were under the rule of the father and the husband, and they didn't dare cross them and be independent and think for themselves. And then they decided we want to be a part of the world around us. We want to be educated. We want to have our chance at careers. We want options. We don't all want to be married. We don't all want to have children. We want to be able to make a living without this father or husband.

And then we have seen this male domination go so far that we find women who have been brutalized in their marriage relationships or in their paternal relationships, and they moved out to what may *seem* a perversion of love— they found a bonding with other women. This is very obvious in our society today. It existed before, but we kept it hidden. We closed it off. We didn't want this to be a part of what the world knew about us, because then we became pariahs and were thrown aside.

It is a long way up for women from the status of women in ancient times, say in the time of Jesus, when a woman could be brought before Jesus and accused: "This woman was caught in the act of adultery, and Moses said stone such a one to death. What do you say?" I think that is the first move toward woman's liberation, when Jesus says, "Well, any man who has never sinned and who is not guilty of any woman, let him pick up the stone and throw first." He didn't say, "Where is the man who was with this woman?" He didn't say, "Well, I don't believe there should be one kind of standard or two." He just said, "Let the man without sin cast the first stone." And he looked around and all these men had moved away. He said to the woman, "Woman, where are your accusers?" She said, "Sir, I have none." He said, "Well, neither do I accuse you." In other words, "I know nothing about you.

I haven't been guilty of it. So you may go on your way, but don't sin any more."

Freibert: What are the differences in black and white southern women's relationships then and now?

Walker: Well, I think we have gone through three or four stages. And I am sure that white women as well as black women have advanced. First of all, in those days of slavery, nobody thought about educating women. We didn't have women's suffrage. The women's movement in this country has paralleled the black movement or the struggle for black rights, whether they were civil or human rights. And as the women's movement became a national movement, at first the southern white women were not a part of it. And as the northern women sought to bring the southern white women into the movement, they ran into conflict over the question of race. The southern white women were the last to accept the black women into the movement.

Even important women like Susan B. Anthony and others who were friendly with Ida B. Wells wanted her to back off, saying, "Don't come and march, don't stand and speak, because our southern sisters will be offended." The movement broke in two between the white northern and their southern white sisters who objected to the inclusion of the black women. Three or four very important black women rose up, not only Ida B. Wells and Mary McLeod Bethune later, but Sojourner Truth was a very great leader in the women's movement, and Harriet Tubman was in the movement. Ida B. Wells was one of the most outspoken, and at the turn of the century we had that kind of crisis.

Then we came to the very great drive of women all over the country, except in the South, where black people as a whole had been disenfranchised. Black men were not voting en masse, and black women had no voice. But white southern women were fighting for the vote, too, and when that vote came in 1919, black people still did not have the vote. There was friction and conflict in the women's movement over these issues. Anti-lynching was the great cause that Ida B. Wells was fighting. She was fighting lynching, but she was writing, too, along with Mary Church Terrell and Mary McLeod Bethune, great organizers of the National Council of Negro Women and the Federated Women's Clubs movement. They were talking about the lack of voting privileges of all black people.

I forgot to say that at the turn of the century Ida B. Wells was preparing to go to the first big international conference of women held in England. She

expected to go as a delegate for women from this country, and there was a
great protest made. The southern women were outraged, and the northern
women compromised by asking Ida B. Wells not to go and not to speak. She
went, of course. She was asked on another occasion when they were demon-
strating for the vote not to appear, but she did appear. That is the kind of
racial conflict we've had within the women's movement.

Even today the aims and imperatives of the women's movement are not
the same for black women as they are for white. The white woman in the
past fifty years has sought to be liberated from her husband and from a patri-
archal bond. The black woman never felt that kind of pressure. The black
woman was always a working woman from the days of slavery. All the days
she had been in this country, all the years, she has been a working woman.
We do not have the same kind of conflict between marriage and career that
white women have. I remember somebody's saying to me once that marriage
was nothing more than being a kept woman, and I was surprised to hear that,
because women in my family had always been married women, working
women, mothers with careers. I go back to my great-grandmothers. Vyry was
a slave and having babies with the threat of being separated from husband
and children, but always working. Then my grandmother was married to a
minister. When he died my grandmother was forced to work. At first she took
in sewing, and then she took in washing—washing and ironing. And these
black women have always been very strong women, but not necessarily taking
the places of men.

We never felt threatened in our homes by the fact that we had to work at
our careers. Nowadays we hear a great deal about whether a woman should
work when the children are small. My mother said she was at work teaching
when I was six weeks old. At my first job I did stay home fourteen months
before I went back to teaching, but with the next child my husband asked me
to stay home two years. I stayed home three. At the end of those three years
I had another child, and I didn't wait two years. He—the third child—was
nine weeks old when I came to work at Jackson State. The fourth child was
born while I was on a Ford Fellowship, and when I came back to work, I
brought that child with me two weeks short of three months old.

I always had some help. I brought someone in. I had a person come in to
cook and clean. I didn't like very much having someone do the cooking
because I preferred to cook myself, but I would be so tired. And to this day I
have always had somebody to come in and help with the cleaning. Anyway I
have learned that black women have never been free to pursue the same

aspirations that white women pursue. The white woman has had to fight the
father and the husband for the right first to go to school, second to become a
part of the professional world, third to be a working mother, and even so the
pattern of the white woman is that she generally stays home with the child,
with the baby, for so many months or so many years before she goes back to
work. That couldn't work with the black woman. Many times there was no
man in the house. There was no man there. She had these children in the
fields. She had these children on the job. She had these children one day and
then went back to work the next day. So the aspirations and aims of white
and black women in the same women's movement have not been the same.

One thing that I think black and white women agree on is that women need
to be paid the same money for the same work or the same jobs as men, but
that has rarely happened in our society. I wrote a piece—I think part of it is
in Claudia Tate's *Black Women Writers at Work*—in which I said that my
mother, my sisters, and I have all suffered in academia. Men with the same
degrees, the same training, made more money. Men doing the same work got
more money. This has prevailed in the society. And even though there is a
federal law against it now, the law is frequently violated. It is rare that a
woman receives promotion, rank, and pay with men. The society still doesn't
abide by that rule.

Freibert: How does your experience as a black woman writer compare
with that, say, of Zora Neale Hurston, Nella Larson, or Gwendolyn Brooks?

Walker: I guess I have had some of the same problems they have had. You
should compare me with a white woman writer, because there is where the
great difference has been. I'm not an unfulfilled person in the same sense that
Zora was. Zora was certainly a very great storyteller and very bright, a brilliant woman, but she didn't graduate from Columbia with a doctorate under
Papa Boaz. Not that she wasn't as smart as Margaret Mead or Ruth Benedict.
They were white, and she was black. There's where the contrast is. She didn't
get the doctorate in anthropology. Well, I can say that I went to school, and I
got the doctorate. Very few black people had done it at Iowa before I did,
and very few have since, but I went back where I had gotten a master's and,
though it was difficult, I managed to fulfill the requirements. And I got it.
Therefore, that's one thing that Zora was frustrated in. I've not been frustrated.

Zora was married twice very briefly. Her marriages did not work out. I was
married thirty-seven years to one man, and I have four children, eight grand-

children from that union. In that sense I am not frustrated at all. I know only one other person who has been married as long as I have to the same man, and that is Gwendolyn Brooks. Gwen was married to Henry Blakely in her very early twenties when first I knew her. They had a very brief separation, but while they were separated I think Gwen must have realized that Henry was always very good for her. They had two children together, a son and a daughter, and in that respect we are alike. Gwen is still married to Blakely. My husband is dead.

I never knew Nella Larsen. I saw Zora as a child, but I never saw Nella Larsen and knew little about her until I was an adult. I read Zora's books as they came out. I have since read Nella Larsen's *Quicksand* and *Passing.* I don't care for her as much as I do for Zora, but I think she's a fine writer. I know almost nothing of her personal life. Zora was accused of sodomy, taken into court, and although she came out of it and was vindicated and proved innocent, it literally ruined her life and career. And I have not had that kind of awful situation.

There are three women from Georgia—two white and one black—whom I put in the same bag: Flannery O'Connor, Carson McCullers, whom I knew at Yaddo, and Alice Walker. I never knew Flannery O'Connor, but she went to the same school I went to in Iowa, and they told me about her. Those three women are from the same neck of the woods in Georgia. They are all three women of gothic imagination, all three writing of the violent South. It was Flannery O'Connor who wrote *The Violent Bear It Away.* Carson was writing things about grotesque people in *Ballad of the Sad Café,* and in *The Heart Is a Lonely Hunter* and *Reflections in a Golden Eye.* I would say even in *Clock Without Hands.* Flannery O'Connor's "Artificial Nigger," *The Violent Bear It Away, Everything That Rises Must Converge*—they can all be compared with Alice Walker's *Third Life of Grange Copeland, Meridian,* and *The Color Purple.* I'm not like any of those women. Those women have a different imagination. Those women have a different perspective. They have a different philosophy. I think they are all remarkable writers. I think that it will take many more years before we say these women were great artists. They were great craftswomen, virtuosos, but I don't think any one of those women can stand up now to the test of what I consider the great test of an artist—that you are willing to go back and read their books over and over again. I don't know. I do not personally enjoy reading them over and over again. I'm repelled by Flannery O'Connor's "Artifical Nigger." I don't think much even of *The Violent Bear It Away.* I think one of her best things is

Everything That Rises Must Converge. Carson McCullers, who is around my age, died very much younger. I read *The Heart Is a Lonely Hunter* and liked that, but there were things in it I didn't like. And then she came out with *Reflections in a Golden Eye.* I would never read that book again. When she came up with *Clock Without Hands,* it was so painful I could hardly bear to read the whole book.

I had great difficulty with Alice Walker's *The Color Purple.* I do not like the book for many reasons. I think Alice's best work is *In Search of Our Mothers' Gardens.* It's a very beautiful book and a book that I can relate to and understand. *The Third Life of Grange Copeland* for me has many problems. The book *Meridian* includes my name, and I'm there as a character, and I don't exactly appreciate that. I can hardly make myself go back and look at *Meridian.* I think I feel about those books the way I feel about Faulkner's *Sanctuary.* At first I was just repelled. I like the kind of macabre humor that Faulkner uses, but then again, it is that same gothic imagination.

Now I find myself able to read and reread Eudora Welty, and she has a gothic imagination and she does sometimes deal with the grotesque and with things almost gruesome, but her *Delta Wedding* reflects that Delta language and you can hear that speech. Her folk things are truly authentic. I think she is a great artist. You see the difference? I can read her any time. I would say that Eudora Welty's immortality is assured. I'm not sure about those three women from Georgia. I think that way up the road, they are going to be like Kate Chopin.

Freibert: She's back now. My students love her. They loved *Meridian,* also.

Walker: A lot of people love and like Alice. I have known Alice, but I think that *The Color Purple* is a reflection on the black family as a whole, particularly on black men, that it is not even complimentary to black women, and certainly to black children. And I agree with those women out in California who said that it is not good reading for pre-adolescent children, that it should not be required reading in the grade schools and junior high schools.

Freibert: I don't think it was intended for that.

Walker: But when the fight came up, the question came up as to censorship, and all of us are opposed to that. So you see there is a fine line there.

Freibert: That is the most difficult thing to decide.

Walker: And that's what I'm saying. It is like saying Henry Miller is a

great writer in *Tropic of Cancer* and *Tropic of Capricorn.* There is some
filthy stuff there. There is some filthy vile stuff there. Now it depends on how
you are judging. And I don't think literature should be judged on moral
grounds. I think it should be judged on aesthetic grounds, and then you might
say Henry Miller is a great writer.

Freibert: Young writers like Nikki Giovanni and Sonia Sanchez rate you
among the greats. Sonia calls you "a strong gust of woman."

Walker: Sonia is like a child of mine. Nikki and Sonia and Alice are my
daughters' generation. Sonia is older than they by a few years, but they are
still young enough to have been my daughters. I like all three of them personally.

Alice and Nikki and Sonia can write what I cannot write. I want to write
very much about the Vietnam War, the sixties, and the seventies, but I ask
myself over and over again, "What am I going to do with that vocabulary?"
because it is a shocking, brutal kind. And the four-letter words, the drug
scene, the violence and crime, the black nationalism, all that stuff. It's really
not my cup of tea. I want to write about it because it's my son's generation.
He went to Vietnam, and I think there needs to be a record of that. I don't
know whether I am ever going to be able to put it down, because I cannot
use the four-letter words and the language, and I cannot deal with the shock
bit.

Freibert: To skip backward a minute, what is it about Gwendolyn
Brooks's *Annie Allen* that so appeals to you? You have spoken so highly of
that work.

Walker: Well, I'll tell you what I liked about *Annie Allen* when I read it.
I had read *A Street in Bronzeville,* which shows Gwen's talent very clearly,
and it's a very good first book, but *Annie Allen* reflects very careful discipline, hard work, knowledge of the craft, and such an understanding of that
adolescent girl as she does in *Maud Martha,* that I think the book is nothing
short of superb. "The Anniad," which is in there, is to me a great piece. I
have argued with Dudley Randell when I say it's written in rhyme royale. He
says it's not the Chaucerian stanza, but I say it is. I think I know as well as
Dudley. It is the Chaucerian line and stanza. And that's a very difficult stanza
to write. I think Gwendolyn Brooks proved in *Annie Allen* that she was capa-
ble of most difficult forms, that she could write in the strictest meters and
still keep the very wonderful flavor of black life and folklore. I think that's
what's in *Annie Allen.* I think, too, that that book is a very well-crafted book.

I think that Gwen is at her very best in *Annie Allen.* I think in this book she fulfills the promise of *A Street in Bronzeville.* You see in *Annie Allen* that she is an artist who understands the craft of poetry and the art of writing. And I think that aside from a number of the very flavorsome pieces in there, you don't see anything like again until she comes to "Mecca." "Mecca" is another very fine piece.

I haven't seen any recent things of Gwen's to say that I like this or that, but Gwen wrote nine volumes of poetry. She says some of the stuff was for children and then did *Maud Martha,* which I think is a sensitive portrait. I wish she had done more of that sort of thing, but *Annie Allen* is superb. I think I have said it somewhere.

Freibert: I'd like to get back to your poetry for just a moment. The French feminist critics talk about "writing from the body" these days. Early in the forties you wrote,

I want my careless song to strike no minor key; no fiend to stand between
my body's southern song—the fusion of the South, my body's song and me.

Is there a connection here?

Walker: Well, I don't know whether I was thinking in the feminist vein when I said that, because I have said it over and over again, in both "Southern Song" and "Sorrow Home." What I am saying, in a very sensuous, not sensual but sensuous, way is that I'm a creature of the South. When I wrote this I was in cold Chicago, and I didn't see grass and hay and clover in bloom. I didn't see red clay. I didn't smell the earth after the rain. All of this comes back to me, so I write about the South, and then I contrast, as I do frequently in poetry and prose. (I do it a lot in the Richard Wright book.) I contrast the ideal beauty of the land, the ambience of the South, and the horror of its violence and racial conflict. When I leave the physical beauty of the South, and when I talk about "my body's southern song—the fusion of the South, my body's song and me," I mean that I am a part of this whole process of nature, that when we come together I am complete and it is complete because it is a part of me and I am part of it. Now I want to see the dichotomy closed, the split ended. The social horror and the physical beauty are constantly there, and I talk about that in everything I write—the beauty of the South and the horror of this other society.

A Writer for Her People

Jerry W. Ward, Jr. / 1986

From *Mississippi Quarterly* 41 (Fall 1988): 515–27. Reprinted by permission of *Mississippi Quarterly.*

JW: Dr. Alexander, I would like to take the road less travelled by, as Frost put it, to talk a little about your life, literature and culture in the Eighties, and the future as you see it. Can we begin with place, the sense of place, the South? You've lived and worked in Mississippi since 1949, and you wrote in the poem "Jackson, Mississippi"

> I give you my heart, Southern City
> For you are my blood and dust of my flesh,
> You are the harbor of my ship of hope,
> the dead-end street of my life . . .

How important is Mississippi as a place in what you choose to write?

MWA: I think I told a writer quite recently that Mississippi is the epicenter of my life. I was born 250 miles away from here in Birmingham, and after I was ten years old, I lived for the rest of my childhood and early adolescence in New Orleans, 200 miles from here. And I have spent over half my lifetime now in Jackson, Mississippi. Mississippi spells for me all my roots gathered in one place. My great-uncle Jim came to Mississippi at the time of the Compromises and started a school in Greenville in the oldest black Baptist church there. My grandfather and grandmother, the Minna of *Jubilee,* brought their first child, born in Alabama, to Mississippi; they came to help him in that school. My grandfather taught with his brother-in-law there. But my grandmother didn't like Mississippi, so they soon left and went to Pensacola, Florida, where they spent a large portion of their married life and my grandfather was pastor of two or three Baptist churches there . . . among the oldest. But Uncle Jim stayed in Greenville until he died, and he's buried there. In the Twenties, my father and mother came to Mississippi to teach in Meridian, and I went to school for the first time in Meridian. Then in the Forties, my sister Mercedes taught at Prentiss. I think she taught there for about two years. That was her first teaching position. And in 1949 I came to Jackson.

So, you see, when I say in the poem "You are my blood and dust of my flesh," that is literally true.

JW: Because of the ancestral history . . .

MWA: In Mississippi. But the next two lines are rather pessimist I'm sure. "You are the harbor of my ship of hope"—this is where I put in from the sea. I put down roots here; I came to stay here; I looked at Jackson, Mississippi, like a harbor. After going from place to place and literally tossing on the sea of life, I put in at this harbor. And it has sometimes seemed like a dead-end street, that I'm going no farther. This is my place.

JW: But it hasn't been a dead-end street, in spite of vicissitudes, for your creativity.

MWA: I have done more in Mississippi than any place else. I came here the author of one book, and I have written six more.

JW: That's a good record, considering that you worked as a full-time teacher at Jackson State College.

MWA: And raised a family. When I came to Jackson, my third child was nine weeks old. And my youngest child was born in New York five years after I came to Mississippi . . . when I was on a fellowship. They tease me and say my first child should be called Rosenwald and my last child should be called Ford. But Mississippi is the birthplace of three of my grandchildren. My two daughters-in-law were both born in Mississippi, honor graduates of Tougaloo College, and their children have been born here.

JW: Much of what occurs in this state is grist for writing, but it seems rather tragic.

MWA: It depends upon the imagination of the writer. I received at Christmas time a calendar book of Alice Walker's. Alice has two things to say about Mississippi. When she first came, she said she'd stay awhile because the stories were knee-deep. And she wrote a great deal in Mississippi. And then she decided that she couldn't write any more in Mississippi, and she had to leave. She went to Arizona one summer, and she wrote there, and she came back with the full determination to leave Mississippi permanently. She didn't know how she could write any longer here. So she went to Brooklyn, and she stayed there awhile. But I think it's very interesting that she says before she could write *The Color Purple,* she had to leave Brooklyn. She went out to San Francisco. She says as soon as she got there, all these voices of these characters came up. She knew she could write *The Color Purple* there. I think that's interesting about a sense of place.

On the other hand, Alice has a Gothic imagination. She's truly Southern Gothic. There's been nobody more Gothic than Alice. Faulkner had that kind of imagination. Eudora Welty has it. Carson McCullers and Flannery O'Connor had it. And Richard Wright had that Gothic imagination.

JW: And Erskine Caldwell . . .

MWA: Erskine Caldwell, yes. Don't leave out Alice Walker. You can't understand her at all if you don't understand that Southern Gothicism. But I don't have that kind of imagination. I belong to what we call in the South the Sentimental tradition. I sometimes think I could write better if I had the Gothic imagination, but I don't have it.

JW: It's good for sales; it might not be good for you.

MWA: It would not be my way of expressing myself at all. But I feel the Sentimental tradition is as much a part of the South as Southern Gothicism. I feel, too, that I can express a different point of view, a different sensibility, and a different imagination. For me, it is a positive, religious, maybe sentimental . . . but more optimistic, not necessarily Pollyanna, but it is rooted in that other feature of the South, what we call a religious tradition or this business of being in the Bible Belt. Nothing has influenced my life more than the Bible, and religion has a lot of different meanings in the South as it has all over this country. I'm a believer, and for me, faith, family and community are keystones of my life. I don't have that Gothic imagination.

JW: No. Yours is much more generous, much more open to a full range of human possibilities . . .

MWA: I don't think that I have even a great sense of the comic any more than I have of the tragic. Nothing to me is hopeless. Everything has possibilities. I believe in the goodness of the future. No matter how hard things may seem at the moment . . . the political clouds may gather, the racial problems, poverty, even sickness and death. I'm almost a Pollyanna in my belief in life, in love, in the goodness of my fellow man. No matter how horrible he may seem or what terrible crimes he may commit, every person has within him the possibilities of good. God is in everybody. There is a sacred inner self in every man. Whether it's developed, or whether it has its chance or not, it's there. And I believe that so strongly. It crosses color lines, it crosses racial lines, it crosses class lines. It's part of my heritage of the Judeo-Christian belief.

JW: And through your work the legacy that you give to us?

MWA: That is part of it. I feel that that expresses the kind of imagination I have, because the key word in my life, I discovered, is *vision.* I believe in vision, and I'm a visionary. Every part of my life that I've expressed finds some connection with vision. I think that's true in more than the religious sense or the poetic sense. It's also true in terms of history, in terms of what I hope and believe and feel for my family, what I hope and believe and feel for my people as a race. It's vision. My creative world, my inner life, is guided a great deal by that sense of vision.

JW: So that is what you called, in another context, the "figuration and configurations of concepts, thoughts, and ideas [that] are the keys to the inner thinking of the creative artist."

MWA: Yes, and I think, too, when I talk about figuration and configurations I begin with that concept, that picture in the mind that is the beginning of an idea. A number of pictures come together, a number of concepts come together to give you a complete thought. And a number of complete thoughts come together to develop an idea. You see the relationship between the word and the sentence and the paragraph. And in poetry, it's the same way, only you are dealing with phrases and words in a different pattern from that of prose.

JW: When you talk about vision and describe the inner working of the mind, it is a way of addressing the visual imagination which seems to inform the writer's imagination. I know, for example, a number of artists are your friends. I wonder how important has visual art been for you?

MWA: You know, it's a strange thing. I think always that music has been uppermost in my mind, and in all of my thinking and writing all my life. But I didn't have early instruction in art. It was not until I went to Chicago that I had a chance to see many art exhibitions. I remember being so awe-struck and excited at the Art Institute of Chicago. I saw great paintings and great masterworks of art for the first time. I heard a symphony for the first time when I was seventeen in Chicago, and I heard José Iturbi playing with the Chicago Symphony. The Art Institute and Orchestra Hall were the experiences of my Chicago years. Although I had heard a lot of music in my home, I had never heard a great symphony live. Those pictures at the Art Institute, and the recitals and music at Orchestra Hall, seemed to bring together a lot of the yearnings of my childhood. I felt these things very deeply but had never had the great experiences of art as I had in Chicago. So, I don't know

that my images have ever come out of created art. I really think that my
visual perceptions began and were shaped by the Southern landscape. I think
from a child I have had the feel of the South in my blood. I say it in my
poetry—"Warm skies and gulf blue streams are in my blood." The climate
of the South seems to me a home for my very heart. In almost everything I
have written, I have chosen my images out of the Southern landscape, from
nature in the South. I remember the steep hills of red clay where the train
plowed through, going from Birmingham to Meridian, or from Meridian back
to Birmingham. I have never forgotten how you looked out and saw almost a
mountain of red clay. I don't remember seeing that red clay looking exactly
that color anywhere else. The red hills of Georgia, yes, a different color red.

JW: But Alabama red is very special.

MWA: Alabama red from Birmingham to Meridian, down through those
mountains. You come right down through the mountains from Birmingham
to Meridian.

JW: So, that's the earliest image?

MWA: Yes, I must have been five or six when I saw that. I don't remember
too much about the train ride that I took when I was four to Pensacola,
Florida. I remember my grandmother's house and her latticed-in back porch
and the jardiniere and the hat-rack in the front hall, but I don't remember the
landscape. I didn't remember Florida as it is until I went back as an adult.

JW: When you were doing research for *Jubilee?*

MWA: Well, I saw Florida for the first time as an adult . . . yes, in the
years before I finished *Jubilee.*

JW: This interview reminds me of how rich and revealing conversations
can be to people who really want to understand the artist and the artist in
relation to other people. Now, *A Poetic Equation,* your conversations with
Nikki Giovanni, is a widely read book. And I know you are interested in
doing a dialogue with James Baldwin should fate so grant that . . .

MWA: Do you think that's going to happen?

JW: I don't know, but I was wondering if you had ever considered doing
similar conversations with Sonia Sanchez or Amiri Baraka?

MWA: Well, I've done one with Sonia, and I've had the pleasure of talking
a number of times with Baraka. He came down here in 1977 . . . I think that
was the first time while I was at the Institute for the Study of the Life, History,

and Culture of Black People. And then I've been up to New York in his class and at his school. I think the closest I've come was not in a conversation with him but with Michael Simanga for *The Black Nation.* Baraka obviously sent Simanga to see me.

JW: But would you like to do a dialogue with Baraka?

MWA: I think that would be most exciting. Everytime I see Baraka, I'm chiding him about something he has not done. So I don't know how he would feel about it.

JW: He's had many favorable things to say about you in his writings . . .

MWA: Oh, he thinks I'm a great writer. He thinks I'm a great poet.

JW: And it's a genuine sentiment coming from him.

MWA: I feel that Baraka is himself the embodiment of what we talk about all the time as black genius. We have had a lot of great writers, a lot of profound writers, a lot of . . . shall we say scintillating, brilliant writers. But I really believe Baraka is unique as a black genius in that he has been the leader of what I call Revolutionary Black Drama. He began with that play he got the Obie for . . . *Dutchman.* I think that he is an example of the kinds of changes that have gone on in black literature, especially in poetry. He starts out with the Beatnik generation, with Kerouac and Kaufman and Ferlinghetti and Ginsberg. He belongs in that group very definitely in his early poetry. Then he moved away from that to a far more serous note. I think that his great contribution to the black consciousness movement was in drama. And then . . . have you read his autobiography?

JW: Yes, I have.

MWA: The contribution there is in a special vernacular, which is his own speech pattern out of his childhood and adolescence. That's Alice Walker's best contribution to *The Color Purple,* the language that is her childhood and adolescent language and that we have a feeling constantly is an unconsciousness expressed. This is something coming out of her inner life, and she hears herself talking.

JW: She either hears herself or she's hearing relatives.

MWA: Yes, all of them. You can hear them speaking in *The Color Purple.* You hear Alice, you hear her family, you hear her generation, you hear her mother's, her grandmother's, and her great-grandmother's generation. That's language. I think, despite the fact that some people feel that some of the characters and the idea of family emerge in a very positive fashion . . . I don't feel that way about the characters of the family idea, but I feel very strongly about the language.

JW: And that is what comes in a different genre for Baraka, the autobiography?
MWA: Yes, in his autobiography . . .

JW: And perhaps in that slightly autobiographical novel *The System of Dante's Hell.*
MWA: Yes. When I think about Baraka, I see those three very different genres in which he has excelled and given us some splendid things. The early Beatnik poetry, the Revolutionary Black Drama, and the language of that autobiography.

JW: Indeed, we *must* have a conversation between you and Baraka. Now, you have a great deal of unfinished work. Your autobiography, which I think is going to be a magnificent contribution to Afro-American literature . . .
MWA: I hope so. I wonder if I can live to finish it. I keep feeling it should be the best thing I've ever done. It should be a very good work. I wonder sometimes if the beauty I feel I have experienced in my life can be beautifully expressed there. Somebody criticized me once about *Jubilee* and said my style was awful, that I didn't sound like a poet. I worried about that for a while, and then I learned afterwards that this was just malicious criticism. It didn't matter too much, because other critics said I was singing a folksong in *Jubilee.* They heard the rhythms in the work. This book about my life will not be confessional. It won't be purely social and intellectual history. But I do want it to be a song of my life.

JW: A kind of Whitmanesque song . . . a celebration?
MWA: That's exactly what it should be. It should be more than just a celebration of life, but that is big enough if I succeed. I think it should be a song that all men and women can hear singing in their own hearts.

JW: That will be a great song. There are many other songs to be sung, the short stories for the collection to be called *Goose Island* and . . .
MWA: I always planned to break up that flawed and half-written, not very good novel into a number of short stories, because I had such remarkable characters there. You know, of course, it was a slum story. I say over and over again, though people don't believe me, and it sounds conceited, that

Richard Wright got the idea for *Native Son* from *Goose Island*. I was writing about social conditions in Chicago and what they could do to a very talented personality. My character was a woman. She was a very talented musician. She married, and her life went down the drain into prostitution. She was a very interesting character, but then there was the pimp who was another very interesting character. And there was the man who was a narcotics dealer and a smuggler. That was another character. There were the shoplifting young girls. This was a life of crime on Division Street. I always wanted to take five or six people and develop them as a part of *Goose Island*.

JW: The stories in *Goose Island* will be very different. When you first created the characters that was Chicago, Depression, 1930s. If you write about those characters now, they come up to the 1980s and will be very different characters.

MWA: Yes, but they will be more familiar to everybody than they were to men then. That was a very limited world. But it is now a world that we see in all our communities all over the country. That to me is very sad.

JW: But it has to be dealt with. There are two novels left, *Minna and Jim* and *Mother Broyer?*

MWA: There are four novels left. The sequel to *Jubilee* is one and *Mother Broyer* is another. There is a novel of the Sixties, Seventies, and Eighties. There's a novel that deals with the period of the Vietnam War, the Civil Rights Movement, the drug scene and the youth subculture. It really deals with the experiences of one of my children. It follows the autobiography and *Minna and Jim,* but it's still family story and Southern-based. And then I've been thinking—I'm not going to rush to do this next one—but, of course, out of the awful experience and fiasco of the litigation surrounding *Jubilee* and *Roots,* there's another novel about this person who wants to get up and over on top without either the integrity or the talent, and what that's like. There's a mighty interesting story there. How you write a blockbuster if you don't have a blockbuster mind.

JW: You'll give us an answer, just as John A. Williams gave us another answer about the world of publishing in *!Click Song.* You have finished the poems for *This Is My Century.* I hope that collection is nearing publication.

MWA: Yes, you know, I wrote a poem in August, "For Farish Street." I think it's one of the best poems I've ever written. I sent it on to the publishers for the collection. I had three or four additional poems . . . I'm not sure I sent all of them. I had a tribute for Robert Hayden, a poem for Owen Dodson, and poems for Sarah Webster Fabio and Margaret Danner, two of my dear friends who are now deceased. Those four poems will be added to the collection I've already done. The piece on Farish Street (it may be done in a little brochure soon) I sent to Charles Rowell for the special poetry issue of *Callaloo,* and I sent one out to Iowa for an edition by poets who've been in the workshop out there. "For Farish Street" is written without the intricate symbolism but in the form T. S. Eliot used in *The Waste Land.* It has seven parts. The first part is called "The African Village." The second part is "A Patchwork Quilt." The third part is "Small Black World"; the fourth, "The Crystal Palace"; the fifth, "The House of Prayer"; the sixth, "Black Magic," and the seventh part is "The Labyrinth of Life."

JW: The number seven is fascinating, numerology . . .

MWA: I believe in seven. My autobiography will talk about seven in my life. I was born on the seventh day of the seventh month of the year. My mother was her mother's seventh child, and my father was his mother's seventh child. I am the child of the parents of seven, and my grandmother said, "You are born lucky." Seven is my lucky number.

JW: Perhaps that explains something about 1937—"For My People"— and what I hope will be a celebration "Fifty Years: For My People" in 1987 in Jackson. But you have such a great amount of work left to do. Have you set any timetable for completing it?

MWA: I pray a lot. I told my doctor several years ago that I would like to live to finish my work. Some days my health seems very good. Other days I wonder if I can live out the year. You never know. Life is a gift everyday. Every morning is a gift. A long time ago I decided to do something that Benjamin Franklin did. He was remarkable in that he was so well organized. He planned every day of his life. I work with one day at a time. I'm grateful when I wake up in the morning and know that I'm here for another day and hope I will live to see that day to the end. I try to do as much as I possibly can every day. I try to do some writing, with the understanding that when the time comes to leave this life I probably will have something unfinished on my desk. But I will have done the best I can and the most I can with what I have. That is my constant belief. I think I'm fairly well-organized, because most of the things I want to do I've organized on paper already. I haven't done too much with that novel about the Sixties, Seventies, and Eighties. And I have not done anything to organize the *Roots* fiasco. I did take the poem that I had about it out of *This Is My Century.* The poem serves as a kind of outline for the novel. It brings up the images and talks about the kind of people who will be in the novel.

JW: What is the title of that poem?
MWA: "Ripoff *Roots* Style."

JW: Are you planning to collect your essays and speeches?
MWA: My editor and I put together about twenty-five speeches, essays and articles covering a period of about fifty years, from 1932 to about 1983 or 1984. The best speeches I've given, the best articles, seem not to be in the Thirties, Forties, and Fifties but in the Sixties, Seventies, and Eighties. So, we have five decades of speeches and articles, and we have a publisher, but we haven't finished editing the book. Now, the interviews . . . we're off to a good start. The book I'm most excited about is Myriam Díaz-Diocaretz's *Fields Watered with Blood,* a collection of critical essays on my work. That is most exciting. At first, I thought there weren't many critical pieces, but Myriam gathered maybe a dozen, and then is adding unpublished work. I was so proud of the piece Ron Baxter Miller has done on Biblical typology in my work and Southern history. Paula Giddings had long since done that article entitled "A Shoulder Hunched Against a Sharp Concern." I like that very much. And the two pieces in Mari Evan's *Black Women Writers* by Eleanor Traylor and Euginia Collier. Those are two very fine pieces. Then Phyllis Klotman has an article. There's Dilla Buckner's work on folklore and James Spears's article on folk elements in *Jubilee* from the *Mississippi Folklore Register.* I think Myriam has asked Sonia Sanchez to write something, and Maryemma Graham, Stephen Henderson, you, the West Indian writer Michelle Cliff, and perhaps Adrienne Rich. It's going to be a very fine book. And I asked Myriam to ask Paul Brennan to write a piece. The book may be published in 1987.

JW: You mentioned Ron Baxter Miller's article on your poetry and the typological unity there. Now, is it an ideational unity you are seeking in *This Is My Century,* a unity based on a synthesis of Du Bois, Freud, Einstein, Marx and Kierkegaard?
MWA: To a certain extent, yes. But there is something else. I have dealt with a number of these figures, and I add five black men to that: Du Bois, Garvey, King, Malcolm X, and Frederick Douglass. I am thinking seriously about a half dozen figures from the Civil Rights Movement that I did not

write about in *Prophets for a New Day.* I think I have John A. Lewis there, and I had Benjamin Mays, Bayard Rustin, and two or three poems on King. I wanted to do the firebrand of Samson setting the tails of the foxes afire, for Stokely Carmichael. I never did it. And I have been over and over thinking of a good text and a good poem for the mass leader that Jesse Jackson has become. I want to make him a Biblical figure, but he doesn't seem to fit the eighth-century prophets at all. He seems to fit . . . not one of the Gospels, not one of the saints, but . . . I'm not sure whether he belongs in the orthodox canon or the unorthodox, such as the Apocrypha or the Pseudepigrapha. Sometimes he's like Saul and Paul. I know he's the preacher. He's not Koheleth; he's not the average one. I think sometimes he belongs with the Maccabees. He's an Apocryphal figure. I keep working with it, because I want to do a piece on Jesse. Sonia Sanchez did a piece on Jesse in 1984, and I have watched him with great interest. I think Jesse is a very great man. He seems so much of the ordinary that people forget how *extraordinary* he is. There's a duality there: Saul/Paul. He's so much like Paul and he's so much like Saul.

JW: And what do you see for the future?

MWA: When you talk about the future, there is that brave new world.

JW: Yes, you mentioned that in your speech "Religion, Poetry, and History," but it's not the Shakespearean brave new world . . .

MWA: I say "in the 21st century our progeny will raise their eyes to more than a vision of a brave new world." In my autobiography, I say that we move toward a beatific vision that is beyond our wildest imagination.

JW: One final question. Is political action beyond writing a special price that black writers in America pay if they are not content with art as Art? Is that, as Baldwin has it, the price of the ticket?

MWA: I don't know that I understand Baldwin there. I'm not familiar with that quote. I do know that ever since Chicago days I have been committed to a life of the artist for the people. I think that's the one thing I got out of my association with Wright. It may have been unformed before then, but it came out of the South. I think I've always had Black Nationalist feelings and yearnings. I grew up a time when we talked about race pride, and in my family, in my house, we were always reading *Crisis* magazine and *Opportunity.* My father's friends were Garveyites. My mother believed in Booker T. Washington, but my father believed in W. E. B. Du Bois. And King was the kind of man that my father was in an intellectual way. When I look at Malcolm X, I think about my brother, my uncles, the men in my family who went through—some of them—some difficult experiences, but at the same time had a real philosophy of hope for black people. I remember Nikki saying to me when I mentioned the Communists didn't like me. . . . They rebuffed me. I couldn't have even had a full flirtation with the Communist Party, because they simply rejected me. They thought of me . . . now I realize I was considered *petite bourgeois,* Black Nationalist deviationist. I was never going to follow a set party line. And, of course, they accused Wright, and rightfully so, of not being a Stalinist, of being a Trotskyist. He was! And he had a reason. I learned then that the ivory tower was no place for a black writer. And black writers who kept saying, "Well, I don't want to be called a Negro writer or a Negro poet or a black poet"—what else were they? They were poets mainly, but they were Negroes first. They were black men before they began to write. They came here male, and the next word was *black.* I have no desire to separate myself from what I am . . . from my race, from my gender, from my nationality, and from my consciousness. I'm black, woman, writer; I'm very Black Nationalist.

JW: That is, I think, a very fitting end. Thank you for giving me the pleasure of this interview.

MWA: Well, I enjoyed it.

An Interview with Margaret Walker Alexander

Kay Bonetti / 1991

From the *Missouri Review* 15:1 (1992): 11–31. Copyright © 1991 American Audio Prose Library, Inc. Used by permission. All rights reserved. This is a print version of an interview available on cassette. For more information call 800-447-2275.

Interviewer: Ms. Walker, when you were a teenager, after you'd finished two years of college in New Orleans, Langston Hughes told your parents that their daughter had talent and that they should get you out of the South. Why?

Walker: Langston was saying that I couldn't get the kind of education I needed there. The summer before I went to Northwestern, some Jewish friends of my mother and father took my poetry to a professor of English at Tulane University, Richard Kirk. I dared not walk on that campus. At that time the only black people who could go over on Tulane's campus had to be maids and cooks and janitors. He wrote me a nice little note, said he thought I had talent, if I was willing to work.

Interviewer: How did you decide on Northwestern?

Walker: My mother and my father had gone there. It was a Methodist school and Methodist ministers could send their children there cheaper—they'd get a rebate. It cost about six hundred dollars a year, and they took off a hundred and some dollars of each semester for us. When I left school I still owed some of the money. I paid it though.

Interviewer: After you finished school you stayed in Chicago for a time working on the Federal Writers' Project of the WPA. At the end of that time you made a most interesting statement. You said, "I felt the thing that I had to do then was to go to graduate school and get a teaching job back south." Why did you want to go back?

Walker: The South is symbolic—the violence of the South, the protest, the struggle, all of that. The South is both an historic region and a mythic ideal. All my images, in my poetry, come from out of the South, where I was a child, where my imagination was formed, and where I was an adolescent. I never felt at home anywhere but in the South.

Interviewer: And yet, why do you have to live there to write about it? Look at all the southern writers who have left.

Walker: I'm one of the few black writers who lives in the South and writes there. Alice Walker told me she had to get out of Mississippi. She simply could not write there. I don't feel that I have to be in exile to write. I wrote at Yaddo. I wrote at Cape Cod. I wrote in Virginia. I wrote in North Carolina. I wrote in New York. I wrote in Chicago. There is no place that I can live where I can't write. Maybe if I were in New York or Chicago my stuff might be considered better than it's considered as a southern woman living in Jackson. But I don't care about that. Those places were too cold, the pace was too fast. I just like living where I *live*.

Interviewer: You began *Jubilee* in your senior year at Northwestern, worked on it for thirty years and published it in the sixties. Where do you think it fits on the continuum of twentieth-Century African-American fiction?

Walker: *Jubilee* is a folk novel and an historical novel. In every sense of the word, regardless of period, time and circumstance, *Jubilee* can be defined in that way. I used folk ways, folk sayings, folk philosophy, folk ideas, folk everything. Vyry is a folk character. At the same time, no one can deny the historical accuracy of what I have written—the Antebellum South, the Civil War, and the period of reconstruction and reaction.

Interviewer: How was it received when it came out?

Walker: My southern salesman said if I had been a white woman writing that book I would be a rich woman. He went to a bookstore in Atlanta to get them to have an autograph party and when they discovered I was black, they told him no. He came to one of the church bookstores in Jackson, I think Southern Baptist, and although I had been a regular customer and had bought many, many books, they refused to have the book autographed in their store. But a big department store that has stores over Louisiana and Alabama gave me a wonderful autograph signing. The woman in that store said she sold more of that book than she had sold of any book in twenty years.

Interviewer: Were black people buying it, or white people?

Walker: Black and white. People in the South ate up that book quickly. In many schools it's required reading and it's on various supplementary reading lists. The book is twenty-four, twenty-five years old, I guess, and it has never gone out of print. Next year, *Jubilee* will be twenty-five years in paperback. That's where it's sold most.

Interviewer: Did you have trouble finding a publisher when you finished it?

Walker: My publisher was waiting for it when I finished it. I signed seven book contracts without an agent, but I tell all young people now that if they want to have a career, the best thing to do is to get an agent. I don't need an agent now. My books have made their own reputation.

Interviewer: Beginning with the Yale Younger Poets prize after you got your Masters at Iowa.

Walker: I tried the Yale Younger Poets competition off and on about five years. Stephen Vincent Benét encouraged me. My book was rejected in '40 and '41 and I was not even going to send it in '42, but he asked me about it. He immediately gave it the award, but said that the publishers were not anxious to have a black woman published at Yale. I had not expected to find that kind of prejudice there. When I went up to Yale, I stayed first in the Y, and the woman told me that they had no discrimination there. I said, "Well, I didn't expect to find it here." She said, "Why?" I said, "Isn't this the cradle of democracy?" But I did discover there was strong prejudice and racism all over this country.

Interviewer: Do you see *Jubilee* as a novel about African-American experience?

Walker: I take that for granted. I'm an African-American woman, and I write about being a black person.

Interviewer: Where do you see yourself in terms of that tradition?

Walker: I was a child at the time of the Harlem Renaissance. I knew most of those people, read them as a child. But I belong to the school of social protest of the thirties. I was influenced by Wright, by what he wrote and what he said. I worked with him for three years.

Interviewer: The social protest writers were pretty radical, weren't they?

Walker: I'm in one or two anthologies that reflect that. One is called *Writing Red.* I said to someone, once, "I didn't know I was that radical. I never published in any left-wing magazines. They wouldn't have me. I published in *Crisis.*" They said, "Yes, and that was black, wasn't it? But it was considered red, too." I didn't realize that, but I did know that was the decade of socially conscious writers. And that is where I belong. Despite the fact that *Jubilee* appeared in the sixties, it's influenced by the thinking that I acquired in the thirties. My poetry was written in the thirties and forties, published in the forties. But it's socially conscious poetry.

Interviewer: During the mid-thirties, after you graduated from Northwestern, you stayed in Chicago where you worked on the WPA and were a member of Wright's South Side Writers Group. Did you know Jack Conroy during that time?

Walker: The first time I saw Jack he had just come to Chicago to revive and organize the new *Anvil,* because the old *Anvil* had gone under, about that time. I thought Jack Conroy was a very, very wonderful person. He tried to help young writers. He tried to publish people in the movement—not just the labor movement, but basically the labor movement. He had a tendency to appreciate, shall we say, those with a leftist radical orientation. He had great, great stories of the working class, of mines and of the workers, the farmers, everybody.

Interviewer: Conroy tells a funny story about having to send a rejection letter to J. D. Salinger. He and Nelson Algren had run out of money and were writing rejection notes on mortuary stationery, because it was all they had. J.D. Salinger wrote back and said, "Thank you for your nice letter, and I'm really sorry that you can't publish my work. I have to say, I hope it's the only rejection slip I ever get from a mortuary."

Walker: They were very thick. I think Wright thought a great deal of Jack, too, and Jack liked Wright then.

Interviewer: Jack Conroy said that he never really knew what happened to break up the friendship, that Nelson Algren just turned on him, and he never knew why.

Walker: He didn't have to do anything. I knew Nelson before Jack came to the job. Nelson was a gambler. He must have made two or three fortunes, with the book and movies, and he gambled it all away. He even gambled away the money he made at the Iowa workshop.

Interviewer: You and Richard Wright were very close during those years.

Walker: I knew Richard Wright three years. I was always at his desk. Everybody seemed to feel that I was trying to marry the man, and that kind of thing. I don't think he ever asked me, and I don't think I was asking him. We talked about marriage, and I told him, "I hope when you're ready to marry the woman you want to marry will want to marry you, because I think that's what's important." I knew when our friendship ended that he had used me in Chicago. He had used me. He was not my sweertheart. We were never romantically involved. He was not a lover, as people have said. They saw us together, and put their own interpretations on it. What I have said in *Richard Wright: Daemonic Genius* is as true as if I had put my hand on the Bible and raised my hand up and said, "I swear to tell the truth."

Interviewer: You have your journals, too.

Walker: I have the journals. And I have his journals, too. That's part of the problem. Mrs. Wright sold Richard Wright's letters and papers and journals to Yale University for $175,000. In those papers she had forty pages of letters that I wrote to him, of which I have no copies. I had no idea I was going to write the biography. It so happened that I went to Atlanta, to speak for the Institute of the Black World, and there I saw Horace Cayton. He was going to Paris that month, December, and then he would be through with his research and ready to write his book about Wright. We spoke in a Baptist church that night, and I talked about Wright's negative treatment of women, and implied that his treatment in fiction was the way he felt about women. That caused a furor. I think I do the same thing in my book, although I didn't say in my speech that he was bisexual, that I had actually seen him on the bed with another man in New York. That was the reason for the breaking up between us, not my going there trying to get married to him, as Michel Fabre and Ellen Wright said. They didn't know what they were talking about. But I got it from the horse's head; I saw the two men in the room.

Interviewer: You were set up. A woman took you up there, so that you would see, but she didn't know you were too naive to understand what you were seeing.

Walker: I was stupid as the day is long. I didn't know anything about a ménage à trois, which was also going on then.

Interviewer: You say in your biography of Wright that his work is a line of demarcation in African-American literature. Can you explain what you mean by that?

Walker: We had some very fine writers, like James Weldon Johnson and W. E. B. Du Bois, Paul Laurence Dunbar, and Charles Chesnutt, long before Wright. Wright comes after the Harlem Renaissance, when we had a great school of black writers, but the writers of the Harlem Renaissance believed that black people were really what white people said we were: some kind of exotic, that we laughed in our suffering because we were not without laughter, as Langston Hughes wrote. None of those writers had the real conception of the problems of black people being basically economic and political. Wright wrote with the understanding that we are basically a powerless people because we do not own the means of production, and the political system is manipulated by those who do own the means of production. As a result we have very great difficulty with the system. All the problems we face—of substandard education, substandard housing, problems of health—all of these problems go back to the basic problems of politics and economics. That was his thesis.

Interviewer: And what do you think then followed?

Walker: After Wright we have a school of writers who not only were naturalistic, as he was, but who sought to deal with a consciousness that came out of an understanding of the problems. That school was most evident in the late thirties through the forties and fifties. In the sixties the Black Nationalist Revolution colored our thinking so that our best writers were the ones who understood the changes we had gone through. Both Ralph Ellison and James Baldwin were influenced by Wright, but I don't think they were as consciously naturalistic as Wright. A woman like Ann Petry, who wrote about the street, was doing the kind of writing, based on sociology, that much of Wright's writing was like.

Now, I'm very much refreshed with the knowledge that black women in the eighties were really the key to the best literature in the country, that we had a group. I don't know that these women were that much influenced by Wright, because I think Wright was very chauvinistic. Most of the black writers up to his time were chauvinistic. Langston Hughes and Countee Cullen and Sterling Brown belonged to the Harlem Renaissance, but so did Zora Neale Hurston, and she was a wonderful writer. Great imagination, marvelous storyteller, and just as talented as the men. But they gave her a hard time.

Interviewer: It's interesting that you don't think the black women writers of the eighties were influenced by Wright. They were influenced by Zora Neale Hurston, who in turn influenced Wright, as you argue so persuasively.

Walker: Zora Neale Hurston definitely influenced Wright, though he talked about her terribly. I don't know whether all male writers are like the black male writers, but they certainly have shown a jealousy of the black woman writer.

Interviewer: Toni Morrison has said, "Nobody can tell me that those books that I grew up with, by people like Langston Hughes and Jimmy Baldwin, weren't beautiful. But those books were written for you, and I am writing for somebody else." Do you think there's any validity to that?

Walker: Yes. Wright said that, after all, the critics are white and the audience was white. Their books didn't sell that much among blacks.

Interviewer: Toni Morrison feels that now, because of their heritage, black writers are free to write . . .

Walker: What they want to write. And to write for a black audience as well as for a white audience.

Interviewer: The thing that strikes me about much African-American literature that's come along in the last twenty to thirty years is a strong strain, like you see in Alice Walker, of Christian existentialism. I think you see it in *Jubilee,* as well. Vyry's strength is that she refuses to buy into hatred. She elects choice.

Walker: Vyry is conditioned by what she learned in the quarters, what she learned from black and white people, and she belongs in the Judeo-Christian tradition. *Jubilee* grows out of my family beliefs. I'm the daughter of a minister and the granddaughter of a minister. I'm a Methodist and my background is Christian. I think you can't get away from that when you're writing. Vyry didn't believe that hatred would solve any problem. I say exactly what Vyry says, "Yeah, a lot of white people are evil, but every white person is not evil." My father used to say, "We should respect a man's belief. If we don't, we don't respect him." I can't write a book that is not influenced by Christian theology and by Christian faith.

Interviewer: What led you finally to write *Daemonic Genius?*

Walker: After I was in Atlanta Vincent Harding said, "Margaret, you better get ready to finish this book." I said, "What book?" He said, "This book about Richard Wright." I said, "Are you crazy? Why would I write a book about Richard Wright?" Well, he says, "Can't you see our brother Horace will not be able?" A month later, fifteenth day of January, 1970, Horace Cayton was dead in Paris. That's the day I knew somebody had to write the book. I was sure Ellen Wright and Michel Fabre were satisfied that everybody was dead who had attempted to do this. Then they began to court me. Fabre wanted to come and see me. And I sent word I wouldn't be available.

Interviewer: Was this after he had written his book, or while he was writing it?

Walker: Before he had written it. His book didn't come out until '73, and Cayton died in '70. I saw him in Iowa in '72, and met him then. Then when his book came out in '73 he had all this mess in there about these women who were Wright's girlfriends.

Interviewer: And you knew that didn't make much sense, given what you knew about Wright.

Walker: Right, and not just what I knew. Both the marriages had failed. But Ellen Wright is mad because I put all that in the book.

Interviewer: About the bisexuality?

Walker: The bisexuality. The fact that his marriages didn't last. The first one was gone in less than a year. During his second marriage, to Ellen, Wright was moving around the world. In 1952 he was a whole year in England writing *The Outsider,* in '53 he went to Africa, in '54 he went to Spain. This kept right up 'til '57, and then they were going to move to London, but the English would not let him stay—he came back to Paris and she stayed. I said to Abraham Chapman, "Why would Mrs. Wright stay in England when her husband was denied a visa and came back to Paris?" He said, "But Margaret, their marriage was over two years before Dick died. That marriage was over." That's the first time it had even crossed my mind.

Interviewer: What was the basis of Mrs. Wright's lawsuit?

Walker: In 1971, Charles Davis asked me to come to Iowa to participate in a seminar on Richard Wright. "How I wrote *Jubilee*" had been published in *New Letters* and included excerpts from letters Wright had written to me, which gave it great authenticity. When I began to write the book, I naturally planned to use that as a nucleus and core for the book. My essay was published in '71, published as a book in '72, and then in paperback. During those three publications she did not say a word. Fabre did not say a word. They didn't say anything until in '82 they heard that I was doing a biography. Then they began to say that I was using the letters and those had not been published, and therefore couldn't be used. I said they'd been published, and I can prove they've been published. I wasn't using any letters that were not published. The judge said I had a right to do everything I did. The case was decided on the 19th of September, 1990, and I won.

Interviewer: Yet they're still fighting it, even though the book's already in print.

Walker: I haven't gotten a penny out of the book, and probably never will because it's been tied up in that suit. They're using the royalties to fight the legal battles. This black woman has been through two copyright infringement suits—lost one and won one. Now everybody figured that Ellen Wright was going to beat me in court because she was a white woman, and she was saying I couldn't use her husband's stuff. But the judge gave me the benefit of the doubt. Papers in the country headlined the fact that I had won that suit; they said this is a boon to authors.

Interviewer: There seems to have been controversy about both of your very large books, the Richard Wright biography and *Jubilee.* Can you talk about the problem with Alex Haley and *Roots?*

Walker: To tell the record straight would take three full big books. In 1977, when I sued Alex Haley, I had never heard the term "fair use." I didn't know what the laws on copyright infringement were. I studied them for two years. I went through *Roots* and found every plagiarized thing. Fifteen scenes from *Jubilee* somehow showed up in *Roots.* I wish you could see the book, because it's all the way through.

There are six characters, most of them with the same names; Chicken George is born on a page in *Jubilee.* There are one hundred and fifty some-odd verbatim expressions. Some part of four hundred pages of *Jubilee* appear in *Roots.* My friends said, well, so what? You wrote "Goose Island" and Richard Wright took it and made *Native Son.* You turned around and wrote a book about him. What's the difference?

Richard Wright was a demonic genius, and I won't say what I generally call Mr. Haley. We went to court and the judge said that I was wrong, even though he said in his opening remarks that it was a foregone conclusion that copying had gone on. Then he assigned us to magistrate court. The magistrate sent word back that there was every evidence of plagiarism, that there had been complete access, but she did not have the authority to declare it a case of copyright infringement. The judge must do that. It went back to him and said, "I'm going to make a ruling on this case in ten days, and then I'm going to retire from the bench." A man in mid-life, in good health, federal judge for life, got off the bench after rendering the decision in that case. Then he said, "Alex Haley hasn't copied anything from anybody. There are similarities, but they're strained, and there's nothing there." Well, the public had seen what was there. They saw it on television in 1974, two years before *Roots* was published.

Interviewer: Weren't there other suits against Haley?

Walker: There are one hundred books, not just mine, where something has been copied out of them and used in *Roots*. A man named Harold Cour-lander hired lawyers, just like I had. Two months after the judge said that mine wasn't copied, another judge said there were three paragraphs copied out of Courlander's book, *The African*. That's all. And he won. They settled outside the court. It was rumored that he got $750,000. A month before I sued there appeared in a magazine called *New West* a story about an editor at *Playboy* named Murray Fisher who said he not only put together the book *Roots* for Alex Haley, but he put together *The Autobiography of Malcolm X* for Alex Haley. He said he did that one for free, because Malcolm X believed that all white people were devils, and he was proving that he was a white man who wasn't a devil. But he wasn't going to do *Roots* for free, because there was too much money in that, and they would either have to pay him or put his name on the book. Alex Haley wrote Doubleday and said, "You'll have to settle with Murray Fisher, because you can't let his name go on the book. People are going to say I didn't write this book anyhow." *New West* said Murray Fisher was paid a quarter of a million dollars, cash, flat, plus ten percent of the net proceeds from the sale. What shocked me most was that here comes a man from England, named John Rolling, who said Kunte Kinte was his story. He had a book named *Kunte Kinte*. So, when people look at me like I'm crazy, an agitated old woman making up something, that's just the superficial stuff.

Interviewer: I'm just burning with curiosity about some of the historical circumstances of *Jubilee*. How much did your great-grandmother tell you about her father, who served as a model for Randall Ware?

Walker: I knew that he was Randall Ware, and I kept that name. His name is in the courthouse in Dawson, Georgia, now, as having owned practically the whole town of Dawson, a black man. It's very hard to separate fiction from fact, when you've worked with this thing imaginatively over such a long time. But my grandmother told me that her father was a rich man.

Interviewer: In "How I wrote *Jubilee*" you speak of the year that your father died, when you and your husband decided to cut back around through Greenville, and trace backwards your grandmother's journey as a child with her mother, from Dawson, Georgia, to Alabama. You found your grandmoth-er's youngest sister who gave you Vyry's chest. Had your immediate family lost touch with these great-aunts who descended from Vyry's second mar-riage?

Walker: Two or three of the half-sisters had been down to see my grandmother when we were in New Orleans. The youngest was Martha. Martha lived to be ninety-nine years old. She was born when my grandmother was having her first child so Vyry was having her last child when her first child was having her first child. When Vyry died my grandmother said her mother's things had been sold all over two hills, Baptist Hill and Methodist Hill. Martha had done away with most of her mother's things, but she carried that Bible and chest with her to Detroit, where she died. When I went to Detroit, Uncle Henry's granddaughter had the Bible. I made Xerox copies, and got some information that I wanted. She would not turn loose that Bible under any circumstances. She resented my grandmother's side of the family because Martha was one of the second man's descendants. There was feeling there.

Interviewer: Among the two sets of children. I wondered about that.

Walker: My grandmother never said anything against any of her sisters, because they were all her mother's children. I'm the only one in the family, other than a cousin who died three years ago, who kept up with records and births and deaths. About three years ago, a white woman in Greenville called me on the telephone and said she had read *Jubilee* and people there remembered my great-grandmother, and that her people, her folk, had a farm nearby. This woman came to see me, in Jackson, and brought me three documents: my grandmother's marriage license, dated December of 1876, Jim's marriage license, and my great-grandmother's will. Vyry's will is documented in the courthouse in Butler County, Greenville, Alabama. They begin the sequel to *Jubilee.*

Interviewer: How did she come by that stuff?

Walker: It's in the courthouse. She said she was doing research and she was interested. I know what she was doing. She was hunting up that property, because her people had taken it over. She was looking me up to see if I had sense enough to know she has no business with that property. I'm not concerned about her people taking the property. That's happened to black people all over the South.

Interviewer: How does it happen?

Walker: Black people had land all over the South, just like Randall Ware had all that land. All of that land got taken over by wealthy white people in the town. They're wealthy now, they weren't wealthy then.

Interviewer: You've said that you conceived *Jubilee* as a series of episodes with titles drawn from your grandmother's sayings. Did those sayings provide the concept for each episode?

Walker: No. What I did was to write a sentence outline. If you wrote a complete sentence, and left it there, twenty-five years later you could go back to that complete sentence and the thought that sentence expressed would return to you. I wrote that outline in 1948, complete sentences. Some of them were things my grandmother had said. Some were not. When I sat down to the typewriter I had my topic sentence. But a sentence is not an idea. A sentence is a group of words expressing a complete thought. A thought is only the beginning of an idea. A paragraph expresses an idea. A concept can be symbolized by just one word.

I know this for a fact: every artist begins with a concept. He begins with an idea, whether he's a painter, a graphic artist, a plastic artist, whether he's a musician, whether he's a writer. Creative thinking is nothing more than having the concept out of which the idea grows. It doesn't matter whether you're writing a poem or a piece of prose. It begins in the idea.

Interviewer: What was your vision? What was the idea of *Jubilee,* to you?

Walker: Oh, I don't think it was one big thing at all. It was a lot of little things that we put together which makes the big book.

Each chapter has what each poem has, unity. Unity and coherence, and emphasis, which I was taught as a child. What gives it lasting value is it's not a story you've ever heard before. It's a different story. It's unique. A lot of people, however, will say, "That's the same story my grandmother told me. I heard that story." But nobody had ever put that story down.

Interviewer: Why did you want to do it?

Walker: Because my grandmother talked about it all the time, and when I was a little girl, I told her, "When I grow up I'm going to write that story." I'd ask, "And where did you go, where did you live after that?" I had the feeling that it was an important story. The older I got, the more I realized that I had a very great story. And I had a document, a living document. I knew that the society in which I have grown up and lived, the segregated society, didn't want to believe that story. They had another story that they were always telling, *Gone With the Wind.* And that wasn't my story.

Looking Back: A Conversation with Margaret Walker

Alferdteen Harrison / 1992

From *Margaret Walker's "For My People": A Tribute,* photographs
by Roland Freeman. Jackson: University Press of Mississippi, 1992.
Reprinted by permission of University Press of Mississippi.

*What do you think is the importance of Roland Freeman's photographic trib-
ute to you on the fiftieth anniversary of your first publication?*

This is the first time that I can recall any illustration or depiction in photographs of what I was saying in the poem. I have always depended on the
energies of the poem itself to communicate to people what I was thinking.
Now after fifty years, this is a wonderful tribute to the book *For My People,*
covering not only the title poem but the twenty-six or more poems in the
book as a whole. This is something different, and I hope that it will help to
remind many people of what my commitment has been to my own people
throughout these fifty years.

Roland Freeman has done the same thing with his photographs that many
black writers have tried to do with their poetry or their stories. He has gone
through the South and shown the life of our people in all areas, and this has
been not just from the standpoint of race, but of class: poor people, working
people, people whose opportunities have been limited and who have struggled on for some kind of existence. That is what his photographs represent.

I am very proud and pleased and honored to have Roland Freeman do this
book. I think it will be a further step toward popularizing the poetry. People
generally don't like poetry, but everywhere I have gone and read my poetry
people have liked it, and I think these pictures will enhance its popularity. I
am grateful to Roland because I think he has the right concept—he understands the social significance of what I try to say. And therefore it pleases
me very much.

*So, to have this photographic tribute fifty years after you wrote your first
piece is—very appropriate.*

What strikes me is that I wrote these poems for the most part in the decade
of the 1930s. It was a period of depression—economic depression—and

black people suffered along with everyone else from lack of jobs, from lack of standard housing, from lack of appropriate schooling. We were literally outcast from the general society. But then there were poor white people, too, and poor working people. It was a time when the unions were struggling to have collective bargaining, to have a forty-hour week, and all these entered into the picture of economic depression. A number of my poems indicate that. In fact, all through my poetry, from the thirties through the eighties, you will find concern for poor black people.

So this is a really fitting kind of collaboration, tied together in the nineties?

I think so. I think it is a kind of document that gives a picture of fifty years of struggle. And I have some poems in the book, that first book, talking about our struggle, about our problems, economic problems more than political, but seeing them as basic to the problems of racism. I think that Roland's pictures go along with the poems: they are companion pieces. And I find in them certain subjects that are clearly the subjects of the poems. For example, Roland's photographs say a great deal about the family, and I have poems that call attention to members of the family. Not just the children or the parents or the grandparents, but the extended family—that has always been one of the subjects in my poetry.

I'd like you to reflect back to the circumstances of publishing this work. How did you choose a publisher? How did you come to publish this book?

This is a nice and interesting story. I was a student at Northwestern University when I first heard of the Yale Younger Poets competition. I knew the reputation of Yale University, and I knew something about university presses. I have now had three books published by university presses. For me they stand for a kind of quality, not necessarily true with all commercial publishers, and frequently the university press is not interested in making money as such, but in finding the quality of life that I especially wanted to express in my poetry.

I entered the Yale Younger Poets competition five years before I received the award. The first time I sent my manuscript of poetry away, I must have been twenty or twenty-one years old, and that was before I wrote the poem "For My People." The manuscript came back as fast as I sent it, and I realized that it didn't get any further than the press before they turned it around and sent it back. In 1939 I was studying at the University of Iowa, and I discovered that a number of people who had been at the university in the writer's workshop had entered that contest and some had won. I didn't know at the time that my teacher, Paul Engle, had won that award ten years before I did. But I decided on my own to send my manuscript again. In January of 1940 I again sent my manuscript to Yale, but this time I wrote a cover letter to the editor, who was Stephen Vincent Benét, and I sent the manuscript and the letter directly to him. For the first time the publishers there did not send it back without his seeing it. It was his personal mail, and he got a chance to read it for the first time. Almost six months passed before I heard from him, and then he wrote a very encouraging letter, saying he regretted that I did not win the prize but that he was very impressed with my work and hoped that, if I had not published it in another year, I would sent it back. I graduated from Iowa with a master's degree that summer, and the next year I sent my manuscript back, in 1941. That was the third or fourth time I think I had sent it. And he wrote again another apologetic letter but pointing out that my work was valuable and that I mustn't be discouraged: it would eventually be published.

The next year—1942, the year I won—I did not even submit my manuscript. I was convinced, as Richard Wright has said, that Yale wasn't going to publish any black writer. So I didn't send it. I was surprised to hear a colleague tell me at a college language meeting that Stephen Benét had said I was going to win the prize that year. I was surprised because I had not even submitted my manuscript. But when I went back to work, I received a telegram asking me to send it to him at his summer address, if I was still eligible, and also to wire him in New York that I had done so. And that is the way I got it published.

That's a beautiful story. How did that make you feel?

I think that I must have known, as young as I was, that to publish with a very prestigious publisher would not only add luster to my work, it would give me a chance to be better known. I was in my twenties, and fifty years later I realize that was the auspicious beginning of my career. For a long time after that I didn't publish any poetry, and people assumed I was a one-book poet. But my teacher at Northwestern told me I didn't have to rush out and publish again right away, that the book would last the rest of my life, and if I didn't do anything for the next fifteen to twenty years, it would be time enough. That was precisely what I did.

So, how did you arrive at that title, "For My People"?

It is the title of one of the poems—the title poem—most of which I have often said I wrote in fifteen minutes on a typewriter. I think it was just after my twenty-second birthday and I felt it was my whole life gushing out—as I had felt about my people all my life. "For My People" was just the way I started the poem. It was what I wanted to say, it was that and nothing else. But at the end of six or seven stanzas I didn't know how to finish it. I kept wondering what the conclusion should be. Nelson Algren was on the writer's project in Chicago, and I let him read the poem. And he asked me, "What do you want for your people?" And that gave me the answer, and the last stanza. Even fifty years later I am satisfied that what I said then is what I still want now.

Did the publishers want to change the title?

I have been very fortunate with the books that I have written. I know that often publishers change titles, but nobody talked about changing the title of that book. It was the title of my thesis for the masters degree. When *Jubilee* came along, the publishers wanted to change that name. I held fast to *Jubilee,* and when the sales conferences took place they asked the salesmen if they didn't think we should change the title, because they had researched and found about a half dozen—six or seven—other books with the title *Jubilee.* But the salesman told them no, they could sell that book with the title *Jubilee,* and the publishers had to abide by that. I have never had a book with the title completely changed. It is always what I choose. I know that doesn't happen with many people. I happen to know Richard Wright's books were not named by him, that publishers typically named them because he did not have a name for them. But I always had my own titles and I won't let anyone change them.

What are some of the highlights, or pivotal events, that have either affected your career or that are significant about black life since your first publication?

I have had a very great struggle over the fifty years to try to be a writer, as well as teacher, and a wife, and a mother, and to go on lecture tours, and it has been a struggle in more ways than one—largely financial. But I was determined to do certain things and I took chances. Unfortunately, I pushed myself always too hard and I was always ill as a result of it. But I was fortunate in winning prizes. For the ten books I have written, I have received at least ten prizes. The first was from the Rosenwald Foundation for the book *For My People,* and then I received two Ford Foundation grants, one for *Jubilee* and one for the Richard Wright book. I have received money from the National Endowment for the Humanities, a senior fellowship to do re-

search on the Richard Wright book, and I discovered that the wonderful Lyndhurst prize I received four or five years ago was given to me because of the
Richard Wright book. Every book has been financed by another book, and
cash prizes are not always the usual thing. I have had a lot of honors, but the
cash prizes have financed my creative work. I couldn't have done it on my
teacher's salary, and I had nobody to serve as a patron, but government and
foundation sources paid for my creative career.

*I think that is an excellent statement for your career of fifty years. The final
area we want to pursue is what do you see, other than this illustrious career,
that has been generated as a result of* For My People*?*

I think that there are two ways to measure the success of a book. The
general public wants to know right away how much money you made. That
has always been a joke because ordinarily books just don't make a lot of
money. My books have sold well, however. *For My People* went through
eight printings before it went out of print, and when the University of Georgia
collected my poems and reprinted them, that meant the ninth printing of *For
My People*. Even though it might not have sold for much at first, it started
out at two dollars and a half and later sold for five dollars. I discovered a
printed edition that sold for eight dollars, and people have told me they have
gone in old bookstores and found copies selling for as much as thirty-five
dollars—not coming to me of course. But I think for a writer's first book of
poetry to have sold nine printings is very good indeed. It doesn't happen all
the time.

For My People got off to a very illustrious start. Winning the Yale Award
for Younger Poets was a distinction in itself. And when I went to New York
to promote the book, I was invited to the *New York Herald Tribune* Book and
Author luncheon at the hotel Astor where I read my poetry. That began my
career as a lecturer. Everywhere I went and people heard me read my poetry,
the word spread to others that I could read my poetry well. I have never
lacked for engagements; I simply couldn't always fill them.

Jubilee has been a tremendous success. I understand three million copies
have been printed and the publishers admit that they have sold a million
copies of *Jubilee*. It was a bestseller in France where they admitted printing
100,000 copies at a time. So *Jubilee* has seemed to make a fortune. I didn't
get to be a millionaire by any means, but the royalty checks were wonderful
Christmas presents. The Richard Wright book has not made a lot of money
because of controversy around it, but I had already secured in advances and

grants at least a hundred thousand dollars so I did not worry about how well it sold. Now that it is coming out in paperback, I feel that it will make some money.

The commercial value is not to be compared to the literary value of at least three of my books. *For My People* has stood out through these fifty years as a fine example of a black woman's poetry, and *Jubilee* has gone around the world and I never hear anything from people except that they liked that book and couldn't put it down until they finished it. The Richard Wright book has had remarkable coverage, not all of it positive, but not all of it negative, and it has gone through two precedent-shattering court cases, which make it a book that cannot be forgotten. The commercial value of my books has never been as great as the literary value. My books have been popular—that is, they have been successful with the people—and that is all I could wish.

That is a crowning statement for a career. What do you envision as an epilogue, so to speak?

I have had ill health all my life. They told my mother I would never live to be an adult. And my husband used to tease me and say, "Look how old you are. You weren't supposed to get to be thirty-five." Everything under the sun has happened to me, but I always have been optimistic. I really think I have had divine guidance and providential support because people tease me now and say, "Margaret doesn't have nine lives—she has twelve!" I'm like the cat with the nine lives. I have had five surgical operations, five pregnancies, and a stroke, but I am very optimistic about the future and I don't think I am going to die until my work is done.

The Fusion of Ideas: An Interview with Margaret Walker Alexander

Maryemma Graham / 1992

From *African American Review* 27 (Summer 1993): 279–86. Copyright © 1993 Maryemma Graham. Reprinted by permission.

Margaret Walker is the prize-winning author of *For My People,* the first collection by an African American writer to win a national award. Published by Yale University in 1942, the volume celebrated its fifty-year anniversary as Walker herself turned 77 in 1992. This interview took place in Jackson, Mississippi, on July 14, 1992, in the home of Margaret Walker who, in addition to being a poet, is a novelist, biographer, and critical essayist. Informed by Walker's decidedly historicist approach to literature, the interview covers Walker's lengthy career, politics, and current projects.

Graham: I'd like to talk about the book *This Is My Century* as a representative text.

Alexander: From my early adolescence, I've been dealing with the meaning of the century. I was born when it was barely fifteen years old, and now we have less than ten years left in this century. So the body of my work— whether it's *Jubilee, For My People, This Is My Century,* or *Richard Wright*—springs from my interest in a historical point of view that is central to the development of black people as we approach the 21st century. That is my theme, and I have tried to express it, both in prose and poetry. I feel that, if I've learned anything about this country and century, I've expressed it already in the books I've written. There are a few more I'd like to do, and that same theme is there. For example, I think that, when you look at the Civil Rights Movement and remember the violence of the 1960s and the legislation that came out of it, we make a mistake to think that the protest movement of the '60s was an isolated decade in itself. Protest, for black people in this country, is more than a century old. It began right after slavery, but particularly toward the end of the 19th century, and from the beginning of the 20th century with Du Bois and the NAACP, and the Urban League, in the first ten years of this century. The whole issue for black people was protesting the treatment received from the government and the question of whether we had equal rights. When I was born, we were in the very beginning of World War I. This country had not entered into it yet. And, basically, what we had at the beginning of World War I was reflected again in World War II.

Graham: What is it that you're saying we saw in both wars?

Alexander: Well, the problems that World War I stirred up and left started World War II. And we can go further than that. During the 20th century, this country has engaged in war on four continents other than North America. The century really began with the Spanish-American War, and we were dealing with nations south of the border. I remember reading in the newspapers almost every day when I was a high school student about a new revolution taking place south of the border. We went through some fifteen years of that. I don't recall the Russian Revolution, because I was only about two years old, but it was a big and important issue of the 20th century. And then World War I was fought for control of land, people, and money. Telling the folk that it was a war fought for the benefit of democracy was a slogan. This country banked the raw. They not only sent people to France to die over there—they loaned them money. And when the war was over, everybody owed this country. Some of them paid it, and some didn't. And as a result of fifteen years of bad management, the country entered the Depression.

If you look at the period in America after each world war and each foreign war, you will discover five issues: the health of the people, the education of the people, the economy, the political ideas that develop the world's economic state, and the whole nature of the state vs. the church. The issues that we face everyday in Congress are issues that have come out of these five things.

Every time we have a war, we have to change the economy. My mother said that, before World War I, you could go with a dollar and buy groceries for a family. You could take 25 cents and buy meat. Nickels and dimes counted. But, after World War I, pennies, nickels, dimes, and quarters did not count anymore. I can recall that, prior to World War II (and I mention this in the poem "Youth and Age" in *This Is My Century*), I bought three pounds of onions for a dime; look at how much it costs to buy three pounds of onions today. You could buy a loaf of bread for a nickel or a dime. When I was a child you could buy a pint or quart of milk for 11 cents. You see the difference in the economies.

I was married during World War II, and when my husband and I came to Jackson, I could buy a week's worth of groceries for $15. When I moved into my present house after the Korean War, $100 would buy two weeks' groceries. When I came back from Iowa, I couldn't expect my grocery bill for the same family of six to be $25 or $35 anymore—it had moved up, until it got to the point where I couldn't expect to get a week's groceries for less than $100. It hasn't gotten any less than that since.

Graham: Would you say that *This Is My Century* is a protest against or in response to conditions that black people have faced throughout this century?

Alexander: Well, for black people, the 20th century has been a century of protest. And in all my work I look first at the historical perspective. I'm always looking back in order to understand what's happening today, and what may happen tomorrow. If we understand yesterday, then we know what's happening today, and we can reasonably predict what will happen tomorrow.

Graham: There's a general view, which a lot of us in literature are trying to fight now, that protest is a dated mode of expression, and that it does not good literature make, or does not good sustained art make. This is a real problem in terms of arguing the motivation for or inspiration behind black writing. How would you speak to this issue?

Alexander: Consider protest in terms of politics and policy. When I first realized that we live by protest and not just propaganda, it was way back in the 1930s. I lived through the march from the Depression in this country and saw a liberal administration under Roosevelt. I saw that. And I believe the television political correspondent who says, "This conservative country has thrived and lived on liberalism, fighting it all the time but living with it." The things that happened during the 1930s and the Civil Rights Movement have been the gleams of light that poor black people have looked to in terms of social and liberal legislation.

I believe that every issue in the country now boils down to race. Whether it's education, unemployment and labor, health, politics, religion, or the family—all the social institutions are now affected by this country's attitude toward race. And to protest the gradual encroachment of the conservative and fascist youths behooves the liberal.

It's now that we have administrations under men like Nixon, Reagan, and Bush that we are told that those of us who believed in Roosevelt, Johnson, Truman, Kennedy, and Carter were dirty liberals. Every 20th-century social movement in this country emerged from liberal thinking, and the conservatives who are standing up claiming everything have carried us into a morass. There is no way we can look ahead and see the future of this country without realizing that we are on the bottom in terms of economic development. Things like housing, education, the professions, and the arts do not receive funding. Instead, we must spend our taxpayers' money on arms, military assemblages, and in support of foreign nations like Israel and South Africa? I can't believe that we are looking toward a healthy future.

Graham: And you don't believe that the writer's responsibility in relation to all that you have said has changed in terms of giving voice?

Alexander: Well, it hasn't changed for me, and it hasn't changed for the people I've known and worked with through all these years. It has always been my understanding from my school days that the writer's responsibility is the same as that of the social scientist or philosopher: to be like God and show the way. And certainly this consists of telling the people . . . not only analyzing what is happening to us everyday, but showing the way we must go for a better life, a healthy economy, better education for our children, physical health and fitness. These are the things that we should think about.

My father used to say that money has no intrinsic value but to a miser. You could only do three things with money: save it, spend it, or give it away. If you saved everything you had, you were a miser; if you spent everything you had, you were a spendthrift; and if you gave everything away, you were a fool. And so you were supposed to do something of each of these with any dollar you had, and then you should spend money for the conservation of life's highest values. You have to spend money for shelter, food if you want to live, and education. You should also spend money for recreation and health. Then you should save some for a rainy day. I was raised that way—to believe that money itself has no intrinsic value, but what you do with money leads to life's highest values.

Graham: Let's look at the books you have coming out in the next year or two. Why are these books important for you to do?

Alexander: I expect to have at least three books published next year—two are in the publishers' hands—and I'm waiting on the fourth. The first book that is already in production and should be out in January of 1993 is the book about Sister Thea Bowman's life. It's a deeply religious and spiritual book called *God Touched My Life*,[1] and that is what Thea Bowman is saying. I believe it is an interesting book because she talks about life in Mississippi as a black girl and what it was like in Canton going to the public schools before the Catholic sisters came and started an educational institution. She talks about the Civil Rights days when Martin Luther King came through Canton, and life in Washington at the height of the 1960s and early '70s when she was doing graduate work at the Catholic University. Here is a woman who comes from a certain background—her father was a doctor and her mother a school teacher. She lived in a deeply earthy, black religious culture, surrounded by churches of every denomination. A Southerner in part, she is transported to a very white, rich, Northern, cold culture. When she went to the convent to be a nun, she said there were about three black people present, and they were strangers. Everybody was white, the climate was cold, and it was very hard for her. Then she contracted tuberculosis. How she overcame so many things, how she lived for ten years or more with cancer, what happened to her parents, and how she went around the world preaching the gospel—that's the story of that book. I think it's a very inspiring story.

I have another book that's not quite in production stage, but it ought to be by the fall of the year. It's in the process of being read by a number of readers. It's on Jesse Jackson and his relationship to black politics in Mississippi and the nation.[2] We don't see Jesse as the black messiah, or that hustler from Chicago, but we do see him as a very magnetic political leader of black people from 1983 to 1988.

Graham: So this book concentrates on that period of his life?

Alexander: On those two presidential campaigns. It will include his speeches announcing his intention to run for the presidency and the ones he gave at the conventions. Then we have interviews with some of the key leaders in Mississippi black politics. We also focus on the chairman of the Democratic party and how he has come up through the ranks of this political party, working with the NAACP, and Senator Eastland. We have Aaron Henry, who has been the chairman of the state NAACP for 25 years. Leslie McLemore has an article from his book on Fannie Lou Hamer, whom he sees as a catalytic agent for social change—a very important woman. And then we have Senator Henry Kirksey, whom we call a political gasline. We also deal with what happened in Mississippi from 1964 to 1984.

Jesse Jackson says his interest in politics began with the challenge to the Democratic Party by the Mississippi Freedom Democratic Party (MFDP) in 1964. Fannie Lou Hamer was there; we have a list of the people who were there. He says that he realized the Voting Rights act of 1965 was the beginning of a need for voter registration, and we know that Jesse's actions in several cities caused us to get black mayors in Chicago and in New York, and had something to do with a black mayors' being elected in Washington. We see Jesse Jackson in Mississippi with what he called the Southern Crusade. It began in Memphis and came to Tunica, Mississippi, where there was a ditch in people's neighborhoods where they were suffering.

Graham: Sugar Ditch?

Alexander: Yes. Then we see the people who were around Jesse and followed him through Mississippi, were the lieutenants of his first campaign. People like Louis Armstrong have advanced to the city council in local politics. Leslie McLemore has run for Congress and several other offices, although he's not been successful in being elected. He is a political scientist and one of the editors of the book. Mary Dellareese Coleman has provided major assistance.

We think that the book is important, not just for a look at Jesse Jackson as a national political leader of black people and an international presence, but to show what it has taken in redistricting—getting rid of gerrymandering, voting and challenging the status quo—to change politics in America, and to work for the rights of black people. What Jesse Jackson is all about was not just to be President of the United States, but to create social change, and that's what he did.

Graham: But isn't there an issue that one has to consider in terms of the relationship between the MFDP, which was in essence outside of the mainstream two-party system challenging that system, and Jesse, who became a nominee for one of the parties?

Alexander: He really didn't become a nominee until later. He was never nominated, remember, although he came close to it.

Graham: What I'm saying is that the MFDP seems to have had aims that were more radical and revolutionary . . .

Alexander: That's an interesting point that you're raising, because as I look back to the 1930s and remember a decade of what they called social change and radicalism in this country, I remember the CIO was a hallmark in the 1930s. Black laborers were not in the unions; they were scabs, because the AFL would not admit black people to the unions, and a man like John L. Lewis came south with the automobile workers and the miners and organized unions from Philadelphia to Birmingham, Alabama, in the '30s. And that changed the picture of American labor. Now in the Republican counter-revolution, we have seen how the aim of the Republicans is to break the back of the unions. Why? Because we are the bulwark of American labor and the economy, and when the unions are broken and you have no backbone for the economy, what happens? You're looking at unemployment, homelessness, and chaos.

Graham: I was just trying to get at the MFDP model.

Alexander: The MFDP was not purely a moderate thing. It was a revolutionary movement that was outside of the usual political strategy.

Graham: Yes, it was. There'a question I've always wanted to ask, and I think it's a good time. In your poetry, you celebrate the average man and woman in the "For My People" tradition, whereas in the books that you've written—biographies, histories—you celebrate individual figures that are prominent, who had some really significant roles in terms of leadership. There's an interesting kind of contrast there between the representation of the masses of people and those in leadership positions. Will you talk a little bit about that?

Alexander: That's not what I'm after. What I have always tried to do in my poetry—even before I was conscious about revelation, freedom, social gains, or any of that—was to look at the Southern world around me, to appraise the Southern landscape, the physical world of beauty around me, and the social climate. I begin with that. I talked about lynching very early. When I wrote *Jubilee,* the theme in the book was freedom. I'm talking about freedom from slavery, and freedom from oppression. My poetry continues that theme of getting freedom for our people. I talked about freedom in "For My People"; I talked about freedom in "Prophets for a New Day"; I talked about freedom in *Jubilee* and *How I Wrote* Jubilee. I attempted to understand what it meant to have social change and its benefits for black people and their rights in the 1930s. I think that I have consistently stayed on that theme.

Now, I don't think that individual freedom and mass revolution can be separate. I think they go together. I said once in an article that I wrote—I think it was on the humanistic tradition in Afro-American literature—that some of us are too old to understand the kind of social change we need in this country, but our children are not too young. We owe them another world; we owe them another mind to face the future. We hope that the 21st century will not be so racist, fascist, and sexist as the 20th century. Black women writers, and particularly myself, have faced three main problems or conflicts in all our work: racism, fascism, and sexism. I think I have been fighting them all my writing career.

Graham: Last question—what other books are there to be written by Margaret Walker?

Alexander: Well, I hope to live to finish about four or five more. I don't know. I write so slowly. I'm trying now to finish my *Black-Eyed Susans,* which is about Jackson State College, where I worked for 30 years—and where two students were killed in 1970. That incident is the core of the book. I have decided to expand it to show what has happened there on the campus, why violent things could happen, and what we are going through now which tells us it could happen again.

Graham: So it's sort of a fictional text based on social history?

Alexander: That's right. I thought at first that it would be just about 150 pages. Now it looks like it's going to be a longer book because I think you have to go back through the history of the black college to understand how the racist environment started, and what it was like from the beginning.

Graham: Haven't there been any books on the black college experience?

Alexander: Nobody has done the kind of story that shows the conflict in the society as being racist—the conflict between black and white. All black people in the South feel that education for the black man is still a matter of white control, and those whites who control it are not necessarily liberal in their attitudes toward blacks. They are very conservative and fascist. They are very reactionary. And how the black college has lived in that environment is amazing.

Graham: Well, what do you think about the survival of these schools?

Alexander: The ones that will remain will be the ones that were privately founded in the beginning.

Graham: That's interesting. So the state colleges are going to have difficulty?

Alexander: The state colleges are going to strive more and more to become white institutions, because the white citizen doesn't want to pay taxes to educate black people, and we are constantly fighting that. Black people don't have the money to keep their state schools up. I think we're going to lose a lot of them in the deep South. I don't know what their future will be, but we've already seen this happen partially in Missouri, West Virginia, Kentucky, and Texas. The school doesn't have to be a little school or a big school, just a school that's growing and flourishing and very visible.

Graham: So here again, in *Black-Eyed Susans,* you're taking a piece of the black experience that has heretofore not been explored and giving it to us . . .

Alexander: Well, I'm also very anxious to have a lot of humor in it. There's a lot of humor, but there's also plenty of gossip. And I don't just talk about the black school, I also talk about the white schools surrounding it, and how some of the same things that are leveled as criticism of the black schools go on at the white ones as well. But they are never out in the news.

Graham: And another book? Your autobiography, perhaps?

Alexander: Well, that autobiography has been waiting more than 25 years, and in the last few years I've learned a great deal about autobiography. I've read two of James Olney's books on autobiography. At one time, it was going to be a book about vision. But then I began to think about Cassandra as I talk about her in *Richard Wright.* I once said I would think of the book as *I Am Cassandra,* but I'm very reluctant to use the pronoun *I* at the beginning of the title. I think I'm going to call it *Call Me Cassandra.* It emphasizes several things—my feelings of vision, and ritual and ceremony, and some of the myths and legend. It also deals with family history.

Graham: Have you actually started on this book yet?

Alexander: I've been putting down notes and writing outlines and thinking of my life over seven decades—looking at the first decade, the second, the third, the fourth, the fifth, the sixth. I have a historical feeling for it, but I also would like it to have spatial organization, and not necessarily chronological. I think that's going to be difficult, but I think I'll write it like I would a novel or a poem.

Graham: Will it be a sort of *This Is My Century* in prose?

Alexander: It'll have images out of the South, because my life's been in the South, but also the experiences at Iowa, Northwestern, and Yale.

Graham: It must please you ever so much to be living, alive and very well, in a period when black Southern literature is really coming into its own in a different kind of way.

Alexander: Well, I think I said this one night when we were talking about Southern literature in the libraries and also said it in the Richard Wright book. Every section of this country has been celebrated in literature: from the time of the Transcendental movement in New England; the Midwest with Hamlin Garland, Sherwood Anderson, Hemingway, Sinclair Lewis, and that group.

There's been a Southern revolution, but it's been of a different kind. I think more than any other part of the country, the South has made a turn. I wouldn't say to the right or to the left, but it's made a definite turn. And it has been so much influenced by the Civil Rights Movement that nobody thinks now of sending out an anthology on the great writers of the Western world without including black writers. And I can't tell you how many black women writers who were never in these books before are now included. It is gratifying to pick up any one of these books in any state in this union and see not only your own work but that of many other black writers that you know. That didn't happen prior to the Civil Rights Movement, and it has continued to happen ever since the Movement.

To kill the Civil Rights Movement was one of the great desires of the conservatives, fascists, and Republicans. But they can't completely destroy it anymore than they can burn all the books. It's like saying they're going to take the vote away from black people; they can't do that now, although they might make it unpleasant, as they did before, to participate and become active in seeking political office. The same thing is true in literature. The white people in this country claimed for many years that all American literature was Eurocentric, and since we didn't belong to the Anglo-Saxon tradition, we had no part in such Eurocentricity. There are a few people still out there fighting, but basically they're being overwhelmed not just by Afrocentricity but by what they choose to call mutli-culturalism, where the Asian-American, Mexican-American, and Black American must all have a seat at the fellowship table, and feast.

Notes

1. *God Touched My Life* is a biography of Sister Thea Bowman of Canton, Mississippi. A well-known nun and charismatic leader in the Black Catholic religious movement, Sister Thea died of cancer in 1990. Despite Walker's optimistic prediction, *God Touched My Life* remains in the initial publishing stage.

2. The Jesse Jackson volume is currently in press at Wayne State University.

Margaret Walker's Reflections and Celebrations: An Interview

Jacqueline Miller Carmichael / 1992

Walker: I wrote from the time I was eleven years old. My father gave me a notebook which I have in my file. I went to high school when I was eleven and a half years old, so I was writing poetry during my three and a half years, I guess, of high school and that was at Gilbert Academy. I finished Gilbert when I was fourteen. I went to college for two years in New Orleans. Then when my sister had finished high school and I was seventeen, I went to Northwestern.

Carmichael: Who was the teacher? I know you said your father was your mentor and Langston Hughes, but was there a teacher who influenced you?

Walker: No one teacher. My English teachers throughout high school and in college were kind and sympathetic. At Northwestern there was one teacher, that was Professor Hungerford. But my education got its foundation in my home with my mother and father. My mother taught me how to read and write. Daddy was the person that I modeled things after. We talked about authors and he had books that I liked. He taught philosophy, psychology; my father was professor of religion and philosophy, and he taught psychology and anthropology and sociology. He was quite a scholar.

Carmichael: How did your brother and sisters react to your writing?

Walker: My sisters and my brother are all just as talented as I am, probably with more genius. My sister in New York is a trained musician, a concert pianist, a composer. Mercedes taught for a while in black colleges in the South and she was turned off by them. She said they were so horrible to their faculty people. She went North to New York and taught for a good twenty-five years in the public schools of New York. She is now retired. And she has always played for a church; she started when she was seven and she could always play whatever she heard and when she was about fourteen years old, she had her first public recital.

Carmichael: Was that in Mississippi or Alabama?

Walker: No, that was in neither place. We went to New Orleans when I was ten years old and we stayed there until I was seventeen. In fact, my other sister and my brother live in New Orleans now. Both of them have taught in the public schools of New Orleans. My sister worked nearly forty years there and she has retired, and my brother worked thirty years and he has retired. My brother is a fine musician, a jazz man. He is working every week now, sometimes he works on weekends and one or two nights in the week. But he has been to Europe and the Islands and has played in New Orleans for many years and has been a member of the musicians' union since he was eighteen.

My sister Gwen in New Orleans, who taught school, was strictly the teacher. She always wanted to teach little children, and that's what she played. I played with dolls and house and with imaginary playmates, because my sister next to me, who was a musician, didn't want to play dolls. She didn't care anything about dolls and she didn't want to play house and play momma. So I went out under the big tree with my big felt hat on and I put my coat on in the wintertime, and I would go out under that tree and play by myself. I had all these imaginary people that I would talk to and had fun with them, because I didn't have anybody else willing to play. They didn't want to play.

My sister in New Orleans had polio when she was eleven months old but it has never been a handicap to her. She finished college at seventeen; she went to the University of Chicago and got her master's in child psychology, and then she went to Columbia and spent a year in primary supervision, and then she took another master's at Loyola of the South, teaching math and science. She recently was named Woman of the Year by her chapter of the American Association of University Women. Then she got the sectional Woman of the Year and the National Woman of the Year. What she has done in community service and education in New Orleans equals anything I've done in Jackson. So they—each one had his own field. My brother arranges jazz music for his own little combo band and he writes some of the things himself, composes. But he is strictly a jazz man.

Carmichael: When did you begin keeping a journal?

Walker: I started a journal when I was thirteen. Yesterday we were cleaning out the cabinets there. I've got boxes and boxes, manuscript boxes, like the one on the floor, filled with notebooks that go back to age thirteen. I am going to take some of those journals and excerpt some for *Sage* magazine

[*Scholarly Journal of Black Women*] in Atlanta, and then I am going to use some of them in my autobiography. Because as young as I was, my journals always reflected not only my own feelings, my emotions, my ideas, notes on works in progress, but comments on current events. I have always been interested in history and current events, and that was one thing I had in common with my husband. One of the things we always talked about together— politics and current events. The one thing he read every day was the newspaper, and then we would talk about it. Some things he'd ask me questions about—what happened to cause this—and we'd go back into history and into the news journals.

Carmichael: Were you able to write freely? Did anyone interfere with your writing?

Walker: Nobody ever stopped me from writing. Nobody ever could. I would get up in the morning and go and sit on the side steps and write poetry or write in my journals. My grandmother told my mother that I never cracked a book to study. I finished high school second highest in my class when I was fourteen, and I finished college with a B average, though I had transferred from New Orleans to Northwestern. I was not in the lowest sections of the class; I was in the middle to the highest. I went to Northwestern and I was, according to the tests that we had to take, I was in the upper third of the junior college at Northwestern at the time.

When I was a freshman in college, as an example, my father had been trying to find out who won the freshman English prize, because he knew I was a freshman in that class. The woman teaching it was this white woman and she knew he was trying to find out. She kept it so quiet that even up until the day before—Daddy prided himself, he and Momma, on knowing everything that was happening at the college—they hadn't been able to find out. So that morning they decided that they weren't going to let me go to commencement, because I would embarrass them with not having won the prize, you know. Nobody was supposed to do better than I; I was supposed to do the best. And my grandmother said, "How can she do all that when she doesn't crack a book? All she does is sit around and write poetry in those notebooks. She reads novels and writes poetry; she doesn't study any books. How can she do it?" Well, they laid me out. I was perfectly willing not to go, because I didn't have anything nice to wear, and my stockings were ragged. I said I didn't have any. You know, I was getting to be—I was a teenager and thought I was a young lady. I had had my first pair of high heel shoes. I was fifteen and I was tall, about as tall, almost, as I am now. Well, a friend of ours, who later became the head of surgery at Meharry, a young doctor whom my father had taught in high school and college, rushed home to tell me, "Margaret, you won the prize!" He came before Momma and Daddy came. He said, "You won the freshman English prize." Matthew came to tell me that, and I said, "I did?" He said, "Yes." I said, "Well, they laid my soul to rest this morning because I hadn't won." He said, "They didn't know." Anyway, I won.

Nobody ever stopped me from writing. I wrote mostly on the typewriter. I started typing when I was twelve and that's when I started writing prose, that is, long pieces of prose. I wrote my first prose composition when I was only ten years old. It was a piece I wrote on Thanksgiving for school, probably for seventh or eighth grade. From age thirteen I was writing that prose all the time in my journals. And I kept—I wrote poetry almost every day, and all I ever was interested in doing after I went to New Orleans (seems like in Birmingham I played a lot, and I remember the woods).

But when I was nine years old I organized a children's operetta with the children in the neighborhood and performed and presented that on my ninth birthday. My mother said she had told me that I wasn't going to have any birthday party that year, because she had been giving me birthday parties the last two, three years; I wasn't going to have a party. So I got this thing together and decided to have it on my birthday. My grandmother said that it would be a shame not to fix some ice cream and cake. And we pulled the piano out on the front porch and used the lot next door, put Japanese lanterns across and my sister Mercedes played the music, and I directed it. I had the little boys who were in there to go to the woods and to help get all this stuff to make the background for it. One little boy was singing the lead song and my sister Gwen was a butterfly and I was a rose. It was called, I think it was "The White Rabbit Who Had Lost His Golden Whistle." One little boy sang a song. "Alas, alas, O woe is me / What evil has my pathway crossed / This summer day grows dark and drear / My golden whistle has been lost." And next door was the AME Church where they had that day a fish fry. We assumed nobody was coming and interested in our play. We looked up and the people had all left the fish fry and they were standing all out in the streets listening to our play.

Carmichael: Do you have a copy of that—in writing?
Walker: No, I don't think I have. But then I was looking in my notes and

journal the other day and I remembered something my mother wrote when I was a child called, "The Visit of the Note Family," and with which she was teaching little children how to recognize music notes. And she had this thing with singing—there was the quarter note, the half note, and the whole note, the eighth note, and the sixteenth note. They would all come in and they had their heads covered with the head of the note, and then there was this long part and their arms would be the stem. That's the way we learned notes and that must have been when I was seven or eight years old, Momma was doing that. I remember when we were in New Orleans, Momma gave a wonderful pageant; she gave pageants in Birmingham, in Meridian, and in New Orleans. That's where I got the idea of giving big, big programs. The pageant that she gave in Birmingham was called "The Princess of Poppyland," and then in Meridian it was "The Passing of the Kings," and in New Orleans she wrote the pageant "Climbing Jacob's Ladder." So, I inherited that from my mother.

When I started teaching, my father used to give plays. I remember in Birmingham when I was a little girl five or six years old, not quite six, he gave the play *Julius Caesar* from Shakespeare. When he went to New Orleans, he gave two plays: *Passing of the Third Floor Back* and *Nothing but the Truth*. Those plays—I remember going to these plays that my father [presented]—my mother and father believed that education was more than what you got out of the books, that you had to perform, and that the debating society, the dramatics clubs, the music department [were very important]. They put on programs and that was for the edification of students and it meant just as much as the books. Momma did it in Meridian, in Birmingham, and in New Orleans. Daddy did the same thing.

I grew up with that, so I had the idea when I started teaching, and nobody taught me this, I never had it in any school, but in our black colleges I think you will find that's a tradition. Every year the students participate in some kind of dramatic or musical activity. My mother had charge of the glee clubs and the male singers and the choruses. She even directed a small orchestra in New Orleans. She could play the piano and the organ, and she taught vocal music. When an artist came to town, a singer or a violinist, Momma played the accompaniment for them. So I grew up with that kind of thing, plus my father's books. To me, I didn't think it was anything when I was in it, and my mother was constantly saying that we were poor and didn't have any money. But I never felt that we were dirt poor. We were not mired down in poverty and we certainly were not ignorant. I grew up with a very rich cultural background, but I didn't realize until I was out of college and having careers that I had an unusual family background.

It wasn't just *Jubilee*. Jim in *Jubilee*—whose story comes next, his story, Minna and Jim will form the sequel to *Jubilee*—when he went to Selma, he met a man from his own hometown who became his best friend, and he introduced him to Minna, his sister, and they were married. My grandfather graduated from Selma and so did Jim, and these are the first schools after slavery. My grandfather was a preacher; Jim was the teacher and he was the preacher. In 1975 I went to Pensacola, Florida, and went looking for the church where my grandfather had pastored. I realized that when he was nineteen years old, he was called to that church, and when he was twenty, he married my grandmother. So he already had that church and he was only a young man, nineteen and twenty years of age. I saw the program where they were celebrating in 1975; they were celebrating one hundred years of that church. They said the first pastor of this church was Edward Lane Dozier; that was my grandfather. He pastored the curch for seventeen years. I went up to Greenville, Mississippi, where Jim went, and I found in the courthouse a record of the land that he [Dozier] owned, and they took me to the church where he started a school. I found out that those black Baptists up in the Delta were the beginnings of Jackson College where I taught for thirty years.

I think I have a very rich background, and on both sides. My father's people—my father was West Indian, and he said, "You must remember that Jamaica and the West Indian Islands ended slavery thirty-five years before it was done in this country." So his parents never knew slavery. They had no taint of slavery and they were all highly educated. His brothers and uncles went from the schools in Kingston to Cambridge in England and to McGill in Canada, and he wanted to go to Cambridge, but his father wanted him to become an Episcopal rector, which is the church that he had grown up in. But he was converted to Methodism in a Wesleyan revival, and he wanted to be a Methodist minister. So he came to this country and got his divinity training at Gammon and Northwestern.

My father had a master's in biblical literature from Northwestern University in the 1920s. I'm very sure that very few people, black or white, have that kind of scholarly background. I believe that you may not be born with all that talent, but you're bound to have the environment that gives you the predilection for it. The home environment and the school environment led me to have a desire for a scholarly education and career.

I don't think my fellow black writers regard me too much as a scholar; most of them don't regard me too much as a poet; and many of them feel that with one novel, I'm not a fiction writer. But I'm all three of those. I'm a poet; I'm a novelist. *Jubilee* proves that somebody liked it. It's been in print twenty-six years and never gone out of print, and Bantam says they intend to hang on to it. It's being discussed now in Hollywood for a movie—two or three times it has been discussed. But, of course, the man who produced *Roots* fooled my friends into thinking he was going to do *Jubilee,* and that's why so much of *Jubilee* is in *Roots.* I sued Alex Haley. I probably shouldn't have sued him, because I probably should have sued David Wolper and Stan Margolies and Fred Silverman. They were the three white men where it began. And I would not know how to sue Time-Warner because they're my publishers now, and they took that to help me win the case against Richard Wright's widow. And I won. Warner's the biggest company in the world; they have the biggest communications industry in the world. And although I did not win the Haley case, my son kept saying, "Think about the lesson you're learning today." And I said what is the lesson—what did I do? I didn't do anything to these people; why are they doing this to me? Way down the road, as we say in the Negro Spiritual, "You'll Understand It Better By and By." I understood.

I learned in those two years that that was a diversion from my Richard Wright writing—writing about Wright. I learned all I could find and read about fair use, about copyright infringement. I learned what it was that the judge had used against me and what case had been against me. I learned it so well that there was not a drop—not a bit of copyright infringement in the Richard Wright book, and I used both published and unpublished stuff. And I went to court; they sued me and I went to court and won. I won both in the district court and in the appellate court. That's something that has never happened before. It's a precedent-setting case and it's changing the attitude of values and copyright infringement in the publishing world in this country.

Carmichael: Congratulations.

Walker: I'm very proud of that decision. I worked fifteen years on that book. I was altogether twenty years from the time that it was first mentioned to me to do it. There again my journals helped me. I had letters from Wright and I had my diaries in which I talked about him and his coming to Chicago and our seeing each other and my going to New York. There's a section in the *Native Son* chapter that came directly out of my journal—out of my diary. That's what that is. So my journals have been put to use—to good use.

Carmichael: Do you have advice for others on keeping a journal?

Walker: I have a tendency to keep notebooks or journals or diaries. My

notebooks are journals. I have in those notebooks notes for works in progress;
I talk about what I'm going to write or what I want to write. In looking
through my journals and papers yesterday, I found a character chart that I
made for *Jubilee.*

Carmichael: True to form? You followed through on it?

Walker: Well, in 1948, I made a sentence outline of the entire book of
Jubilee. Many of the chapter headings came directly from that outline. I teach
my students theme writing and tell them to make an outline, make a sentence
outline, write a full sentence and you have a complete thought, and you're
ready to work from that—you lift out those sentences. They can become
topic sentences or they can be leading sentences, but you know what you
were thinking and you go right back to that idea or that thought. That's the
way to keep it on paper until you're ready to use it.

I taught my students about different kinds of sentences, different kinds of
paragraphs, how to organize a theme, beginning, middle and end, and in later
years I was teaching them different ways to write about literature. I didn't
teach my students anything that I hadn't put into practice myself. I taught
creative writing, and I blundered through that the way I had blundered
through my own learning. But I believe that you can't teach a person who
doesn't have any talent how to write—you can't do that. The person has to
have the desire and the predilection or the inclination, but you can teach
structure of all the forms. Once they are familiar with the structure and they
know how to do that creative thinking, you can turn them loose and they can
do their own job.

Carmichael: I've gone through your manuscript [*Jubilee*] and it's in such
great order, very easy to follow, even with the missing pages I was able to
go through it. And I was concerned about the dialectical changes.

Walker: You mean—not dialectical changes—I notice somebody said that
they didn't believe I had made changes in the dialect. Oh, yes, obviously.
The antebellum speech is so archaic and obsolete that nobody could read that
today. I wrote largely in that slavery-time, antebellum dialect, and the copy
of that [Ph.D. dissertation] is in the library at the University of Iowa. My
thesis for *Jubilee* is full of the original speech. It's not just sight dialect, it's
based on spelling and sound and orthography—it's spelling. They never said
it; it was *hit.* That *h* was in front of many vowels.

Carmichael: And *I* was *ah,* the pronoun *I?* I think you wrote *ah.*

Walker: Not always, but g-w-i-n-e was *gine.* I'm gine downtown. Even
today we call it *gwine* but *w* is silent. It's *gine.*

Carmichael: So that was your decision to change it?

Walker: No, no. Within three weeks, within two weeks, my thesis copy went to the graduate office early in May, and as fast as my typist could do that same manuscript over—I don't know whether it took her ten days or two weeks or what. It was seven hundred and forty-one pages, and we sent that to Houghton Mifflin where I was already in contact with my wonderful editor there, Dorothy de Santillano. She's dead now. Her husband, Giorges de Santillano, was a scholar at MIT; he was a medieval scholar. I had a wonderful letter from Houghton Mifflin. I was introduced to her by my teacher at Northwestern. She came to Chicago to have a book party for one of her authors, John Gardner. Because Professor Hungerford had taught Saul Bellow and John Gardner, he told her about me—told her that I had a wonderful book. He called me and told me he'd found somebody to help me, because I had told him that there was a string attached to getting a doctorate or a master's in creative writing—that is, using a creative thesis to get the master's in English or the doctorate in English. I had discovered it when I was getting my master's, and I learned in time what the requirements were. They tell you, "Yes, you can do a creative thesis for your master's and you can do a creative dissertation for your doctorate, but they must be of professional caliber." Well, when a thing is of professional caliber, the publishers buy it. It's sold. If they have no reason to believe you're going to be published, they don't give you that degree.

I learned that in 1939 when I had written to Stephen Vincent Benét and he wrote back that he had kept my manuscript [*For My People*] out of seven, trying to make up his mind which one should get it [the Yale Younger Poets award]. He told me to send it back the next year, and he kept encouraging me. What I didn't know was that Yale was so racist they didn't want a black woman published. He finally persuaded them. It was the last book he ever edited. He told them if they didn't give it to me he wasn't going to work with them, with that, anymore, and he wasn't going to give it to anybody else. So he forced them to give it to me.

When it came to the doctorate, I was back out at Iowa in that same workshop. It was my feeling that there was the best place to go if you wanted to do a creative thing. When I had finished my comprehensives, had taken all my examinations except the oral on the dissertation—in fact, I had not written the dissertation, I was still working on *Jubilee*—I went to Chicago and talked to Professor Hungerford and told him I had passed my comps, and he said, "Well, we're going to celebrate; we'll roast a leg of lamb." And his wife and he had me out to dinner to this wonderful lamb dinner. He said, "Well, Margaret, I never thought—this is a great accomplishment; not only are you getting a doctorate, you got this book." I told him, "Well, I'm not going to get the doctorate, I'm not going to get that piece of paper if I don't publish this book." He said, "What do you mean?" I told him what had happened before. He didn't say anything else, but he kept it in mind, and when Mrs. de Santillano came, he told her about me. That's the way I got a publisher.

Carmichael: You were always at the right place at the right time.

Walker: Well, it seems like God takes care of babies and fools and I was a double responsibility. I had three children. [She glances over at the plants in her study.] Oh, my corn plant is so pretty, isn't it?

Carmichael: It's beautiful.

Walker: It's just doing so well there. That light is perfect. And for my Norfolk pine and my sansevieria—they're all doing well. I must have gotten a florist room full of flowers when I was in the hospital. Every day they came with flowers. I couldn't keep all the arrangements because they died—oh, roses and carnations and mixed bouquets. Alice Walker and her daughter sent me a gorgeous bouquet. The potted plants—I've kept most of them. I have some beautiful things.

Carmichael: You were hospitalized about a month ago?

Walker: I became ill on the seventh day of April and on the eighth day of April, I proceeded to go downtown and receive the Governor's Award for Excellence and I couldn't stand alone, I couldn't walk, and I couldn't get my equilibrium. So I had to hold on to somebody, but I held on to everybody until I received my award. Thursday, April 9, I got in the car and I spent the night in Nashville and went on to Knoxville where the College Language Association was meeting. This was my fiftieth meeting—fifty years since I joined CLA, and I had been going off and on as much as I could. I had spoken for the banquet, I had been on different programs; they gave me an award. I still couldn't walk and I couldn't stand alone.

I went back to Nashville on Saturday and Sunday, friends came and took me out to dinner to Crestwood, Creekwood, or whatever it is, and Monday morning I had a master's class in poetry for Tennessee State, and Monday night I dressed and went downtown. I sat in a chair and gave this speech on "How I Wrote *Jubilee*." Tuesday I went to Vanderbilt. Dr. Jimmy Franklin came and took me. I held on to him and I gave a speech on Richard Wright at Vanderbilt. Then I went back to the hotel. Tuesday night, Dr. and Mrs. Hefner at Tennessee State took me to a dinner party and it was an Easter gala, and I enjoyed that.

And Wednesday, I went to Fisk and the wife of the president of Fisk had me to lunch, and she had this marvelous lunch—cornish hen and wild rice and all kinds of vegetables. I knew not to eat the dessert, because it was lemon icebox pie. I know not to touch that because it's too sweet, and I'm diabetic. But I drank the tea that was sweetened; I shouldn't have done that. Then I went and sat in Jessie Carney Smith's office and she autographed a *Notable Black Women* book for me. I had taken over the rest of my lunch from Miss Ponder, and I ate that.

Then I went to dinner at Mrs. Hefner's, the president's wife at Tennessee State, and she had invited about twelve women, ten or eleven, to come and play bridge, because I love to play bridge. That's my recreation, my one outlet. It used to be I didn't do anything but go to church and school, but I found I needed a little recreation, and I love cards. Bridge is my favorite. I play contract, auction, and duplicate bridge. Every year at Christmas I have a bridge party here at my house. I play with two clubs when I'm home, basically three, because I get invited to the three, but I belong to two. I entertain them at Christmas in addition to my regular times in the year. So she knew—I had given her a bridge party when she was leaving—she knew I loved bridge. And they came with all these lovely gifts. Oh, I had so many presents! Everywhere I went the people were handing me, "And I brought you this, and I brought you this." Oh, all over the country, AKAs [Alpha Kappa Alpha] and LINKS [a service club committed to community work through educational, cultural, and civic activities] have made it their business to give me some of the loveliest things for, oh, fifty years.

Well, anyway, I got to Mrs. Hefner's, and I was sitting there with the ladies just before dinner and she passed this tray of rosé wine. And I never drink wine, but I picked up that rosé and it felt so cold and it smelled so good, and it wasn't any more than just a drop—wasn't a fourth of a cup, might have been an eighth of a cup—and I drank that wine. Then I went to dinner. She had cornish hen with wild rice and gelatin salad and a gelatin dessert and green vegetables, and I ate like a pig. I pigged out! Then I sat down to play bridge, and I had the worst catastrophe. I got through three rounds of bridge; I was on the last progression and the last hand when I began to feel sick. I said, "Call Mrs. Hefner," and when she came I said, "Help me to the bathroom; I think I'm getting sick." And I got to the bathroom and I went in and I stayed so long she said, "Are you all right?" I said, "Yes, I'll be out in a minute." I should've stayed longer but I went out. I didn't feel too much better.

I sat down to the table and my head hit the table, and as I came up with my head, I regurgitated. All that food I had eaten—all that cornish hen and wild rice—oh, I was so sick! And I mean it didn't stop until every drop of it was out and it was on her floor. Thank God it wasn't carpet; it was vinyl. That room had vinyl. The rest of the house was full of carpet. Oooh, Lord, I thought I'd die! I said, "This has never happened to me before." I was so embarrassed. I kept saying, "Oooh, I'm so sorry. I couldn't help it!" They called the doctor. The doctor said he believed I had a middle-ear infection, the reason I couldn't stand and couldn't walk. I stayed on her bed. I said, "I'm going to stay here tonight anyway." She said, "We wanted you to stay." So I stayed on at her house. Siggy [Walker's son] went back to the hotel.

The next morning when she got up she said, "What do you want for breakfast?" I said, "The doctor told me to eat light today," and I said, "We're going home." I said, "I'm going to take a cup of decaffeinated coffee, nothing in it, a slice of whole wheat toast, and a half of a grapefruit, if you have it." She said, "Oh, yes, I sure have it." That's what I had for breakfast, and that was perfect on my stomach. I took my insulin the night before and that morning I took insulin, and I took medicine the night before. I felt like I could make it the next day. Siggy got out—we went to the hotel and checked out and we got on the road between eleven and twelve o'clock, about eleven-thirty, and he had me at my door by seven o'clock. [Earlier, I had] said, "I have to eat something in the middle of the day, but I don't want anything too greasy. I might be able to eat fish." So we stopped and we got fish sandwiches, and I said, "Not a lot of that tartar sauce—very little—I don't want it rich." I got home with . . . well, I got home and I said, "I'll be in the doctor's office tomorrow morning."

I [had] told him on the phone Tuesday . . . Siggy [had] called him and told him I wasn't getting any better. I still couldn't walk and I didn't have my equilibrium and I had headaches. I was still having headaches, and I was taking Tylenol and I was taking anti-vertigo pills and I was taking my kidney pill—antibiotic. I think that's what—those things kept me going. I was taking [Tylenol] two and three times a day. But I had told the doctor Tuesday, "When I get home, I'll be in your office Friday morning," and I was there. This daughter, this same who who just called, Marion, had called me and she said, "Momma, have you had a stroke?" I said, "No, why would you ask that? Not that I know of." She said she detected a slight slur in my speech, just a slight slur. But my speech was not affected, and my thinking was not affected. It was my motor on the left side. Anyway, she called the doctor. She said that in the middle of the night . . .

[At this point Siggy knocked on the door and entered to bring his mother's medicine. He was followed by the young woman who came to give Walker her bath. Walker asked if I wanted to remain and resume the interview. I agreed, delighted that she did not choose to stop there].

Walker: I had five operations. My husband and I both had operations. One year we had them ten days apart. Illness—I've been sick most of my life. I had all the childhood diseases. I had what you call dysmenorrhea, every month I went to bed. I couldn't eat, and I couldn't drink water. Everybody said, "Have a baby and you'll be fine." That's not true. I had the babies and I still had dysmenorrhea. I had low blood pressure and anemia for years. Yesterday [30 June] my pressure was only 120/60. I have generally a slow pulse and low blood pressure, and I have an open place on my side that's been there eleven years. . . . I've had pneumonia, viral pneumonia, and on top of it, now I have this illness.

But I'm still trying to write. I don't know whether I'm going to finish these last four books or not. If I live to do it, nothing but by the goodness and grace of God will I manage to do it. I told my daughter the other day, a woman has asked me to write eight lines of poetry and send them to her and she will send me a check for fifteen hundred dollars. I need that fifteen hundred dollars, but I can't make myself write those eight lines. I know I can do it. I got three ideas in my head and I say I'm going to sit to the typewriter, but I haven't been able to type for a year and a half. So you see, I'm handicapped. My fingers—I had a fungus on my finger last year. I had to have—I had three nails [removed] last year. How do I do it? It's not me, must not be me. I was writing novels, I started writing novels when I was twelve years old. That first book I never finished. I looked the other day and I discovered the novel that I wrote when I was on WPA [Works Project Administration, Chicago], *Goose Island.* I still have that manuscript.

Carmichael: Why wasn't it published?
Walker: Well, it wasn't really a good novel. It wasn't well written; it wasn't organized. See, I learned how to write a novel on *Jubilee. Jubilee* really was the way I learned to do it. I spent fifteen years, from the ages of

ten and eleven, until I was twenty-seven learning and doing that craft of poetry, and I had that book published. My first book was published when I was twenty-seven. This year I'm seventy-seven. It's fifty years. You see those pictures of that man—he's the Richard Wright that I was writing about. But I married the most handsome man I ever knew in my life. He was a good-looking man [Walker's husband died on 26 October 1980].

Carmichael: That's what Mrs. Bernice Bell [the curator of Walker's papers] said.

Walker: That I married a handsome man?

Carmichael: She said Alex was good-looking.

Walker: He really was. Women turned around in the street to look at him.

Carmichael: How did you react?

Walker: Well, I just was very proud. The only thing in the whole—all the years of marriage—we were married thirty-seven years. After we moved in this house, after we fixed the house, after I got my degree and he had gotten his business going—he did well in the business. Seven or eight years before he died, it was nothing for him to make seven hundred dollars a week. And he had not been able to work.

Carmichael: What was his business?

Walker: Interior decorating. He made—he hung rods for commercial and residential customers. He made cornices and covered them and he hung draperies. [Walker greets her grandson.] This is my grandson, Khari, "Kingly Warrior." He's not quite sixteen but you see how tall he is? He'll be sixteen on the twelfth of August. He was four years old when his father and mother came in this house. My husband said to them—my husband died of cancer—he knew he was dying. Before he went to the hospital the last time, he called Siggy and Norma, my son Siggy and Norma, sat them down to the table up there and he said, "I want you all to take everything you have in that apartment and come and store it in the back of this house, and I want you to come in here. I don't want to leave Margaret in this house alone when I go to the hospital." Every time those boys went to the hospital, my husband said, "And take care of your mother, and take care of your mother." He told me, he said, "I know you're going to miss me because I would miss you. I want you to know that we've had some wonderful times together. I always wanted my last days to be my best days, and they are; they have been. I want you to continue to be a lady, hold your head up high, pay your bills, and try to live." I said that was a sign of his love for me, wasn't it? He was going to look after me when he was gone.

One day I walked out to the door, and I was always getting money, but I found myself getting ready to go to Texas and I said, "I need two or three hundred dollars." I walked into the hallway there and said, "Oh, I need two or three hundred dollars today. If Alex were here, if he didn't have it, he'd go out and get it and give it to me." And just as clear as a bell I could hear him say, "But I left it there for you." I called my son; I said, "James, I want you to go downstairs in the bank there and tell that man . . . that I want my money today." He said, "What money, Momma?" I said, "That your daddy left." I said, "I have the bank book." He said, "You can't do that without opening up the estate." I said, "Yes I can. He died without a will; I'm his wife. It says, F. J. Alexander and I'm Mrs. F. J. Alexander. That's my money," and all the money I needed to go to Texas was there. Isn't that uncanny? It's almost like you're psychic, isn't it? "But I left it there for you."

I have had more since he's been dead than I had all those years we were married. For twenty-five or twenty-six years since *Jubilee* was published, I've never been broke at Christmas. I used to be borrowing from Christmas to Easter and from Easter to school closing and from school opening to Christmas. I would get up in the morning and say, "Where can I get a thousand dollars today? Where can I go borrow five hundred dollars?" Wherever—I was in Iowa one day and I said, "Lord, I need a thousand dollars today. Where must I go?" I walked right straight into the business office, financial aid of the university, and they handed me that thousand dollars.

[The interview is interrupted at this point by a telephone call. Walker permits me to take photographs of her talking on the phone. Her daughter-in-law, Norma, comes home for lunch and joins in the photographing session by taking pictures of Walker and me. The interview resumes with a statement made by Elsie May Chambers, state editor for the *Clarion-Ledger* and one of the local reviewers of *Jubilee* when it was published in 1966.]

Carmichael: She was the one who wrote that the editors made you change the dialect.

Walker: What I said is that the thesis copy in the University of Iowa library bears no resemblance to the book, because Mrs. de Santillano said, "Most people can't read this. The white people can't read it, and black people will be mad about it. So you have to modernize the dialect." And I changed most of it—the sight dialect and the spelling, and took away all the apostrophes and took *h* from in front of all the vowels. I spent weeks with that. I got a contract in July and in, I think it was October or November, I sent it back ready for the printer. I worked on it very hard and the typing took a long time. When she read the book the first time, she cut out 100 pages—right at a clip. And then later, they cut out one or two more chapters so that the book is less than 500 pages. It was 741 pages in manuscript; it is now 400 and some odd pages printed. They took out the speech Henry McNeal Turner made.

Carmichael: Yes, I saw that.

Walker: They took that out, which was historical for black people, but not acceptable to white people. She took out a story I had on the black panthers that my grandmother had told me. That was a slavery-time story; and they said, "Oh, people will connect it with the present-day Black Panthers." And they were very prevalent then. I had it in Alabama and Black Panthers were really thriving in Alabama, the political group. I wasn't talking about that political group at all. I was talking about an actual and real animal that was a black panther. I took it out—I had to take it out. That reminds me, the fact that I may go back and make a story out of that. That's a by-product of *Jubilee* I hadn't thought about, but it'd make an interesting one. The chapter on Henry McNeal Turner and the letter and the speech he made in the Georgia legislature—it was a great speech. But there were other changes. All of that is still in the thesis copy at Iowa.

Carmichael: You originally had about sixty-three chapters?

Walker: I don't remember. I don't remember, but I know that two or three chapters were taken out, and I think the book has fifty-eight chapters. I don't remember that. But there were many questions that my committee people asked that I answered when I had the oral exam. Oddly enough, they were not the things that the publishers were concerned about at all. The academic world is very different from the trade world.

[Walker's call from her sister interrupts her thoughts. She tells Gwen of her condition and describes her medication in precise medical terms. When the conversation ends, Walker changes the subject to her sister Mercedes.]

Walker: Mercedes goes to the reading room and she works in there and she plays for the church and she belongs to a sorority and she belongs to the International Association of University Women and she belongs to the Retired Teachers Association and they're running all the time. I don't run like that. Everybody thinks I'm running. I'm sitting at home. I have time to write. I don't have time to do all that stuff. Somebody asked me, the LINKS in Texas and in Memphis and in California, all the LINKS gave me stuff when I went there. When I was in Nashville the last time, I got this envelope that said, "The LINK, Margaret Walker Alexander." I said, "Am I a LINK?" But I don't tell them anymore. Everybody assumes I'm a LINK. I told the girl when she called me, she's dead now, she asked me if I were interested in becoming a LINK. I told her, "No." She said, "You're not?" I said, "No, I belong to about twenty-five organizations; I can't join any more; I can't go to all those meetings." I sat down one day and wrote down all the organizations I could think of that I belong to, and honest to God, it was twenty-five.

Oh, when I first came, I said I can't do anything but my church and I will go to the sorority meetings, and I did work with the Y at first. When they asked me to join clubs—I belong to a literary club, two bridge clubs, Democratic Women, Methodist Women, University Women, AKA Sorority, you just name it and I belong to it, the National Council of Negro Women. Too many things! All the alumni associations worry you to death for money. I'm a life member of the NAACP, I'm a life member of College Language, and I'm about to become a life member of my sorority, and then I'm going to be through with life memberships. That's all I'm going to be life member of. I do give to the United [Negro] College Fund, and I give to half a dozen charities when I have some money. I believe that for every dollar you have that you're supposed to spend some, save some, and give some away. That's the way I spiritually use money. Right now I have a letter from the Cancer Foundation. I'm supposed to get things on my street for cancer. And I have given to Easter Seals, United Way, Kidney Foundation, Diabetes Foundation; all these I'm interested in because I had all these diseases and my husband died of cancer. So you see, if you have a little money, you put a little money there.

Carmichael: You're getting ready for your boule. You're excited about that, aren't you?

Walker: Oh, I am too excited! Before and after my recent illness, all I could think about was my clothes. I'm on the program. I'm going to be on the public program and I give the luncheon speech for the Southeastern Regional, my region. Plus the fact that the basileus has asked me to sit on the dais with her the night of the banquet when they're closing out. And I have been told that I'll be honored as a Golden Soror. I've been in fifty years. I've already been told that for some of the things I do, and they're going to take my poem, "For My People," which is also celebrating fifty years, and they're printing that. They want me to sign a parchment copy giving all the people in my region a copy when I speak.

The woman who called me just now is saying she used to work with the directorate in Chicago and that she was one of the main people working with the boule when it came to Chicago. She wants to be in touch with the directorate to tell them some way they've got to make an announcement while I'm there of the bill that is up before Congress and see if we can't get support—national support from the sorority for that bill [House of Representatives Bill 3252, 12 September 1989, to provide for the establishment of the Margaret Walker Alexander National African-American Research Center, Jackson State University]. We're also going to try to get national support from the alumni association at Jackson State for that bill. If we can get a few hundred letters written, it will help. There is the bill that was first put up; the second bill is 1252, House Bill. That's very important, not just for my papers, you see the files, I have two lateral files in the next room. I have seven files altogether. And those cabinets are full of papers. I have boxes and boxes in the storage; I have boxes of manuscripts, of galley sheets, of page proofs, and even some of the manuscript that I've done longhand. For the Richard Wright book, I've just got boxes of stuff that would go into the archives as part of my papers. They're trying to get a building suitable to keep the papers of all—as many African American scholars and writers and artists as they can get. But it will also mean a place where people like you can come and do research, and we need it very much in this region. We have nothing down here.

And when I'm told that my papers should go to the Library of Congress, I remind them that all the Library of Congress will do with my papers is take them to the basement where they have all the Indian artifacts. They're not going to process them and microfilm them and set them up for scholarly research. That's what I want done with my papers. Amistad [at Tulane] said they would do it—they would come and take my stuff and organize and catalog and microfilm and do everything. Then if I still insisted on Jackson State they'd give them a copy, but they would keep the original. I told them I didn't think I wanted them to do it at all, because when I was seventeen and going to Northwestern, I could not walk across the campus of Tulane. There was a man there who read my poetry, but Jewish friends had to take it. I couldn't take it to him. And I would feel very bad now, remembering segregation and Tulane, to give them my papers. The white universities don't need my papers; the black students in the black colleges are the ones who need my papers. Ole Miss has an archive and they have a lot of black papers up there including B. B. King's records, but I understand that when they went in there to look, somebody else had taken them all out—had taken some of them away—they're not all there. I was asked by Boston University, and I was impressed with what they would do with the papers and how they would take care of them, and they would buy them; they would pay me for them. But I have no connection to Boston. I stayed there six months and I hated the place. I'm in the last years of my career, maybe the last days or months, I don't know what. And that's too far away from me and from what I have done. I want my papers where I have worked thirty years, the students who know me here, the place where I am known. Yes, they have a street named for Margaret Walker Alexander, a library named for her, and now a research center. That's where my papers belong.

Carmichael: In my week and a half on Jackson State University's campus, invariably I asked students, do you know Margaret Walker? Have you read *Jubilee?*

Walker: Most of them said no?

Carmichael: I was surprised! Most of them said, "I've read *Jubilee.*"

Walker: A lot of them have. I find it very, very pleasant, rewarding and comforting to walk in the grocery stores and have people come up to me. I go to the department stores; I go downtown in the government offices, they say, "Hello, Miss Walker," or "Hi, Mrs. Alexander, I haven't seen you in a long time." I like living in Jackson. "Don't you want to go / Where everybody knows your name? / And they're always glad you came?" I have seen the city grow from a small town city, a big town or small city, to a metropolitan area.

Spirituality, Sexuality, and Creativity: A Conversation with Margaret Walker Alexander

Dilla Buckner / 1995

From *My Soul Is a Witness: African-American Women's Spirituality.*
Edited by Gloria Wade Gayles. Boston: Beacon Press, 1995. 224–28.
Copyright © 2001 Dilla Buckner. Reprinted by permission.

Dilla Buckner: As you know, spirituality is so central to scholarship on women's culture and women's literature that we can't discuss liberation or empowerment for women without also discussing women's spirituality. What does the word mean to you? How do you define it?

Margaret Walker-Alexander: Spirituality is a consciousness of God's presence within us. A consciousness that God is right here. Now. I remember my father telling me that if God isn't in you, then God isn't anywhere. I grew up believing that God is a part of me and I am a part of God. So spirituality for me means being centered in a consciousness of divinity within all the time.

Buckner: What we are finding in today's emphasis on women's spirituality is a new definition of God, or a rejection of God as he. How do you define God?

Walker: God is perfection. God is everything good. And God is everywhere in the Universe and, as I said, within me. Within all of us. For me, God is both female and male which is why I pray to Our Father-Mother God.

Buckner: Your religious background is the same as mine. We are both Baptists and your father was a Baptist minister, so I'm sure that you grew up hearing, as I did, the old saying, "Prayer changes things."

Walker: I grew up in a family that prayed daily and out loud. I don't always pray out loud, however. Sometimes I pray with pen and pencil and paper. I write out prayers. Other times I do a lot of mental praying. There's a very reflective side of me. It's been there since I was ten years of age. When I am working on a project I enter intense periods of meditation. I did that when I was working on *Jubilee.* I lie down and I reflect and I meditate for

long periods of time. Sometimes for days and weeks. And affirmations. I find
that affirmations work for me. When I am having financial difficulty, I repeat
the affirmation, "God is my source. God is my resource." If I am ill or if
there is someone I can't get along with, I use affirmations and many of them
come from Unity. I find that when I am angry, I can't do anything until I get
the poison out of me, and I do that with affirmations. Many of them come
from Unity. I have been reading *Daily Word* since I was seventeen. Affirmations work for me.

Buckner: Do you remember when you became spiritually aware?

Walker: I joined church when I was ten, but my spiritual awareness didn't
come until I was seventeen. I remember wanting to know the presence of
God. I remember the date; it was August of 1932. And I remember the Scrip-
ture of the sermon preached that day: "And sin shall have no dominion over
you." I became very aware of the presence of God in me and because God
was present in me, sin could have no dominion over me.

Buckner: Many women writing about spirituality say that it is not always
experienced in an institutionalized church. In fact, they seem to imply that it
can't be experienced in the church, in organized religion. That it is a very
private and mystical experience.

Walker: Yes. I understand that. But I believe that spirituality is religious.
I don't separate the two. I think once you have an experience which makes
you aware of the presence of God within you, it doesn't matter whether you
are Christian, Muslim, metaphysical, mystical . . . It doesn't matter. You are
religious and spiritual, and I don't think you can ever turn your back on the
meaning of the experience.

Buckner: Is that the case with you? Since your spiritual awakening at age
seventeen, you have remained in the church? You've remained connected to
that awareness?

Walker: No. I went through five years of bitterness and apostasy. I was
disgusted with what I saw in the church and I simply wouldn't go. Didn't go
to church. But I was brought to my knees by circumstances and I returned to
the church. Let me add to something I said earlier about spirituality. I believe
it is a strong force in women's lives, especially Black women's lives, and I
believe spirituality and sexuality are the two strongest forces. Black women
respond to these two forces more strongly than they do to anything else. I
don't separate the two. Spirituality and sexuality. I don't separate the two.

Buckner: Would you elaborate more on that, please?

Walker: Well, I think women have a tendency to fight everything with these two forces. We don't think of sexuality when we talk about spirituality because of Freud's influence on our thinking. Freud limited sexuality entirely to the body and he believed that sexuality was the strongest force in the world. But sexuality isn't just about the body, or mainly about the body. It includes our spiritual selves, our spirituality.

Buckner: Are you saying, then, that women are spiritual/sexual beings?

Walker: Yes. I was reading an article the other day in which a young man said that he was interested in marrying a woman who was strongly influenced by spirituality. I knew at once that he was not separating spirituality from sexuality. He understood that the two go together. And that's the same with great literature and music and paintings. They are influenced as much by our spirituality as by our sexuality.

Buckner: That in our creativity, we express who we are as spiritual/sexual beings. Is that what you are saying?

Walker: Yes. Precisely. We create out of who we are, and we are both—not either/or, but *both*—spiritual and sexual. I recall some years ago doing a seminar on Richard Wright, and a student in the class asked what Wright's sexuality had to do with his writings. And I told him that if he had to ask that question, he didn't know very much about artists. About creativity. Sexuality is a strong force in creativity. It certainly works for me. It works *with* my spirituality, not apart from it.

Buckner: Do you think Black women experience a unique spirituality?

Walker: There is an earthiness to our spirituality and sexuality that comes from our African ancestry. The greatest art in Africa, particularly on the West Coast, was both sacred and secular, or spiritual and sexual. Isn't that true?

Buckner: I quite agree with you. We can't, and shouldn't, always draw a line between the sacred and the secular. I certainly don't in my classes. The two are related. Most definitely.

Walker: We see that in Black music. It is a rhythmic and organic art. It's about spirituality and sexuality. I like what a woman scholar said about Africans. She said they picked up the dust of Africa and carried it with them to the new world. They included it in their music. They believed their gods were in the dust, in the water, in the air, and everywhere. And to them, the gods were spirits. They were a spiritual people. Do you follow that?

Buckner: Yes.

Walker: They believed that they did not leave their gods in Africa, that they took them to the New World. And everything they did in the New World was controlled by what had been true in the Old World. They believed that dancing, singing, and drumming were all spiritual.

Buckner: Are women inclined to be more spiritual than men?

Walker: No, I don't think so. I think that in the New World we were told to be more inhibited and we became more inhibited. We lost some of the earthiness, the connection to nature that we had in Africa. The earthiness that we expressed in uninhibited movement and dance and song.

Buckner: The earthiness that makes our spirituality unique?

Walker: Yes. And we see it in our worship. In our rituals. I think there are certain religious groups that still share spiritual gifts. We see it in the dancing and the singing and the receiving of the Spirit. In an uninhibited way.

Buckner: But you are not saying that we can experience spirituality only in church?

Walker: Not at all. I experience spirituality mostly in a prayerful gathering of individuals or when I am alone with my thoughts and my meditations.

Buckner: What would you like to say before we turn off the tape? I say turn off the tape because I know we will continue talking about spirituality.

Walker: That I am centered in a consciousness of divinity within all the time, and this is what spirituality means to me. God is a part of me and I am a part of God. That is my faith. My children will tell you that I believe I can make it with God. My faith is how I got ovah.

Conversation: Margaret Walker Alexander

Joanne V. Gabbin / 1996

From *Furious Flowering of African American Poetry* by Joanne Gabbin. Charlottesville: University Press of Virginia, 1999. Reprinted with permission of the University Press of Virginia.

Gabbin: Fifty-four years ago, you won the Yale Series of Younger Poets Award for your first volume of poetry, *For My People,* making it the first collection by an African American writer to win a national award. Now you are the dean of African American writers and respected and revered for your work. When did you begin writing and who were the people who most influenced your burgeoning literary interests?

Walker: I started writing poetry when I was eleven years old. My father told my mother, "Pay her no attention, don't get excited; it's just a puberty urge," which made me very angry. By the time I had filled the date book that he gave me I was at Northwestern; I think I'd written in those three hundred and sixty five pages by the time I was eighteen. I told him, "Do you still think this is a puberty urge?" He said, "I guess you're going to write as long as you live." When someone asked me the other day, "When are you going to retire?" I said, "Retire from what? Retire from life?" I'd retired from teaching, and I said, "I will retire from writing when I'm dead. I won't write anymore after I die, but until I do I'll keep trying."

I think my mother's music and my father's books were my first inspiration, but I had wonderful teachers—mostly women—throughout the grade school years, and then in high school a few men. My teachers were always encouraging me. I had little composition books that I wrote in and I wrote poetry in class, but I managed to answer the questions when they asked me: I just looked up and said "so-and-so" and started writing again.

I think the earliest I can remember reading the Harlem Renaissance writers was when I was eleven. The Harlem Renaissance took place when I was a child. I saw a little booklet, *Four Lincoln Poets*—including Langston Hughes and Waring Cuney and Edward Silvera, when I was eleven. By the time I was sixteen I saw my very first living writer. I told my father and mother that when the white president said he didn't think people would pay a dollar to

listen to a Negro read poetry, not even a few people, that he had to have
Langston come to New Orleans. So we wrote eight hundred letters and we
filled the auditorium of that campus. He must have sold hundreds of dollars
of books that night. All the books that he had stacked up went away. I will
never forget it, because it was the first time I had ever seen a living black
writer. It was important for me, and it meant the beginning of my whole
career.

Langston was a friend until 1967 when he died. I had seen him just the
October before, when I went to New York just after *Jubilee* was published.
Langston was the kind of person who would write you a letter of congratulations. He wrote when *For My People* was published, he wrote when *Jubilee*
was published, and I still have those letters. I got a letter from Countee Cullen
saying, "I understand you are one of these unusual poets who can read the
poetry as well as write it."

He said, "The next time you come to New York, my wife and I would like
you to come to dinner." I have that letter. I went to dinner and there I saw
Claude McKay for the first time. Langston of course was there, and there
were others. That was really the beginning of my professional career, with
the publication of *For My People*. I had another wonderful experience at
Northwestern when I met the great Dr. W. E. B. Du Bois. He came to speak
at Northwestern, and afterward I had the courage and the nerve to go up and
tell him, "I write poetry, too." He said, "Send me some." I said, "Where
shall I send it?" He said, "To the *Crisis*." I did, and the next year in May,
while I was still a teenager, the poem came out. Some of my friends who are
very kind critics say that that is the poem I have fulfilled with my whole
career.

I Want to Write

I want to write
I want to write to write the songs of my people.
I want to hear them singing melodies in the dark.
I want to catch the last floating strains from their sob-torn throats.
I want to frame their dreams into words; their souls into notes.
I want to catch their sunshine laughter in a bowl;
fling dark hands to a darker sky
and fill them full of stars
then crush and mix such lights 'till they become
a mirrored pool of brilliance in the dawn.

Gabbin: That's wonderful—"a mirrored pool of brilliance in the dawn." "I Want to Write," also called "Daydream."

Walker: It's had three or four different titles. Every time it's published, there's another title. I got tired of "Daydream"—I thought, "Oh, I don't want to use 'Daydream'"—and then I saw a book *Songs of My People,* and I said, "Oh, there's my poem: 'I want to Write the Songs of My People.'"

Gabbin: You mentioned Langston Hughes, and you also mentioned Du Bois, but there's one other person you met when you were young.

Walker: Well, I saw Langston when I was sixteen, I saw Du Bois when I was seventeen, and I met Richard Wright when I was twenty. Those three men have had tremendous influence on my thinking and on my writing. They were not members of my family and they were not my classroom teachers, but I read them. I read Langston, I read Du Bois, I read Richard Wright. They were men that I always thought of in terms of a great protest movement of black people. People who were constantly writing for the sake of our people—not for art's sake, but for the *people's.* I think they influenced me more than any others. I had wonderful teachers, yes; and my parents encouraged me. I was fortunate to that extent. But those three men represented for me everything that we try to do when we write. They represent the *humanity* of black people; the fact that every individual is a human being. Nobody can be *more* than a human being, and nobody can be less. That is what I taught my students all those years.

Gabbin: A major theme in your poetry, in your fiction, your essays is freedom. Stephen Henderson says in his seminal work *Understanding the New Black Poetry* that the overarching theme of our literature is liberation, and you consistently use that theme in your writing. Why have you stayed with it?

Walker: When I was about eleven years old—I guess eleven and a half—I went to high school, and one of the first things I studied then was the French Revolution. I had already read about the American Revolution, but for some reason Patrick Henry and George Washington didn't excite me.

But when I read about the French Revolution—Robespierre, Danton, Marat—I was excited. I heard them saying *freedom*—"égalité, fraternité, liberté." It became a motto for my life, and it began when I was only eleven. I was much older when I read about the Russian Revolution. In school they talked about "the barbaric Russians"—"the Communists," they called them. They had pictures in the book that showed you these people with shining whiskers and they were devils; they told you these people were no-good people.

One of the first books I read after meeting Wright was *Ten Days That Shook the World.* If you ever read that book and you are not moved to think in terms of freedom for people who were living under the terror of the czars, even going beyond the Kerensky government—something is wrong if you aren't affected by it. I was tremendously impressed, and when I read the short stories that Wright wrote in *Uncle Tom's Children,* you've got the essence of what we were in the thirties, the writers of social protest. That's what he was saying in everything. Baldwin and the postmodernists look down on those writers of social protest. They're not popular anymore, and our black men are not writing social protests; they're doing . . . what is it, "deconstruction"?

Gabbin: "Deconstruction of the language," "tropes," "analysis of texts" . . .

Walker: I've been reading some of the postmodernists. One man is a marvel with language, and he doesn't ever have a plot. He doesn't *believe* in a plot. He says, "Language is everything." The writer knows that the word is powerful, that it has more than emotional and intellectual meaning. But I am still a student of the old school of fiction; I believe you have to tell a story. Postmodernists are very wonderful writers, but they'd be better if they had a plot.

Gabbin: You know, I've been trying—and I know my story's probably like a lot of other people's—for many years to write down a story that's really important in my life. In fact, it's the story of how I met my husband . . . I've been trying to write this story, about our meeting, and every time I put down the facts, they don't come alive. They're just there; it's not a story. How do you do that? I know other people want to know.

Walker: That was my problem with *Jubilee* for years and years and years. I wrote those first 300 pages when I was nineteen at Northwestern. Then I looked at that stuff and I said, "Oh, this is not right." I didn't know what was wrong with it, but nobody there could tell me what to do. In the fifties I went up to Yale, and I worked with Normal Holmes Pearson, who had co-edited the *Oxford Book of Verse* with Auden. When I left in May I was still not understanding what to do, and Professor Pearson said, "You're telling the story but it doesn't come alive. You're telling it but you're not showing it." I left Yale deciding I would not stay there and try to get a Ph.D., that I'd go back where I learned to put the poetry together and had written the ballads for the first time. I'd throw my hat in and see if Paul Engle would let me come in, because we fussed all the time.

Anyway, when I went back, I spent a summer working under a man who taught me how to do it. His name was Verlin Cassill and he had a little book on writing fiction. I think he's done more potboilers than prize winners, but he absolutely is the most marvelous teacher of fiction I ever encountered. He told me, "You've got to read Chekhov. Not the plays"—I had read *The Cherry Orchard* and *Three Sisters*—"but read the short stories and see how he puts incidents together." What you're talking about is what was one of Wright's greatest assets. That was the ability to dramatize the material. What do we mean? Well, what is a plot? A plot is a series of related incidents that tell a story. Through the actual dramatization of material, taking the facts and making fiction by showing the action, by actually getting the person reading it to see the action. What is going on? What are they saying, and what does it mean? If they're walking, if they're thinking, if they're acting—actually dramatizing that material means showing the story rather than telling the story.

I thought that I would never learn. I spent eight weeks before I could turn in to him the first chapter, the revised first chapter, of *Jubilee* as you know it. He said, "You got it." I thought about: Here I was now in my late forties, and I'd been fooling around trying to learn that ever since I was nineteen years old. That's why it took so long. I did all the research, I read all the books, but until I learned how to create a scene I could not write fiction. Everybody's got a story. Everybody knows a story. Can you write the story without telling it by showing? It's not easy, and I recommend exactly who he recommended to me: Chekhov. Chekhov's stories show you line for line, page for page, what you have to do.

Gabbin: You know that I've worked with Sterling Brown's work for a long time, and I'm a devotee of the folk tradition. You remember Sterling Brown, don't you, out there? Sterling Brown of "Old Lem," Sterling Brown of "Odyssey of Big Boy" and "Sister Lou." Sterling Brown's work taught me a love for the folk tradition. I know that you are in that tradition as well, and I want you to tell us how you show your debt to that tradition in *Jubilee* and the other writing that you have done.

Walker: I think one of the first conversations I ever had with Richard Wright was on that folk tradition. Both of us were tremendously interested in what we thought at the time was limited to the South, but it isn't limited to the South. It's a part of black life all over this country. It's the way we live, it's the religion we believe, it's our spirit, our art, it's our music . . . It's our daily living, that folk life.

I know you have read Zora Hurston and have read Richard Wright. I don't think Wright ever wanted to admit that Zora had affected him, because he was so chauvinistic that he wouldn't want to say that a woman did that. But she did. You open Richard Wright and read, "Your mama don't wear no drawers." Where did he get it? He got it from Zora. Sterling writes about the working man, the roustabout, the stevedore. Langston writes about the culture of the cities, particularly Harlem; the menials, the maids, the cooks and washerwomen. But all of us know that when we speak in the vernacular of black people we have gone to the root of black life. We are dealing with everyday living, and everyday believing, and the everyday actions of black people. "I talked to old Lem, and old Lem said: They do the so-and-so, and we carry the cross . . . and they get the money."

Gabbin: "And they don't come by ones . . ."
Walker (and others): "And they don't come by twos; they come by tens."

Gabbin: In your essay "The Humanistic Tradition of Afro-American Literature," you developed a line of thinking that I think is essential to appreciate the continuity and the connections in our literature. I'm going to read this: you say that "this tradition began in the ancient Oriental world, in black Africa, in Egypt, some 3,500 years ago with *The Book of the Dead.* The literature of black people, like that of all people, grew out of the cosmogony and the cosmology that developed around the Nile River, and not from Greece or Rome at the end of the ancient world, nor in the Middle Ages with the European Renaissance, nor with the modern expansion of the European man. But black America is tied to her ancient African heritage in all her physical and cultural manifestations. "I want you to talk about that heritage.

Walker: I think that very few English teachers in the Western world have a tendency to tell their students that the descent into the underworld did not begin with Homer.

Gabbin: She's signifying, isn't she, Baraka?
Walker: They failed to say that this is an epic convention that began with *The Book of the Dead;* the pyramids and the coffin texts in Egypt were far earlier than anything Greece or Rome produced. You know, white professors in the white universities—when you talk about pre-Homeric epics, they say

"Was there any such thing?" They don't believe that, because they never read *The Book of the Dead,* and it's very hard for them to bring themselves to realize that these so-called savages understood how to go from this world to the next world without the white man telling them how.

Gabbin: Back in 1975 you did an interview with Charles Rowell. In that interview he asked you about writing a biography of Richard Wright and he said he thought there was no person in this country more suited, more prepared to write that biography than you. Of course, we all know you wrote that biography: *Richard Wright: Daemonic Genius.* However, because of the sensitive and controversial material, it cost you dearly writing that book. I want you to share with us some of the problems, some of the issues, that you dealth with.

Walker: Well, I tell, in the book, of the six areas that he wished to deal with, and the problems were all growing out of that. The first problem was that this man was a card-carrying Communist for twelve years, and if I proceeded to talk about this man's Communism, how was I going to know anything about it when I was never a Communist? That was the first problem.

The second problem was dealing with interracial marriage. In the friendship that Wright and I had together—that was a very close friendship—there was never a romance, never anything like a romance between us. Early in the friendship, he told me that if he ever married, he'd marry a white woman. Since I didn't look white, I knew he wasn't going to marry me.

Then there was the question of money. Richard Wright had two Book-of-the-Month Club selections. Well, did he have a lot of money? Did he make a lot of money? He lived in Europe in a very bourgeois fashion, in a nice apartment; he traveled around the world. But did he ever have a lot of money? That was another question. How did he get along with those agents and publishers and people who helped him to reach a great pinnacle of fame in this country, and in Europe, too?

Then there was the question of the Jewish-Arab conflict. If you started talking about, "This man is a pan-Africanist . . ." Pan-Africanism is really a black thing: most Jewish people are opposed to it, and he was married to two Jewish women. Now how are you going to deal with that?

And finally . . . I have to tell this little bit and then I'll be through with it. Wright's family—his second wife, Ellen—was bitterly opposed to my publishing the book. She spent close to a hundred thousand dollars and wrote letters to publishers like Harper's telling them, "Don't give her any permission to use any of his material," and threatened three publishers with a suit: first Howard [University Press], and then Dodd Mead, and finally Warner, and told them that as sure as I published the book she was going to sue.

Howard was scared to death; they said they'd had enough suits, and they didn't need any more. Dodd Mead was perfectly willing, but they didn't have any money. So finally Warner said, "Oh, we don't mind taking her on." They knew when they took the manuscript that Ellen Wright was going to sue, which meant that I didn't have the authority from the family to write the biography, as Michel Fabre had. Six months after the book appeared—it appeared in November of '88, and in May of '89 she sued. One of our very dear friends who's a critic, and who's been teaching in some of our white universities, said he felt sorry for me, because that was that woman's husband, and I couldn't do anything if she didn't want it done. I got word of what he said, and I had nerve enough to do what I had to do.

I wonder . . . we live through lots of things, and I thought in 1977 and '78 . . . well, Alex Haley published a book in 1976 called *Roots,* and I thought that thing was going to kill me. I thought I was going to die under *Roots.* Everybody talked about that jealous woman wanting this man's money, an agitated old woman; how she ought to go somewhere and sit down, and how "that dumb woman thinks she's going to do thus-and-so," and I said to my husband and my sons, "I don't know what I've done to anybody to deserve this. Anybody can pick up a book of *Roots,* and pick up a book of *Jubilee,* and they can see what's happening there. All you got to do is read it: it's there." You know, we have a saying in the black community: "We'll understand it better by and by." Well, when I wrote the Richard Wright book, and Ellen Wright sued Warner *and* Margaret Walker, I "understood it better by and by."

I had read every book I could find on fair use and copyright infringement. I told Charlie Harris, "That book is clean, there's nothing wrong there, there's nothing in there that anybody can say I've used without saying that I have a right to do this." That's what the lawyers said, and when it went to court that's what the court said. Then despite the fact that her lawyers and her children told her not to push it, she went to the appellate court and the lawyers in the appellate agreed with the lower court. One of them wrote an additional statement about it, which if you read the paperback copy of *Daemonic Genius* you'll see that the appellate court and this extra statement would all be there to explain, and I "understood it better by and by." I couldn't understand why I had to live through the horrible ordeal of *Roots.* I know now. Without *Roots,* I never would have known what "fair use" meant.

Gabbin: In a 1993 interview with Maryemma Graham, you talk about the responsibility of the writer. You say, "The writer's responsibility is like God's. He's supposed to, or she's supposed to, show the way."

Walker: Well, I meant by that not that we are divine to the extent that all human personality is not potentially divine. But I'm thinking in terms of the prophetic nature of the writer. The writer is like the prophet: he has to see the future by looking at the present. He has to understand that what's happened in the past is happening now, and will happen in the future. That is the role of the writer: to write about that future that you do not see, but that is evident in everything you do and hear. You know what's going to happen tomorrow because the seeds of it are happening today.

Gabbin: Talk about what's happening tomorrow. I know you love to write, and you're going to continue to write. What are your projects?

Walker: I saw a young lady here just before we began—Junette Pinckney. She was the person at CBS that had Charlie Rose have an interview with me when the Richard Wright book came out. He asked me, he said, "My, you've done all these things. What are your dreams? What do you dream about for the future?" I answered very flippantly, "All my dreams have already come true." But I will add that some of the dreams are still in the making. I would like to return to the fiction, and I have three short novels—one about education, one about sociology of religion, and one a sequel to *Jubilee.* If I could live long enough I'd like to write those books.

Gabbin: We've been talking about your life as a writer, but we know there are so many other dimensions to your life; I think we'd be remiss if we didn't talk about your work as an activist. You say in *I Dream a World* and elsewhere that the three enemies of black women are racism, sexism, and fascism. How have you personally done battle with these three *isms?*

Walker: There are three examples of actions I took in civil rights sponsorship of the NAACP, we sued to get the Jackson television station WLBT to operate with a staff that is 51 percent black. I was instrumental in changing the "confederate" history book to *Challenge and Change* by Sallis and Loewen. I am gratified to see my grandchildren using this book. I was also one of the first witnesses in the Ayers court trial to desegregate higher education in Mississippi. We consider ourselves loyal, good Americans, and to say that we live under a fascistic system is talking about going to the devil and living in Hell. But fascism is what we have. We live with it every day. It's in every part of our lives. It's not just the judicial system; it's not just that awful Supreme Court; it's not just Congress and that man—what's his name?—Newt Gingrich. It's all of it, and what we have to understand is, that's what we live with. It's racism, it's sexism, it's fascism; and it's the role—and the right—of the black writer to put it on paper, and tell the truth.

Gabbin: In 1988 our literary diva, the brilliant Eleanor Traylor, did an article, "[Border] Measures Crashing Through: Margaret Walker's, Poem of the Century." In this article she equates you with Ogun, or the first artist or forger. And she talks about . . ."

Walker: I didn't know what Ogun was. I had to go and look it up.

Gabbin: Margaret, I did, too. You know, Eleanor coins these words—"Ogunic." She calls your voice Ogunic, and she says in *Prophets for a New Day* you equate biblical heroes with modern heroes.

Walker: Eighth-century prophets.

Gabbin: Yes. Who are those heroes, those modern heroes, for you?

Walker: Well, you know, we went through two revolutions: I don't know whether we got all we needed from either one. Dr. Martin Luther King caused us to see the end of legal segregation—whether you admit it or not, the civil rights movement really ended legal segregation. Then Malcolm X came along and he told us, "Make something of yourself—your manhood and your womanhood are the things out there that matter." We changed our way of dress and our hair: we did everything to deny ourselves as purely Americans and show that we are African Americans. We learned a lot from both King and Malcolm X.

We lost three men through assassination. My neighbor Medgar Evers, killed the same year that the president of the United States was assassinated. Then we lost King by assassination, and we lost Malcolm X by assassination. What greater price can you pay for heroism? Who can you think of that deserves to be a hero who has not given his life for what he believes? They are our heroes. We have had women heroes too. My mother said something one day during the civil rights movement. She said, "You know, we had great women like Harriet Tubman and Sojourner Truth and Mary McLeod Bethune—all these women, but we could not get a revolution going until we had intelligent, intellectual men. The world didn't listen until they heard those men."

Now, I *know* you're not going to say that I'm a woman-basher. I'm not a basher of men or a basher of women. I was married thirty-seven years to a wonderful man; I have two wonderful sons; my father was a wonderful man. I admire men as much as women. I think God intended us to be partners and to get along with each other.

All of us have our weaknesses and our strengths, and we have to strive to be better, to live out our humanity as we reach toward divinity. That is the spiritual destiny of us all.

I don't think we have as many heroes or she-roes as we should have. I think about all the black men in prison who are not in the classrooms, and how many of us work for nothing when we ought to be making dollars. We have a tendency to think if you scrub a floor, you're the floor. Scrubbing the floor doesn't mean you're the floor. I taught my students that it's as important to know how to make a good lemon meringue pie as it is to write a poem because there is *dignity* in all labor.

We cry out for heroes. You walk along the street and you see them every day, and you don't credit them with being heroes. If you live in the Deep South as I do, and you go to church or you go to school, you don't know whose money keeps it going, do you? It's that washerwoman's money. She's the one that does anything that she can do honestly to send her child to school. That's what we do every day; that's part of our life, that's our living. And the day we understand that is the day we'll step a little higher up the ladder.

Gabbin: After all of your years, and all that you've been through—wars and the civil rights movement; attacks on our community in terms of drugs and guns and AIDS; attacks on affirmative action; and the latest assault on our churches, the very heart of our community—somehow through it all, you seem to maintain a kind of faith in humanism; a faith in humanity. I want to know: what is it that keeps you hopeful?

Walker: I think that any day you believe that every human being has a spark of divinity within him, you will not destroy yourself by trying to destroy somebody else.

You will have to believe in the goodness of the future if you believe that we are constantly striving toward a real divinity. We are black people of spirit. That spirit is the basis of animism and ancestor worship in Africa. The African believed for a while in animism, and he said, "Spirit is in everything. It's in the water; it's in the grass and the trees; it's in the wind; and it's in us." We have the greatest amount of spirit in us, and if we don't think positively, how can that spirit live?

Gabbin: Dr. Margaret Walker Alexander, thank you for your poetry, your writing, your essays; for the pool of brilliance that you've mirrored in this part of the world.

Index

AFL-CIO, 148

African, The (Courander), 134

"African Village, The" (MW), 121

Afro-American literature: audience for, 130–31; blacks stereotyped in, 69–71; economic rationale for slavery in, 79; humanistic tradition in, 24, 181; *Jubilee* as, 127; MW comments, 110; overview, by decade, 26, 82, 129–30; revolution and, 82; Richard Wright as pivotal in, 29–30, 129–30

Alexander, Firnist James (husband), 47–51, 64, 155, 166–67

Alexander, James (son), 49, 89, 167

Alexander, Margaret Walker. *See* Walker, Margaret Abigail

Alexander, Norma (daughter-in-law), 166, 167

Alexander, Siggy (son): caring for MW, 164, 165, 166; Republic of New Africa, 89; Vietnam War, 11–12, 57, 111

Algren, Nelson, 75, 81, 128, 140

Ali, Muhammed, 17

Alpha Kappa Alpha sorority, 169–70

Alpha Phi Alpha Fraternity, 43

American culture. *See* society (present day)

Anderson, Marian, 84

anecdotes: birthday party play, 156; "For My People" read in jail, 97; late from school, 34; operetta story, 33, 156; salesman of *Jubilee*, 39, 56, 126; Salinger note to Conroy, 128

"Anniad, The" (Brooks), 111

Annie Allen (Brooks), 60, 111–12

Anthony, Susan B., 106

Arab-Israeli conflict, 15

"Artificial Nigger" (O'Connor), 109

authors, advised. *See* writer, the

autobiography (MW): contents, 68, 119, 151; the future in, 123; journals as source material, 99, 155; process of writing, 101

Autobiography of Malcolm X, The, 134

awards (MW): Ford Foundation grant, 64, 140; freshman English prize, 43–44, 155–56; Fulbright lectureship, 57, 90; Governor's Award for Excellence, 162; Lyndhurst prize, 141; National Endowment for the Humanities, 140–41; Rosenwald Foundation, 140; Ten Commandments recitation, 43; Yale Younger Poets competition, 42, 60, 81, 127, 138–39, 161

Baldwin, James, 117, 123, 130, 179

"Ballad of the Free" (MW), 23

"Ballad of the Hoppy Toad" (MW), 22, 23

Ballad of the Sad Café (McCullers), 109

Baraka, Amiri, 26–27, 117–19

Bell, Bernice, 166

Bellow, Saul, 38–39, 75, 161

Benedict, Ruth, 108

Benét, Stephen Vincent: as discoverer of MW, xi; poetry style of MW, 21, 102; relationship with MW, 42; Yale Younger Poets competition, 60–61, 127, 139, 161

Bergman, Ingmar, 57

Berry, Wendell, 64, 86

Bethune, Mary McLeod, 106, 185

"Between the World and Me" (Wright), 65

"Big Boy Leaves Home" (Wright), 65

Birmingham, Ala., 23, 32, 117

Black and White Women of the Old South (Gwin), 103

Black Arts Movement, x, 26, 27

Black Boy (Wright), 65, 82–83

black college experience, 23, 25, 150–51

"Black Eyed Susans" (concept) (MW), 150, 151

Black Insights (Ford), 22

Black Liberation Army, 13

"Black Magic" (MW), 121

black men: *The Color Purple* as commentary, 110; decision-making ability of, 7–8, 11; hatred of whites, 12; MW vs. Giovanni, 7; rage in, 87; strength of, 8; Wright's portrayal as flawed, 29. *See also* blacks (men/women); men; white men

black middle class aspirations, 77

Black Nationalist Revolution, 57, 123, 130

Black Panthers, 16

Black poetry, 20

black rights movement, 106

blacks (men/women): annihilation beliefs, 15–16; disenfranchisement of, 106; experience of prejudice, 78; hatred of whites, 12, 17; stereotyped in literature black/white, 69; uneducated catered to by whites, 68; whites control of education of, 150